The LOUIS ARMSTRONG *Companion*

The
LOUIS ARMSTRONG
Companion

Eight Decades of Commentary

Edited by

JOSHUA BERRETT

Schirmer Books
New York

Schirmer Books
1633 Broadway
New York, New York 10019

Library of Congress Catalog Card Number: 98–29206

Printed in the United States of America

Printing number
1   2   3   4   5   6   7   8   9   10

Library of Congress Cataloging-in-Publication Data

The Louis Armstrong companion : eight decades of commentary / edited by Joshua Berrett.
     p.   cm.
  Includes discography: p.
  Includes bibliographical references (p.   ) and index.
  ISBN 0-02-864669-X
  1. Armstrong, Louis, 1901–1971. 2. Jazz musicians—United States—Biography. 3. Jazz—History and criticism. I. Berrett, Joshua.
ML419.A75L68 1999
781.65'092—dc21
[B]   98-29206
                                                                        CIP
                                                                         MN

This paper meets the requirements of ANSI/NISO Z39.48-1992 (Permanence of Paper).

Publisher's Note

This book consists of articles, interviews, and reviews that originally appeared in a variety of publications. Except for silently correcting obvious omissions or spelling errors, no changes have been made in the original texts. Where permission to reprint could not be obtained, all best efforts were made to locate copyright owners. Offensive language used by some writers reflecting racist attitudes has been left as an important part of the historic record.

Contents

Acknowledgments

Lewis Porter, associate professor of music at Rutgers University in Newark, deserves much of the credit for initially encouraging me to take on this project, not to mention, offering valuable advice about bringing it to fruition. Dan Morgenstern, director of the Institute of Jazz Studies at Rutgers, was a fount of wisdom and a gentle critical voice. Michael Cogswell, director of the Louis Armstrong Archives at Queens College, City University of New York, was immensely helpful in countless ways, committed to making the richness of Armstrong's legacy accessible. Phoebe Jacobs, vice-president of the Louis Armstrong Educational Foundation and Oscar Cohen, president of Associated Booking Corporation, were vital in providing support and issuing permission to use unpublished material. Ishmael Reed, Arvell Shaw, and Marianne Veidt deserve special thanks for granting interviews. For help of various kinds, my thanks to Mark Tucker, Lila Caimari, Richard Nochimson, Ira Wolff, and my nephew, Colin Baigel. My wife, Lynne, and close family have served as a source of precious support, constant and unfailing. Last, but not least, my thanks to Richard Carlin at Schirmer Books for his patience and guidance in helping produce this book.

Introduction

On July 7, 1971, the day after Louis Armstrong's death, *The Los Angeles Times* published an editorial cartoon depicting him in heaven out-trumpeting the Archangel Gabriel himself. The image was very close to reality. If anything, one could argue, it fell short of the truth. For Armstrong's talents as trumpet player, singer, creative artist with more than eighty copyrighted compositions to his credit, and charismatic personality without peer combined to make him one of nature's supreme gifts to twentieth-century American culture. It was Bing Crosby who said of Armstrong: "He is the beginning and the end of music in America." Duke Ellington added his voice to the chorus with the statement: "If anybody was Mr. Jazz it was Louis Armstrong. He is what I would call an American Original." For Wynton Marsalis the sound of Satchmo's horn "was a pure spiritual essence, the sound of America and of Freedom."

Throughout Armstrong's lifetime his unique place in American culture was underscored by the mythological associations surrounding his birth date: "I was a Southern Doodle Dandy, born on the Fourth of July, 1900." (It does not matter that baptismal records found at Sacred Heart of Jesus Church in New Orleans and authenticated in 1988 have established the actual date as August 4, 1901.) The symbolic "Fourth of July" feels right somehow: as a founding father of American jazz he has left the twentieth century an enduring legacy in his life and music. As jazz critic Leonard Feather points out: "Americans, unknowingly, live part of every day in the house that Satch built. A riff played by a swinging band on television, a nuance in a Sinatra phrase, the Muzak in the elevator, all owe something to the guidelines that Louis set."

Louis Armstrong took a vital cue from his early mentor, King Oliver, who said: "If a cat can swing a lead and play a melody, that's what counts." And swing he did, transforming the very nature of jazz from a music of ensemble improvisation to one defined by a theme-solo(s)-theme format. As the first indisputably great soloist, he helped write the very history of the world of jazz; he led the way by expanding upon "breaks" and embellished melodies to create compelling improvised solos lasting a whole chorus or more—animated by a distinctive "swing" to create a music of passion, excitement, and intensity.

Enjoying a career covering more than five decades, Armstrong lived his credo: "My life has been my music." A master showman known to millions around the world, Armstrong never lost sight of that goal:

> I never tried to prove nothing, just always wanted to give a good show. My life has been my music; it's always come first, but the music ain't worth nothing if you can't lay it on the public. The main thing is to live for that audience, 'cause what you're there for is to please the people.

His stupendous gifts as a master showman could sometimes invite scorn and accusations that he was prostituting his art for the sake of mere "entertainment." To some critics pleasing the people was tantamount to betraying the true "hot" jazz of the 1920s in favor of an effete swing style and glitzy commercialism. Even worse, some critics saw his smiling, mugging, and singing, his acting like a "coon" and "Tom," as symptoms of a deep-seated sense of worthlessness, fueling an insatiable craving for applause. But Armstrong and his music have outlived most of his detractors. In fact, when the motion picture *Good Morning, Vietnam* was released in 1987, more than fifteen years after his death, Armstrong's recording of "What a Wonderful World" remained in the top forty for three weeks.

Armstrong once summed up his life by saying: "My whole life has been happiness. Through all the misfortunes . . . I did not plan anything. Life was there for me, and I accepted it." And his capacity to accept it was reinforced by a very strong work ethic, a characteristic that was embedded in him by the age of seven; for it was then that he began working for the junk-dealing, Russian-Jewish Karnofsky family in the colored section of New Orleans. This work ethic defined his life to the very end. Even though he was then suffering from congestive heart failure and shortness of breath, he did not worry about dying onstage during what was to be his last gig, on March 1971 at the Waldorf Astoria's Empire Room. His dedication to his public was undiminished in its fervor. His personal physician, Dr. Gary Zucker, who attended him in his hotel suite, has recalled feeling a chill go up and down his spine as Louis, assuming the position of holding the horn and looking up at the ceiling, said: "Doctor, you don't understand. My whole life, my whole soul, my whole spirit, is to b-l-o-w this h-o-r-n. My people are waiting for me. I cannot let them down."

The American actress Tallulah Bankhead once said of Armstrong: "He gasses me." Known for her award-winning roles in such plays as *The Little Foxes* and *The Skin of Our Teeth,* she appreciated more profoundly than most the uniqueness of Armstrong's art:

> If I were to try to draw an analogy, I would mention Charlie Chaplin and Mozart. The magic of Chaplin's art is that he illustrates the tragedy inherent in life—man trapped by circumstances and buffeted by fate—by using his own comic personage in the most ridiculous and hilarious situations. The coexistence of the sad and the funny.
>
> Apropos of Mozart, certain undiscerning people think of his [Armstrong's] music as being exclusively gay and frothy; happy music full of laughter. It is—sometimes—but underlying is a profound sadness.

Such is Louis's art.

As a preeminent musical icon of the twentieth century, his image buffeted by the forces of racism and commercialism, Armstrong's reputation has not survived unscathed, but survive it has, despite a welter of half-truths and competing critical ideologies. The man was among the most inclusive and tolerant of music's immortals, displaying an exemplary generosity of spirit: "As far as religion, I'm a Baptist and a good friend of the Pope, and I always wear a Jewish star for luck. Those people who make the restrictions, they don't know nothing about music; it's no crime for cats of any color to get together and blow."

Race-conscious jazz musicians? That was unthinkable for people who really knew their horns and loved music.

The readings in this book represent an attempt to capture the essence of Louis Armstrong's spirit and illuminate his contributions to twentieth-century culture as musician, entertainer, civil libertarian, and human being. They also touch on the more significant formative influences and issues that shaped his career, and on the critical perspectives that have helped determine how we view that career. Some of them were written by his contemporaries, some by our own. Perhaps most compelling of all is Armstrong's own prose, replete with torrents of phrases, at times elliptical, tossed off like trumpet riffs and almost invariably telling a good story. The selections of his prose included here, many of them never published before and none of them ghosted, are presented as close to the original as possible. Occasional misspellings have been corrected and punctuation and connectives have been inserted with the sole purpose of clarifying Armstrong's meaning and allowing him to speak in his remarkably unique voice.

Joshua Berrett

Part One

DO YOU KNOW WHAT IT MEANS TO MISS NEW ORLEANS?

AUTOBIOGRAPHICAL WRITINGS

Armstrong's memories of New Orleans were the most vivid and powerful. They defined his end as well as his beginning, providing the core of his personal values, his distinctive mode of expression, the very essence of who he was as human being and musician. —JB

THE NEW ORLEANS JEWISH FAMILY (1969)

Louis Armstrong Archives Series, Manuscript, No. 1/5

To paraphrase T. S. Eliot, "in Louis's end was his beginning." It was March 31, 1969. Ill in his bed at Beth Israel Hospital, New York, and acutely aware of his own mortality, Armstrong began writing in longhand what would become a seventy-seven-page confession, "Louis Armstrong and the Jewish Family in New Orleans, La. The Year of 1907." Although it is "a real life story and experiences at the age of seven years old with the Karnofsky family" (most likely he was closer to six years of age), Armstrong writes what is a far-ranging memoir that was once characterized by Gary Giddins as "achingly candid." He is deeply shaken by the events of the here and now, pouring out his soul after seeing a comatose Joe Glaser lying in the intensive care unit of the same hospital, and proceeds to dedicate the manuscript to Glaser as follows:

I dedicate this book to my manager and pal Mr. Joe Glaser
The best friend That I've ever had.
May the Lord bless him Watch over him always.
From His boy and disciple who loved him dearly.
Louis Satchmo Armstrong.

Armstrong also thanks his own doctor, Dr. Gary Zucker—"he saved my life at the Beth Israel Hospital—took me out of intensive care twice. Yea." (There are reflections on racial differences and values in the New Orleans of Armstrong's youth, not to mention touches of ethnic humor, all colored by what he had experienced in terms of the civil disorder and assassinations of the 1960s—as well as quirky, gossipy tidbits about the cast of characters who helped shape the drama of his boyhood.

Like almost everything else that Armstrong wrote, there is in this manuscript a thoroughgoing honesty and lack of pretension, coupled with the most acute powers of observation. His thoughts tumble out in elliptical phrases, hinting at jazz riffs. What is perhaps most remarkable of all is the fact that this is the writing of a man with little more than a fourth-grade education who was born to the fifteen-year-old daughter of a slave, Mary Albert (better known as Mayann), and her largely absent common-law husband, William Armstrong. —JB

The neighborhood consisted of Negroes, Jewish people and lots of Chinese. But the Jewish people in those early days were having problems of their own, along with hard times from the other white folks and nationalities who felt that they were better than the Jewish race. And meanwhile they took advantage of every chance that they had to prove it.

Of course, the Jewish folks had a better break than the Negroes because they were white people. That's what was so puzzling to me. Just the same they had had hard times for a long time. The Karnofskys, papa and mama, came from Russia before I was born. The Chinese finally moved into a little section of their own and called it Chinatown, with a few little beat-up restaurants—joints serving soul food on the same menu [as] their Chinese dishes. I used to hear the Negroes bragging about their lead beans and lice [*sic*]. That's the way a Chinese waiter would order it for you. Lead beans and lice [*sic*] wasn't bad at all. Of course the colored people cook the best red beans and rice. But for a change and something different, my mother and my stepfather used to take me and Mama Lucy (my sister) down in Chinatown and have a Chinese meal for a change. A kind of special occasion. And the bill in those days was real cheap. And we felt as though we were having something big. We would also order fried rice and liver gravy with our red beans; and ooh God, you would lick your fingers—it would taste so good.

Russian lullaby song donated by Dr. Gary Zucker, M.D., Beth Israel Hospital, New York, N.Y.

CHORUS
Every night you'll hear her croon
A Russian lullaby,
Just a little plaintive tune
When baby starts to cry.
Rock a bye my baby,
Somewhere there may be
A hand that's free
For you and me
And a Russian lullaby.

This is the song that I sang when I was seven years old with the Karnofsky family when I was working for them. Every night at their house, when mother Karnofsky would rock the baby David to sleep, then I would go home, cross-town, across the track to Mayann and Mama Lucy, my mother and sister.

He [father, William Armstrong] was a freak for being the Grand Marshall for the Odd Fellows Lodge. Especially when they had funerals— then he would go on the hard working job that he had. He was working for a big turpentine company keeping fire in those big furnaces for a very small pay. He also had other children by another woman who lived in the uptown section of New Orleans. I had two stepbrothers, a stepsister, and a stepmother named Gertrude.

I had a long-time admiration for the Jewish people. Especially with their long time of courage and of taking so much abuse for so long. I was only seven years old, but I could easily see the ungodly treatment that the white folks were handing the poor Jewish family whom I worked for. It dawned on me—even my race, the Negroes, the way that I saw it, they were having a little better break than the Jewish people with jobs aplenty around. Of course we can understand all the situations and handicaps that was going on, but they . . . to me we were better off than the Jewish people. But we didn't do anything about it. We were lazy and still are. We never did try to get together, and to show the younger Negroes such as myself to try and even to show that he has got ambitions, and with just a little encouragement I could have really done something worthwhile. But instead we did nothing but let the young upstarts know that they were young—and that was that. Never a warm word of doing anything important came to their minds.

My nationality, Negroes, took advantage of my mother (Mayann) because they thought they were over-smart, meaning Mayann gave birth to Mama Lucy and me. And she had to struggle with us until we grew up both. After grabbing a little schooling and a job at a very young age I myself will never forget, I'll try to forgive. But they were in an alley or on the street corner shooting dice for nickels and dimes, etc. (mere pittances), trying to win the little money his (soul brothers) [had], who might be gambling off the money he should take home to feed their starving children or pay their small rents or very important needs, etc.

Mama Lucy and I used to go out to the front of town when we were very young, among those produce places, where they used to throw away spoiled potatoes and onions into a big barrel. And she and I, among other kids, used to raid those barrels, cut off the spoiled parts, and sell them to restaurants. There was a baker shop which sold two stale loaves of bread for a nickel. They would do that to help the poor children. They could always get filled up, at least on bread. Mama Lucy and I, we had to do it lots of times. Many kids suffered with hunger because their fathers could have done some honest work for a change. No, they would not do that. It would be too much like right. They'd rather laze around and gamble, etc. If it wasn't for the nice Jewish people, we would have starved many a time. I will love the Jewish people all my life.

—

Of course, we are all well aware of the Congo Square, slavery, lynchings, and all of that stuff. Maybe the Jewish people did not go through all of those things, but they went through just as much. Still they stuck together. Most of the Negroes who went through some of those tortures, they asked for it. Those days were like some of these modern days. One Negro who has no ambitions, or any intention of doing the right things, will bring suffering to a whole flock of Negroes that is at least trying to live like human beings. Because they know within themselves that they're doing the wrong things, but expect everybody, just because he is a Negro, to give up everything that he has struggled for in life, such as a decent family [and] living a plain life—this trifling Negro expects him to give up everything just because of his ignorant, lazy moves. Personally, I think that it is not fair. And the Negro who can't see these foolish moves from some over-educated fools, then right away he is called a white folk's nigger. B'lieve it. The white folks did everything that's decent for me. I wish that I could boast these same words for niggers.

I think that I have always done great things about uplifting my race—but wasn't appreciated. I am just a musician and still remember the time as an American citizen [when] I spoke up for my people during the big integration riot in Little Rock; remember?

I wrote Eisenhower. My first comment or compliment, whatever you would call it, came from a Negro boy from my hometown New Orleans. The first words that he said to me after reading what I had said in the papers concerning the Little Rock deal—he looked straight at me and said: "Nigger, you had better stop talking about those white people like you did." Hmm. I was trying to stop that unnecessary head whipping at the time, that's all.

He's the type of Negro who will pan the white man behind closed doors. And the minute he leaves you he will slip over to some white man and tell everything that was said against him, get your head whipped, and he will be the first Negro who will rape a white woman.

It happened in slavery days. The Negroes have always connived against each other, and they still do. They never will be like the Jewish people, I should say not. Half of these young Negroes just don't know what they are getting upset about. If they'd consult the old generation of their families who really witnessed hard times and maybe they will study a little more and do things the right way. Force and brute strength is no good. Not even love and sex.

It's nicer to know and feel deep down in your heart that you have something, anything that you've worked and strived for honestly, than to do a lot of ungodly things to get it. Yes, you appreciate it better.

The Negroes will pan another Negro because he is trying to have a little something half way decent. They'll go as far as to pan you for at least trying. They would rather laze away their time doing nothing or feel, because they have diplomas, which some of them shouldn't have received in the first place, they feel that the world owes them something because of it. And some of them can't even spell "cat" correctly. Just a waste of money to some of the hep cats who graduated. I went only to fifth grade because I had to work along with my schooling. I wasn't fortunate to have parents with enough money to pay. Like some of these idiots whom I see making these big soapbox speeches, etc. I had to work and help Mayann put bread on the table, since it was just the three of us living in this one big room, which was all that we could afford. But we were happy. My mother had one thing that [can't be learned] no matter how much schooling anyone has—and that was good common sense and respect for human beings. Yea. That's my diploma. All through life I remembered it. To me no college in this whole world can top it as far as I am concerned.

I may not profess to be the smartest Negro in the world. But I was taught to respect a man or woman until they prove in my estimation that they don't deserve it.

I came up the hard way, the same as lots of people. But I always help the other fellow if there's any ways possible. And I still say my prayers every night when I go to bed. And I say the blessing when I eat my food.

White audiences from all over the world picked up on my music, from the first note that I'd ever blown. And until these days they are still with me. And they seem to love all the Negroes that has music in their souls. Operas, spirituals, etc. I am very proud to realize that they never let us down with their attendance and their appreciation. I was real relaxed

13

owes them something because of it. And some
of them Can't even spell Cat Correctly. Just
a waste of money to some of the Hep Cats
who Graduated. I'Only 1 to Fifth Grade
because I had to work along with my schooling.
I was'nt fortunate to have parrents with
enough money to pay. Like some of these
I diots whom I see makeing these big Soap
Box speeches etc I had to work and help
Mayann. Put bread on the table, since it
was Just the three of us living in this
big Room (ONE), which was all that we Could
afford. But we were happy. My mother had
one thing that no matter how much
Schooling anyone has—And that WAS
Good Common Sense. (+RESPECT FOR HUMAN DEINGS.) Yea. That is
my Deploma—all through my life
I Remember it. To me, no College in
this whole World Can top it, as far as I am
Concerned.

I may not profess to be the Smartest Negroe
in the world. But I was taught to Respect
a man or woman until they Prove in my
estimation that they don't deserve it.

A page from "Louis Armstrong and the Jewish Family in New Orleans, LA, the Year 1907." Armstrong comments on his fifth-grade education, the value of common sense, and the need to show respect for other human beings. Louis Armstrong Archives Series, Manuscript, No. 1/5.

singing the song called "Russian Lullaby" with the Karnofsky family, when mother Karnofsky would have her little baby boy in her arms, rocking him to sleep. We all sang together until the little baby would doze off.

The Jewish people have such wonderful souls. I always enjoyed everything they sang and still do. Of course I sang the lullaby song with the family. I did not go through every song they sang. But I was a good listener. Still am. That was a long time ago. And I still remember their phrases. When Mrs. Karnofsky would start singing these words to "Russian Lullaby" we all would get our places to sing it. So soft and sweet. Then bid each other good night. They were always warm and kind to me, which was very noticeable to me—just a kid who could use a little word of kindness, something a kid could use at seven and just starting out in the world. My first Jewish meal was at the age of seven. I liked their Jewish food very much. Every time we would come in late on the little wagon from buying old rags and bones. When they would have supper they would fix a plate of food for me, saying you've worked—might as well eat here with us. It is too late, and by the time you get home it will be way too late for your supper. I was glad because I fell in love with their food from those days until now. I still eat their matzos. My wife, Lucille, keeps them in her breadbox so I can nibble on them any time that I want to eat late at night. At Beth Israel Hospital, N.Y. I enjoyed all of my Jewish meals. So tasty. Deelicious [sic].

When I would be on the junk wagon with Alex Karnofsky, one of their sons, I had a little tin horn, the kind the people celebrate with. I would blow this long tin horn without the top on it. Just hold my fingers close together. Blow it as a call for old rags, bones, bottles or anything that the people and kids had to sell. The kids would bring bottles and receive pennies from Alex. The kids loved the sounds of my tin horn. The Karnofskys lived on the corner of Girod and Franklin streets, one block away from the Girod Street cemetery. We used to call it the Girod Street Graveyard in the colored section.

We kids used to clean the graves on Decoration Day for the families of the dead. We used to make a nice little taste (tips). I had a lot of lucky moments with the Karnofskys. After blowing my tin horn so long I wondered how I would do blowing a real horn; a cornet was what I had in mind. Sure enough, I saw a little cornet in a pawn shop window. Five dollars. My luck was just right. With the Karnofskys loaning me on my salary, I saved fifty cents a week and bought the horn, all dirty. But it was soon pretty to me.

—

[The Karnofskys] did a fine job fixing up that house. They had a pretty good size yard. So they started a little business in no time at all. That's where I came in. With [the] little money that they had they bought two small horses, two small wagons, harness for the horses. Their two sons, their ages nineteen or twenty years old, went into business. I alternated with the two sons. One went out in the street buying old rags, bones, iron, bottles, any kind of old junk, go back to the house with the big yard, empty the wagon, pile up the old rags in one place, the bottles, bones, and the rest of the junk, all in separate places.

Soon there would be big piles of everything. There was enough room for piles of stone coal which the older son Morris sold in the streets also. Especially in the red light district, mostly in the evenings, way into the nights. He sold it for five cents a water bucket. To lots of the sporting (prostitutes) women standing in the doorways. Alex would go out early in the mornings on his junk wagon, stay out all day, me right alongside of him. Then I would help Morris at night. The first job that I ever had. So I was very glad over it. Alex would get good money for his junk when he had saved up enough to sell. And pile up the yard again. Going to the bank every week. Both brothers did the same thing with their profits. Being a helper for those boys made me very proud and happy. I began to feel like I had a future and "It's a Wonderful World" after all.

They couldn't pay me much money. But at my age and as times were so hard I was glad just to be working, and very happy so I could help my mother and sister. She had a job at a beat-up paper place where they bundled up old newspapers and made bales with them and sold them to some other company. She was paid fifty cents a day, and [with] my little fifty cents from each brother we managed pretty good. We at least had lots to eat and a roof over heads. And Mayann could really cook good. Ooh she could cook on small money. Mama Lucy was five years old. Too young to work. So we gave her the job [of] housekeeper or the one-room-where-we-lived keeper. She did a good job and was very proud. One thing that I couldn't help but notice about the Karnofskys. As poor as they were they weren't lazy people.

The Karnofsky family kept reminding me that I had talent, perfect intonation when I would sing. One day when I was on the wagon with Morris (we were on Rampart and Perdido Streets) we passed a pawnshop which had in its window an old tarnished, beat-up B-flat cornet. It only cost five dollars. Morris advanced me two dollars on my salary. Then I put aside fifty cents each week from my small pay. Finally the cornet was paid for in full. Boy, was I a happy kid.

The little cornet was real dirty and had turned real black. Morris cleaned my little cornet with some brass polish and poured some oil all through it, which sterilized the inside. He requested me to play tune on it. Although I could not play a good tune, Morris applauded me just the same which made me feel very good. As a young boy coming up, the people whom I worked for were very much concerned about my future in music. They could see that I had music in my soul. They really wanted me to be something in life. And music was it. Appreciating my every effort.

Working for these fine people I learned to be an early riser just like them. I noticed they believed in being on the move. Up early every morning, making hay while the sun shone. In Soulville, where I lived on the other side of town, the Negroes were just the opposite.

—

Honoré Dutrey was one of the finest trombone players who left New Orleans and went to Chicago. I had the pleasure of working with him in Carroll Dickerson's big band. Dutrey was in the Navy in his early days. He was accidentally locked up in some sort of a magazine on the ship.

It left him with shortness of breath. The Navy doctor gave him some medicine to spray into his nostrils, and he played his horn with ease just the same. He used to play the cello parts beautifully. I've never [heard] anyone else yet do that on a trombone, and tone so pretty and all. Dutrey had a brother in New Orleans by the name of Sam Dutrey, another wonderful musician. He played the clarinet. A born genius, yessir.

Here is a short rundown of my idea of the choice musicians in my young days in New Orleans. Also, the cream of the crop at that time. Some of these names are still remembered in our history of jazz. All of them pioneers. They could read music at sight; they might read a flyspeck if it got in the way—as follows:

Henry Kimball, bass violin; Emanuel Perez, cornet; Emanuel and Joe King Oliver played together in the Onward Brass Band. Really something to listen to when they played for parades and funerals. They had twelve musicians in their brass band. Eddie Jackson used to really swing the tuba when the band played marches. They sounded like a forty-piece brass swing band.

The second line is a bunch of guys who follow the parade. They're not the members of the lodge or the club. Anybody can be a second liner. Whether they be raggedy or dressed up. They seemed to have more fun than anybody. They will start a free-for-all fight any minute, with broom handles, baseball bats, pistols, knives, razors, brickbats, etc.

The Onward Brass Band broke up a baseball game over in Algiers, La.

when they passed by the game playing "When the Saints Go Marching In." The game stopped immediately and followed the parade. It happened in Algiers, La. Everybody was so busy swinging and dancing they almost missed their ferryboat back to N.O.

Harry Zeno was a popular drummer during the days of the red light district. He was also a pretty good card player, well liked by people in every walk of life. When he died he had people of all races at his funeral.

My life has always been music. Bill Bojangles Robinson's life was the stage and benefits. He never refused. Always willing. Of course, there were greats on the stage before my time. So it's impossible for me to speak of anyone whom I know nothing about.

It so happened that Bojangles Bill Robinson was passing through New Orleans on his way to open up a theater in Denver, Colorado. We all know how serious he was about benefits and funerals, etc. Bo heard about this old actor who was seriously ill. Passing through and since he had time to go out and view the body—laid out in his coffin at his home.

Bill Robinson, who was a Southern boy himself, knew all about the wakes where everyone can review [sic] the body. People who lined up for the last look at the dead body had their different comments. When Bojangles reached the coffin, touched the man's forehead, he immediately went into the kitchen where the dead man's wife was crying. Bill Robinson said to his wife, he said to her: "I touched your husband's forehead and he seemed a little warm to me." His wife rose up from her crying and said to Bojangles: "Hot or cold—he goes out of here tomorrow!" Takes only Bill Robinson to tell that one. To me he was the greatest comedian and dancer in my race. He didn't need blackface to be funny. Better than Bert Williams. I personally admired Bill Robinson because he was immaculately dressed. You could see the quality in his clothes, even from the stage; stopped every show. He did not wear an old raggedy top hat and tails with the pants cut off, black cork with thick white lips, etc. But the audiences loved him very much. He was funny from the first time he opened his mouth till he finished. So to me that's what counted. His material is what counted. I don't think that there will ever be a Bojangles Bill Robinson again. They might try to duplicate him, but I doubt it. May the Lord bless his soul.

SATCHMO: MY LIFE IN NEW ORLEANS (EXCERPTS) (1954)

Satchmo: My Life in New Orleans *is a personal memoir spanning the years from Armstrong's childhood through the time of his arrival in Chicago in August 1922. First published in 1954 and subsequently translated into a number of foreign languages, it stands as the remarkable document of a man of minimal formal education who was born on a dirt street in the poorest section of New Orleans, very close to the House of Detention. From the age of five until his departure for Chicago Armstrong lived mostly at Liberty and Perdido in the heart of the black vice district—a world of pimps, hustlers, prostitutes, saloons, and gambling joints. His unique mix of personal attributes—toughness, sensitivity, drive, and strength of character helped make possible a truly inspiring rags-to-riches story told by a discerning critic of human nature. As he writes: "Ever since I was a small kid I have always been a great observer." Thanks to these acute powers he is able to vividly recreate many episodes from those early years. The first episode excerpted here describes how, under the tutelage of Peter Davis, he became leader of the band at the Colored Waif's Home, a reformatory run along strict military lines. He had been sent there following his arrest for firing a pistol on New Year's Eve, December 31, 1912. The harsh military discipline could at times be shattering, such as when young Louis witnessed a runaway boy having to "pay for it" by being held down by the four strongest boys in the dormitory and receiving 105 lashes from Captain Joseph Jones. But there were also shining moments. Most notable was when Armstrong became the bugler at the Colored Waif's Home and very soon thereafter the leader of the band. There are also accounts of his caring for his "adopted" son and second cousin Clarence; his experiences playing under Fate Marable aboard one of the Streckfus Mississippi steamers, the* Saint Paul, *and his revealing confession about the importance of being a fat man; his return to New Orleans laden with money and his encounter with six-foot-six drummer, prizefighter, and one-time protector Black Benny*

Williams, who a few years earlier "in . . . crowded places . . . would handcuff Louis to himself with a handkerchief so Louis wouldn't get lost"; and his receiving the call to go to Chicago from his mentor Joe Oliver in Chicago. —JB

As time went on I commenced being the most popular boy in the Home. Seeing how much Mr. Davis liked me and the amount of time he gave me, the boys began to warm up to me and take me into their confidence.

One day the young bugler's mother and father, who had gotten his release, came to take him home. The minute he left Mr. Davis gave me his place. I took up the bugle at once and began to shine it up. The other bugler had never shined the instrument and the brass was dirty and green. The kids gave me a big hand when they saw the gleaming bright instrument instead of the old filthy green one.

I felt real proud of my position as bugler. I would stand very erect as I would put the bugle nonchalantly to my lips and blow real mellow tones. The whole place seemed to change. Satisfied with my tone Mr. Davis gave me a cornet and taught me how to play "Home, Sweet Home." Then I was in seventh heaven. Unless I was dreaming, my ambition had been realized.

Every day I practiced faithfully on the lesson Mr. Davis gave me. I became so good on the cornet that one day Mr. Davis said to me: "Louis, I am going to make you leader of the band."

I jumped straight into the air, with Mr. Davis watching me, and ran to the mess room to tell the boys the good news. They were all rejoiced [sic] with me. Now at last I was not only a musician but a band leader! Now I would get a chance to go out in the streets and see Mayann and the gang that hung around Liberty and Perdido Streets. The band often got a chance to play at a private picnic or join one of the frequent parades through the streets of New Orleans covering all parts of the city, uptown, back o'town, front o'town, downtown. The band was even sent to play in the West End and Spanish Fort, our popular summer resorts, and also at Milenburg and Little Woods.

The band's uniform consisted of long white pants turned up to look like knickers, black easy-walkers, or sneakers as they are now called, thin blue gabardine coats, black stockings and caps with black and white bands which looked very good on the young musicians. To stand out as the leader of the band I wore cream colored pants, brown stockings, brown easy-walkers and a cream colored cap.

In those days some of the social clubs paraded all day long. When the big bands consisting of old-timers complained about such a tiresome job, the club members called on us.

"Those boys," they said, "will march all day long and won't squawk one bit."

They were right. We were so glad to get a chance to walk in the street that we did not care how long we paraded or how far. The day we were engaged by the Merry-Go-Round Social Club we walked all the way to Carrolton, a distance of about twenty-five miles. Playing like mad, we loved every foot of the trip.

The first day we paraded through my old neighborhood everybody was gathered on the sidewalks to see us pass. All the whores, pimps, gamblers, thieves, and beggars were waiting for the band because they knew that Dipper, Mayann's son, would be in it. But they had never dreamed that I would be playing the cornet, blowing it as good as I did. They ran to wake up mama, who was sleeping after a night job, so she could see me go by. Then they asked Mr. Davis if they could give me some money. He nodded his head with approval, not thinking that the money would amount to very much. But he did not know that sporting crowd. Those sports gave me so much that I had to borrow the hats of several other boys to hold it all. I took in enough to buy new uniforms and new instruments for everybody who played in the band. The instruments we had been using were old and badly battered.

This increased my popularity at the Home, and Mr. Davis gave me permission to go into town by my self to visit Mayann. He and Mr. and Mrs. Jones probably felt that this was the best way to show their gratitude.

———

Clarence, my cousin Flora Miles's illegitimate son, was living with us at the time. He was about three years old and still in dresses. Down there all kids wore dresses until they were a real large size. Kids love to wander around a house, and Clarence was no exception. On this rainy day—big sheets of rain were falling—Clarence was playing with some toys I had bought for him. He was in the rear room, which was the kitchen for us, and we didn't notice him when he wandered out of the kitchen on to the back porch, where it was raining terribly hard.

All of a sudden, when Daisy and I were playing records, we heard Clarence crying frantically. So we ran to the rear door to see what was the matter. I was real frightened when I looked on the rear porch and couldn't see him, but I could hear him crying. Then I looked down to the ground, and there was Clarence coming up the steps crying and holding his head. He had slipped off the porch, it was so wet, and fallen to the ground. The average child probably would have gotten killed, but for Clarence the fall only set him back behind the average child.

That fall hindered Clarence all through his life. I had some of the best doctors anyone could get examine him, and they all agreed that the fall had made him feeble-minded. His mind is four years behind the average child's.

I took him to all kinds of schools as he grew. I also enrolled him in a Catholic school; they kept him there several months and then sent him back to me saying the same as the rest said. I got so disgusted with all the running around they were giving Clarence I decided to take over and teach him myself.

And since Clarence has always been a nervous sort of fellow and was never able to work and earn his own living, I set up a routine for him in which he'd be happy the rest of his days. I managed to teach him the necessary things in life, such as being courteous, having respect for other people, and last but not least, having good common sense. I always managed to have someone look after Clarence whenever I had to travel or go to work. The musicians, actors—in fact, everybody whom I'd ever introduced Clarence to—they've all taken a liking to him right away. As we used to say in New Orleans, Clarence never was a "sassy child."

During those days, when I wasn't playing with Kid Ory in a funeral or a parade or an advertising stint, [I] would be at the head of the New Basin Canal, hanging around the charcoal schooners. We youngsters would wait for them to clean the big lumps of coal, put them in large burlap sacks, and then throw the small pieces into a corner of the schooner. We would buy small pieces from them. We would carry them away in big burlap sacks, put them in water buckets and sell them at houses for five cents a bucket. That is how I earned my living when I married Daisy.

Handling and selling charcoal was certainly a dirty job. My face and hands were always black, and most of the time I looked like Al Jolson when he used to get down on his knees and sing "Mammy." But with that job and playing music I made a good living.

It was a useful experience for me to work on the boat with all those big-shots in music. From some of them I learned valuable methods of playing, from others I learned to guard against acquiring certain nasty traits. I was interested in their way of handling money. David Jones, for instance, starved himself the whole summer we worked on the *Saint Paul*. He saved every nickel and sent all his money to a farm down South where employees and relatives were raising cotton for him and getting away with as much of his money as they could, since he was not there to look after his own interests. Every day he would eat an apple instead of a good hot meal. What was the result? The boll weevils ate all of his cotton before the season was over. He did not even have a chance to go down and look his farm over before a telegram came saying everything had been shot to hell. After that David Jones used to stand at the boat rail during every intermission looking down at the water and thinking about all the jack he had lost. I often said to Fate Marable:

"Fate, keep an eye on David Jones. He's liable to jump in the water most any minute."

This incident taught me never to deprive my stomach. As a kid I had never believed in "cutting off my nose to spite my face," which is a true expression if there ever was one. I'll probably never be rich, but I will be a fat man. I never deprived myself of things I thought absolutely necessary, and there are a lot of things I never cared for, such as a flock of suits, for example. I have seen fellows with as many as twenty-five or thirty suits at one time. And what good does that do? The moths eat them up before they can get full use out of them. I have just the number of suits I need, including my uniforms. I have always believed in giving a hand to the underdog whenever I could, and as a rule I could. I will continue to do so as long as I live, and I expect to live a long, long time. Way past the hundred mark.

After the first trip to Saint Louis we went up river to Davenport, Iowa, where all the Streckfus boats put up for the winter. It was there that I met the almighty Bix Beiderbecke, the great cornet genius. Every musician in the world knew and admired Bix. He made the greatest reputation possible for himself, and we all respected him as though he had been a god. Whenever we saw him our faces shone with joy and happiness, but long periods would pass when we did not see him at all.

At the end of the first season on the *Saint Paul* we played our last engagement at Saint Louis for a moonlight excursion for colored people. The boat was crowded to the rafters. After we were under way a quarrel broke out and some bad men from uptown pulled guns. Wow! I never in all my life saw so many colored people running every which way. "This is going to be worse than the scare we had when the lad jumped overboard," I said to myself. Again the captain gave orders to us to keep playing, and again I started looking for an exit. It was real tough that night, but the boat finally landed safely, and very few were hurt.

After we were through playing we went uptown to our hotels. On our way we could hear guys on every corner bragging about the way they had raised hell on the boat. "My goodness," I thought, "that may be their idea of having fun, but it certainly isn't my idea of a good time."

At the Grand Central Hotel in Saint Louis I was a very popular boy. Being the youngest fellow in Fate Marable's band and single too, all the maids made a lot of fuss over me. I thought I was hot stuff when the gals argued over me, saying "I saw him first" and "He's my man" and a lot of blah like that. I was too interested in my music to pay any attention to that sort of jive. To most of it anyway.

He [Black Benny] meant he knew I had plenty of money. He asked me to stand him to a drink, and who was I to refuse the great Black Benny a drink? Nobody else ever did. When the drinks came I noticed that everybody had ordered. I threw down a twenty dollar bill to pay for the round which cost about six or seven bucks. When the bartender counted out my change Black Benny immediately reached for it saying, "I'll take it." I smiled all over my face. What else could I do? Benny wanted the money and that was that. Besides I was so fond of Benny it did not matter anyway. I do believe, however, if he had not strong armed that money out of me I would have given him lots more. I had been thinking about it on the train coming home from Saint Louis. But since Benny did it the hard way I gave the idea up. I sort of felt he should have treated me like a man, and I did not like the way he cut under me. But I did not want to jump him up about it. That would have been just like putting my big head in the lion's mouth. So I disgustedly waited for an opening to leave, and did.

Joe Oliver had left New Orleans in 1918, and was now up in Chicago doing real swell. He kept sending me letters and telegrams telling me to come up to Chicago and play second cornet for him. That, I knew, would be real heaven for me.

I had made up my mind that I would not leave New Orleans unless the King sent for me. I would not risk leaving for anyone else. I had seen too many of my little pals leave home and come back in bad shape. Often their parents had to send them the money to come back with. I had had such a wonderful three years on the excursion boats on the Mississippi that I did not dare cut out for some unknown character who might leave me stranded or get me into other trouble. Fate Marable and the Streckfus brothers had made it impossible for me to risk spoiling everything by running off on a wild goose chase.

After I had made all my arrangements I definitely accepted Joe's offer. The day I was leaving for Chicago I played at a funeral over in Algiers, on August 8, 1922. The funeral was for the father of Eddie Vincent, a very good trombone player. When the body was brought out of the house to go to the cemetery the hymn we played was "Free as a Bird," and we played it so beautifully that we brought tears to everybody's eyes.

The boys in the Tuxedo Brass Band and Celestin's band did their best to talk me out of going up to Chicago. They said that Joe Oliver was scabbing and that he was on the musicians' union's unfair list. I told them how fond I was of Joe and what confidence I had in him. I did not care what he and his band were doing. He had sent for me, and that was all that mattered. At that time I did not know very much about union tactics because we did not have a union in New Orleans, so the stuff about the unfair list was all Greek to me.

When the funeral was over I rushed home, threw my few glad rags together and hurried over to the Illinois Central Station to catch the seven P.M. train for the Windy City. The whole band came to the station to see me off and wish me luck. In a way they were all glad to see me get a chance to go out in the world and make good, but they did not care so much about having me play second cornet to Joe Oliver. They thought I was good enough to go on my own, but I felt it was a great break for me even to sit beside a man like Joe Oliver with all his prestige.

It seemed like all of New Orleans had gathered at the train to give me a little luck. Even the old sisters of my neighborhood who had practically raised me when I was a youngster were there. When they kissed me goodbye they had handkerchiefs at their eyes to wipe away the tears.

When the train pulled in all the Pullman porters and waiters recognized me because they had seen me playing on the tail gate wagons to advertise dances, or "balls" as we used to call them. They all hollered at me saying, "Where are you goin', Dipper?"

"You're a lucky black sommitch," one guy said, "to be going up North to play with ol' Cocky."

This was a reference to the cataract on one of Joe's eyes. The mean guys used to kid him about his bad eye, and he would get fighting mad. But what was the use? If he had messed around fighting with those guys he would have ended up by losing his good eye.

When the conductor hollered all aboard I told those waiters. "Yeah man, I'm going up to Chicago to play with my idol, Papa Joe!"

CAT, DADDY, AND ALL THAT JIVE (1999)

Armstrong's identification with words and expressions that have since become part of the argot of the jazz world help give Satchmo his distinctive flavor and texture. His contribution extends way beyond such familiar examples as "jive," "cat," and "daddy" to include dozens of entries as adapted below from Harold Wentworth and Stuart Berg Flexner, Dictionary of American Slang *(New York: Crowell, 1967). Though Armstrong did not originate all of these words or phrases, his usages are so vividly illustrative as to be invoked repeatedly in this reference work. All citations except the very first appear in his* Satchmo: My Life in New Orleans *(Da Capo), and relevant page numbers are specified in brackets.*

armstrong A high note or series of high notes played on a trumpet, especially in jazz.

blow up a storm To play jazz with spirit and skill. "I first heard Buddy Bolden play . . . [h]e was blowing up a storm." [23]

broken arm Food that has been eaten or only partially eaten after having been served at a meal. "He brought 'broken arms' . . . the leftovers from the tables he served." [29]

bug To be angry or irritated at someone. "I suspected something was bugging her from the way she used to give me hell every time I came home only a half hour late." [164]

bylow Corruption of "Barlow" knife, usually a single-bladed folding knife with a bone handle. "Mary Jack whipped out a bylow, a big knife with a large blade." [74]

cat A man dressing in the latest style. "I had on a brand new Stetson, my fine black suit and new patent leather shoes . . . I was a sharp cat." [164]

chib "The big knife called the chib." [76]

chick A young, attractive woman. "Luckily she was a woman, and a good-looking chick at that." [179] This, incidentally, refers to Daisy Parker, Armstrong's first wife.

chippie A prostitute. "Around the honky-tonks on Liberty and Perdido life was the same as in Storyville except that the chippies were cheaper." [94]

cut out To leave quickly or suddenly. "I was not going to wait. . . . I cut out." [123]

dead soldiers Leftovers, table scraps. "On the way to the kitchen with the dead soldiers or leftovers." [215]

dig To fully comprehend. "Before we could dig what was going on, these tough guys started shooting." [61]

dipper Short for "dippermouth," a person with a mouth the size of a dipper. "Dipper (that was my nickname—short for Dippermouth, from the piece called 'Dippermouth Blues'). . . ." [27–28]

divvy up To divide spoils or profits. "We would pass our hats and . . . divvy up." [34]

drag Person, thing, or event that is boring, tedious, or tiring. "It's a funny thing how life can be such a drag one minute and a solid sender the next." [126]

easy-walkers Rubber soled canvas shoes. "Black easy-walkers, or sneakers as they are now called." [47]

freebie Anything that is free of charge. "That meal was a freebie and didn't cost me anything." [92]

Galilee The Southern States of the U.S., specifically those of the Confederacy. "There was no place for colored people to eat on the train in those days, especially down in Galilee (the South)." [229–230]

gig A jam session or jazz party. "Kid Ory had some of the finest gigs, especially for the rich white folks." [141]

gone Madly in love. "Daisy and I commenced to fall deeply in love with each other. . . . I was so gone over her. . . ." [152]

hep Aware, informed. "By running with the older boys I soon began to get hep. . . ." [25]

hep to the jive Aware of and wise to life. "As the days rolled on I commenced getting hep to the jive. I learned a good deal about life and people." [192]

hot foot To go fast or hurriedly. "The boys would hot foot back to the Home when they heard the mess call." [39]

hustle To work as a prostitute. ". . . [W]hores that hustle all night." [58]

Jim Crow Racial segregation. "It was my first experience with Jim Crow. . . . I had never ridden on a street car before." [14]

jive Baloney, bull. ". . . [T]here was lots of just plain common shooting and cutting. But . . . that jive didn't faze me at all. I was so happy to have some place to blow my horn." [150]

jive Gaudy, cheap merchandise. "When we collected our pay I did not know what to buy so I bought a lot of cheap jive at the five and ten cent store to give to the kids. . . ." [193]

John A man paying a girl's expense in exchange for sexual favors. "Our hustlers sat on their steps and called to their 'Johns' as they passed by." [95]

lagniappe An extra, a dividend, a tip. ". . . I hit her with a few real hard ones for lagniappe (or good measure), which is what we kids called the tokens of thanks the grocer gave us when we went there to pay the bill for our parents. We would get animal crackers or almost anything that did not cost very much for lagniappe, and the grocer who gave the most lagniappe would get the most trade from us kids." [178]

loot Large sum of money. ". . . [R]ich ofay (white) business men and planters would come from all over the South and spend some awful large amounts of loot." [147]

luck up To become lucky. "Before I lucked up on store trousers I used to wear my stepfather's trousers, rolling them up from the bottom so that they looked like plus fours or knickers." [26]

mash Flirting with opposite sex. ". . . [T]o me it was just another mash—that's what we called flirting in those days. We would use the expression, 'The lady has a mash on you,' and then we would poke our chests way out. . . ." [151]

mess around with To insult, tease, harass. "Nobody dared to mess around with slippers. He was a good man with a pistol. . . . He could fight fair and he could fight dirty." [201–202]

ofay A white person. "[H]e had the features and even the voice of a white boy—an ofay. . . ." [238]

old lady A wife, especially one's own wife. "So you've been in another man's house with his old lady?" [122]

old man A sugar daddy or John. "I was so gone over her we never mentioned she had an 'Old Man'—the name we used for a common-law husband." [152]

pad Prostitute's place of business; a crib. ". . . [W]omen walking the streets for tricks to take to their 'pads' . . ." [8]

pass the hat "Singing at random we wandered through the streets until someone called to us to sing a few songs. Afterwards we would pass our hats and at the end of the night we would divvy up." [34]

quail A cornet or trumpet. "Just listen to that son-of-a-bitch blow that quail!" [115]

rooky New in one's work. "They (inmates in Waif's Home) gave me the rooky greeting saying, 'Welcome, Newcomer.'" [37]

round up To arrest and bring to jail. "Fellows were rounded up in a raid on a gambling house or saloon." [126]

scrounge To steal, borrow, or bum. ". . . [S]leeping under old houses . . . and eating what little he could scrounge." [43]

second lining Following someone in hopes of being invited to participate. "When I was 'second lining'—that is, following the brass bands in parades. . . ." [24]

sharp Stylish, smartly dressed. "I had on a brand new Stetson, my fine black suit and new patent leather shoes. Believe me, I was a sharp cat." [164]

sides Artificial padding worn over a woman's hips or thighs. "When she undressed she pulled off a pair of 'sides,' artificial hips she wore to give herself a good figure." [151]

sit in To join a game, usually of cards. "I would sit in with the . . . hustlers who really knew how to gamble." [123]

solid sender Great, exhilarating thing. "It's a funny thing how life can be such a drag one minute and a solid sender the next." [126]

sport Carefree, wisecracking roué. "Those sports gave me so much (money) that I had to borrow hats . . . to hold it all." [48]

sport up Visiting bars, brothels, gambling casinos. ". . . [T]he night Mayann and I went out sporting 'em up. After we left Savocas' we went to Spanol's tonk around the corner." [199]

spring Get another's release from jail. "Whenever a crowd of fellows were rounded up in a raid on a gambling house, the proprietor knew how to 'spring' them, that is, get them out of jail." [126]

sticking Loaded with money. "'You been up North blowing that horn o' your'n. I know you're sticking.' He meant he knew I had plenty of money." [212]

sweetheart To court. "The first person I ran into was Cocaine Buddy Martin, whose sister Bella I used to sweetheart." [56–57]

tonk Honky-tonk. ". . . [T]he cops might close the tonk down any minute." [60]

trick A prostitute's customer. ". . . [L]ots of women walking the streets for tricks to take to their . . . rooms." [8]

wash out To fail or be beaten. "I would sit in with . . . hustlers who really knew how to gamble. I always got washed out." [123]

JOSHUA BERRETT

LOUIS ARMSTRONG AND OPERA (EXCERPT) (1992)

Adapted from The Musical Quarterly, *Summer 1992*

Most compelling about Armstrong's early years in New Orleans is how his odd jobs taught him valuable lessons about music. Working for a junk dealer, delivering coal, and unloading boats brought him into contact with Jewish and Italian immigrant families such as the Karnofskys and Matrangas. These formative experiences helped shape his earliest taste in record collecting—a taste broad enough to encompass selections by the Original Dixieland Jazz Band and performances by opera singers on the order of Caruso and Galli-Curci—these records were to have significant implications for his whole creative process, a topic that is addressed in an excerpt from my article "Louis Armstrong and Opera" (the complete version appeared in The Musical Quarterly, *Summer 1992, Volume 76, Number 2). That article was based on a research project undertaken at the Institute for Jazz Studies at Rutgers in 1988, when, thanks to a grant from the New Jersey Department of Higher Education, I participated in a Summer Institute for Jazz Educators directed by Lewis Porter. —JB*

After I finished my concert at the Neon [sic] Concert Hall I had to rush over to La Scala and stand by those big cats like Verdi and Wagner, and all of them, and take pictures, 'cause they figure our music is the same— we play 'em both from the heart; and they wanted that picture to put up in the lobby, me standing by those big boys there.

Louis Armstrong's words recount one of the many "photo opportunities" on his 1955–56 world tour. His comment that "our music is the same—we play 'em both from the heart" may sound like little more than a sentimental platitude; however, it actually points to a fascinating and important characteristic of Armstrong's creativity. Contrary to popular stereotypes, Louis Armstrong was no American Primitive, although for publicity purposes he did cultivate that image at times; he was, rather, a literate, acutely observant artist whose music reflects a broad listening experience, catholic taste, and a consummate gift for weaving a welter of random impressions garnered from disparate sources into his improvisations.

Traditionally, Armstrong's artistry has been defined largely in terms of a lineage tracing his heredity to such cornet progenitors as Buddy Bolden, Buddy Petit, Bunk Johnson, Freddie Keppard, and Joe Oliver. Tracing his musical genealogy has been a useful but limited approach; it does little to explain his evolution from a young boy singing on street corners to a mature artist. This article takes instead a contextual approach to his work, examining the milieu from which his music sprang and the operatic influences to which he was exposed. These influences, which I propose were deeply internalized and fluently expressed in his brilliant improvisations, contributed to a complex and fascinating cognitive process that we are now only beginning to appreciate.

Before he ever played a note on the cornet or trumpet, Armstrong was singing on New Orleans street corners, making music "from the heart." In his memoir "Negroe [sic] Neighborhood" (part of "The New Orleans Jewish Family" in this volume) he pays touching homage to a major influence in his early life, the Russian-Jewish Karnofsky family who, when he was seven years old, gave him his first job, encouraged him in his singing, and loaned him the money to buy his first cornet. This intensely personal and, in the words of Gary Giddins, "achingly candid" document powerfully describes the Karnofskys's importance to the young boy. "They were always warm and kind to me—something a kid could use at seven and just starting out in the world. . . . When I reached the age of eleven I began to realize that it was the Jewish family who instilled in me singing from the heart."

The role of these early experiences in Armstrong's evolving style emerges in pointed detail in an interview with Richard Hadlock (San Francisco, February 1962):

Hadlock: *I think that maybe some of the youngsters are just starting to think about this again—and that's this singing on the horn or playing like a singer would, giving full value to each note.*

Armstrong: That's all you need in music. I always felt that way, even when I was singing in a little quartet; and even if I put the horn down there would be some spot where I can drive up a little livin'—something—just be around music, because I love a change.

Hadlock: *Did you get that approach from having been a singer?*

Armstrong: In a quartet when a little kid. I sang bass.

Hadlock: *That affected the way you played too?*

Armstrong: I figure singing and playing is the same. Every note's got to have its value. Listening to people like Joe Oliver and them brass bands playing those funeral marches. Just like the symphony would be in that mousy era when they get soft. [Sings opening of "Serenade" from Romberg's *The Student Prince*.] That's jazz. That's the way I look at it. Anything you can express to the public is jazz. But they get too far out. They're goin' to lose themselves . . . but I don't bother about that or about what the other fellow is doing.

Hadlock: *There's a lot of feeling of opera singing.*

Armstrong: Most of it in the olden days—French opera and things like that. Most of that music comes from the opera.

Hadlock: *Bechet had a lot of it in him.*

Armstrong: [Spontaneously bursts out singing the melody of Maddalena's opening line, *"Ah! Ah! Rido ben di core / Ché tai baie costan poco"* from the *Rigoletto* Quartet.] That's the first thing that I used to make all the time.

The excerpt from the *Rigoletto* Quartet is fully consistent with what is known about Armstrong's earliest preferences in music. When he started buying records around 1917 and 1918 he gravitated toward leading pop and opera singers as well as the Original Dixieland Jazz Band, a fact that is borne out by his comments to Richard Meryman: "Big event for me then was buying a wind-up victrola. Most of my records were the Original Dixieland Jazz Band—Larry Shields and his bunch. They were the first to record the music I played. I had Caruso records too, and Henry Burr, Galli-Curci, Tetrazzini—they were all my favorites. Then there was the Irish tenor, McCormack—beautiful phrasing."

This taste in record collecting was formed in part by the environment in which he grew up. Armstrong's initial exposure to Italian singers took place against a background of southern Italian immigrants crowded into the neighborhoods of the French Quarter, Storyville, and environs during the first decade or so of the twentieth century. Young Louis had many odd jobs that took him all over the city of New Orleans, including into the Italian neighborhoods where he had an ample opportunity to hear recorded and live Italian music both in the streets and in customers' homes. On one job, for example, he made the rounds in a junk wagon with his boss, Lorenzo, of whom he writes: "He was a very funny fellow and he did not pay me much, but the fun we used to have going all over the city to collect rags, bones and bottles from the rich as well as the poor! . . . When I was with him I was in my element. The things he said about music held me spellbound, and he blew that old, beat-up tin horn with such warmth." Armstrong also worked for the Italian Matranga family on the docks and in the saloon of Henry Matranga. Tad Jones, who is writing a detailed study of the New Orleans neighborhoods in which Armstrong lived and worked, has ascertained that Louis played in Matranga's saloon on the 1200 block of Perdido, near where the Armstrongs lived at the time. Louis was also a regular in the Matranga home on the 400 block of South Saratoga, where he ate meals. "My mother used to work at his home, just a few blocks away from his saloon, and I used to go to see her there. If I came at mealtime they would make me sit down in the kitchen and eat a plate of their good Italian spaghetti. That family always enjoyed seeing me eat." And Jones speculates that "he may have heard music in the home—more than likely he would have, since his mother worked there. There was probably an old-style phonograph where I am sure recordings were played. That would seem most likely. There were a number of saloons in that area which Italians ran, [as well as] grocery stores. He was in proximity of hearing recorded music, and possibly, in that area, hearing Italian celebrations of some type with music by Italian bands."

Within a broader framework, Armstrong's music represents a unique combination of what he heard and what he studied. His cognitive process was shaped by his underlying values, both musical and general. His position articulated in the Hadlock interview that "anything you can express to the public is jazz" is consistent with his broad-based human values built around a solid core of common sense. These values he in turn communicated to his adopted son Clarence: "I managed to teach him the necessary things in life, such as being courteous, having respect for other people, and last but not least, having good common sense."

Those who disparage Armstrong as an "entertainer," who was somehow of a lower order than an "artist," completely miss his significance.

Dan Morgenstern, in concluding his introduction to *Satchmo: My Life in New Orleans,* says, "Paradoxically, what Armstrong created to entertain happens to surpass in artistry a great deal (if not most) of what self-styled artists have to offer." His artistry drew upon a broad range of experience, but throughout it all he never superimposed hierarchies of "highbrow" or "lowbrow" on his musical taste. He was open to any opportunity, whether playing behind the lead in the bands of Oliver or Henderson, meeting the challenges posed by the broad-based repertoire of Tate's orchestra, playing behind blues singers, or fronting his own groups.

For all their vast differences in style and sound, Louis Armstrong and Charles Ives show an affinity in their underlying egalitarian attitude toward the source of musical material. The following conductor's note to the second movement of Ives's Fourth Symphony—a quotation from an "unknown philosopher of a half century ago" (presumed by J. Peter Burkholder to be Ives's father, George)—would have been readily accepted by Armstrong (though, coming as he did from the Battlefield neighborhood of New Orleans, he might well have questioned whether "all music is from heaven"): "How can there be any bad music? All music is from heaven. If there is anything bad in it, I put it there—by my implications and my limitations. Nature builds the mountains and meadows and man puts in the fences and labels."

In the broader context of American culture, Armstrong's connection with opera can be seen as extending and modifying a practice traceable to the period of Frank Johnson, who was probably the preeminent bandleader in the United States in the first third of the nineteenth century. Johnson introduced the idea of the promenade concert to this country, including on his programs operatic highlights (overtures and potpourris). At dances he performed opera quadrilles and medleys of operatic hit tunes. Around mid-century, George Templeton Strong wrote, "the people are *Sonnambula*-mad." Walt Whitman, writing in 1891, recalled that as a youth he was "fed and bred under the Italian dispensation."

An anecdote by the singer Mabel Mercer attests to the blurring of distinctions between vaudeville and opera and dramatically illustrates a high degree of literacy associated with black entertainers and their performance of black musicals during a period coinciding with the formative years of Armstrong's career. Mercer says that a revue in which she appeared in London around 1916 included an adaptation of a Zulu scene from *In Dahomey,* climaxed by a performance "in flawless Italian" of the sextet from *Lucia di Lammermoor.* She adds, "the audience broke into wild applause, because they were thinking how clever the director was to be able to get these savages to phonetically learn an Italian aria."

Armstrong, too, was stereotypically viewed as a happy savage. However, his uncanny ability to weave effortlessly a welter of impressions from disparate sources into his improvisations, without regard for what was "highbrow" or "lowbrow," is a clear product of his highly sophisticated ear and his careful preparation of material in different keys. Moreover, as the world's foremost jazz trumpeter and vocalist, always intent on pleasing an audience, he was more the prima donna "entertainer" than an ensemble player.

Armstrong's success with the public was made possible by the confluence of many forces discussed here. Particularly important is the fact that during his time jazz was becoming an integral part of popular culture through radio, recordings, and movies; opera too was being popularized, even to the point of comic irreverence, as in the Marx Brothers's classic romp *A Night at the Opera* (1935). In this context we can best see Armstrong's position as a musician who eludes neat categories, with virtually universal acceptance by the public. A major creative artist with more than eighty compositions to his credit, he towers above his colleagues as he assumes his place beside "those big cats like Verdi and Wagner."

Part Two

I'M A DING DONG DADDY

LOUIS AND HOT JAZZ

One of the big events for Armstrong around 1918 was the purchase of a wind-up Victrola, and among the very first records he acquired were those by a five-piece combo called the Original Dixieland Jazz Band. As he once put it: "They were the first to record the music I played." These "untuneful harmonists playing peppery melodies," as *The New York Times* billed them in a period ad, represented a vital early form of "hot" jazz—a raw, gutsy sound replete with barnyard clichés, driven by frenetic rhythms. While they often sound blatantly crude when compared with later groups of the 1920s such as Jelly Roll Morton and His Red Hot Peppers—or, more pointedly, Louis Armstrong and His Hot Five, and Louis Armstrong and His Hot Seven—the Original Dixieland Jazz Band forms an integral part of the history of "hot" jazz. Something of the reaction that this style prompted in the 1920s can be measured by the response of its detractors—musicians such as Paul Whiteman, Dave Peyton, or Erskine Tate. Among the purveyors of "legitimate," "sweet," or "symphonic jazz," these musicians sought to tame the wild beast and "make a lady out of jazz." Active primarily in white ballrooms and fashionable movie theaters before the advent of sound, they fronted sizable bands playing from written

New Orleans saxophonist Sidney Bechet, producer Clarence Williams, and Armstrong in Decca's studios, 1940. Courtesy Frank Driggs Collection.

arrangements rather than simply "faking" their parts. Not for them the improvisation of "hot" jazz, where the development of a melodic theme and its harmony was limited by only the player's imagination.

Although Armstrong played intermittently in Chicago with Erskine Tate's group at the upscale Vendome Theater (performing symphonic staples such as the "Intermezzo" from *Cavalleria Rusticana* or the overture to Rossini's *William Tell*), it was his "hot" solos there and elsewhere that caught the public's ear and were critical in helping make his brand of "hot" jazz the international rage.

Something of the historic significance and stylistic background of these solos is conveyed by the following excerpts from liner notes by Lewis Porter on Armstrong's early recording career in New York, from 1923–25 when he collaborated with Sidney Bechet. Packaged as a two-record set in the Smithsonian Collection of Recordings, these performances reveal a great deal about the burgeoning identity of Armstrong as the quintessential modern jazz soloist, including: his appropriation and adaptation of the New Orleans clarinet tradition as virtuosically transformed by Bechet (later in the decade Armstrong was to have an analogous influence on the "trumpet style" of Earl Hines's piano playing); the seminal idea of composing a solo onstage based on the chord progression (or changes) of a song rather than its melody; the process of drawing upon a "bag" of "licks," some borrowed from opera; his liberation of the soloist, even though he could at times be the consummate sideman playing written arrangements in such groups as the Fletcher Henderson Orchestra; his playing of brilliantly syncopated breaks; and his sensitive accompanying of blues singers. These features made their impact through not only Armstrong's many recordings and live appearances, but also through the publication in 1927 of two albums of his music, *Louis Armstrong's 50 Hot Choruses for Cornet* and *Louis Armstrong's 125 Jazz Breaks for Cornet*. —JB

LEWIS PORTER

LOUIS ARMSTRONG AND SIDNEY BECHET IN NEW YORK, 1923–1925 (EXCERPTS) (1981)

The Smithsonian Collection of Recordings, RO 26

In 1923 clarinetist and soprano saxophonist Sidney Bechet (1897–1959) was the most accomplished wind-instrument soloist in jazz. By 1925 he had been equaled and finally surpassed by trumpeter Louis Armstrong (1901–1971), himself already the beneficiary of playing with Bechet on a number of recordings. The highlights among their collaborations are included in this package, as well as items featuring each player individually. To complete the picture, many of the other recording sessions they participated in during this period are mentioned in the course of these notes.

The fact that Bechet did not achieve anything like Armstrong's position of influence and popularity attests to the capricious nature of the music business. But at least for the brief period covered by this collection, both players, individually and collectively, had a tremendous impact on jazz in New York and, consequently, throughout the country.

Soloist versus Ensemble

The modern image of the jazz soloist—a daring virtuoso free to produce whatever sounds he desires—was not yet a reality in 1923. Jazz musicians soloed, to be sure; but the combined evidence of recordings and oral histories indicates that they generally conceived of a solo as a set piece, an original composition to be worked on and polished up in private and to be played in roughly the same way at each performance. However, this does not mean that there was no improvisation; since the solos were memorized rather than written down, some variation was permissible as well as desirable. (Compare, for example, the two 1923 versions of King Oliver's "Dippermouth Blues" solo: the Okeh version available on *King Oliver's Jazz Band 1925,* Smithsonian Collection R001, and the Gennett version on *Louis Armstrong and King Oliver: 1923,* Milestones 47017). And, on an inspired evening the jazz player would spontaneously come up with new ideas which, remembered afterward, could be incorporated into future solos. Improvisation and composition were, and are, inseparable.

The innovations of Armstrong and Bechet did not represent complete breaks with the past but, rather, changes of emphasis. These two did much more of their composing "onstage" than did their contemporaries, and this proved to be the wave of the future. Today jazz musicians devote much of their practice time to patterns and scales which are applicable to a variety of pieces, rather than planning individual solos in detail.

Another procedure heard in these recordings which proved to be historically significant was that of basing a solo more on the chord progression (changes) of a song than on its melody. This, too, came directly from established jazz conventions. In the New Orleans ensembles that had nurtured the young Bechet and Armstrong, only the lead cornetist was confined to paraphrasing the melody (to use André Hodeir's term), and even he had to be able to hear chords in order to select appropriate ornamental notes. Meanwhile, the trombonist created a slower countermelody based on the same chord progression.

Of the three, the clarinetist was the least concerned with the written melody. He played florid obbligati, somewhat in "classical" style, using scales and arpeggiated chords. Anyone familiar with the frequently recorded "High Society" clarinet solo (adapted from a published Robert Recker arrangement, or Johnny Dodds's solo on "Dippermouth Blues," must relinquish the oft-advanced idea (which I hope never again to see in print!) that the beboppers of the 1940s were the first to play on chord changes.

(The finest recorded examples of the New Orleans ensemble I've just described are commonly held to be to be those of King Oliver's Creole Jazz Band. Their complete Okeh recordings, available on Smithsonian R001, include "High Society" and one of their two versions of "Dippermouth Blues.")

What you will hear in this collection is, first of all, Sidney Bechet's virtuosic [sic] extension of the New Orleans clarinet tradition, then Louis Armstrong's adaptation of that tradition to the cornet. (At this time Armstrong was playing cornet rather than trumpet, but the differences between are so slight that I will not bother to distinguish between them for the most part). In fact, the adaptation process had begun some years before, when both artists were still in New Orleans, according to Bechet's autobiography, *Treat It Gentle* (p. 92, reprinted by Da Capo Press, 1976):

> (Black Benny) said to me one day, "You think you can play. But I know a little boy right around the corner from my place; he can play 'High Society' better than you." So I said, "Well, I'd like to see that boy." He said, "All right, come over with me." And we went, and it was Louis. And I'll be doggone if he didn't play "High Society" on the cornet. . . . It was very hard for clarinet to do, and really unthinkable for cornet to do at those times. But Louis, he did it. So I was very pleased about it.

But Armstrong's biggest influence was, naturally, a cornetist—King Oliver. It was Oliver who taught him how to use his virtuosity with taste, as Armstrong recalled in a BBC-TV interview broadcast on his seventieth birthday:

> I was just like a clarinet player, like the guys run up and down the horn nowadays, boppin' and things. I was doin' all that, fast fingers and everything. So he (Oliver) used to tell me: "Play some lead on that horn, boy." (Quoted in Henry Pleasants, *The Great American Popular Singers*, Simon & Schuster, 1974, p. 101)

What made Armstrong so great was the way he finally managed to combine clarinet-like facility and freedom with Oliver's taste and concern for making every note count, exciting a "new" brass tradition of worldwide influence.

There were other musicians—notably cornetist Bix Beiderbecke—who were working toward the liberation of the jazz soloist during this time, but it was Armstrong, by virtue of his musical, emotional, and personal ebullience, who became the leader of the revolution in jazz. He had found in Bechet a kindred spirit who was already exploring advanced ideas on his instrument. Bechet no doubt influenced many musicians, especially saxophonists and clarinetists, during the short time he was in New York; but he set sail for Europe too soon, leaving Armstrong to carry the message to the jazz world. In achieving new heights of freedom and expression on the trumpet, Armstrong set an example that other trumpeters, as well as trombonists, pianists, guitarists, and eventually even bassists, were to follow. Gunther Schuller has written in the first chapter of his book (*Early Jazz*) of the "democratization" of the beat in jazz; here was the beginning of the democratization of its instruments.

LIL HARDIN-ARMSTRONG

LIL AND LOUIS: *SATCHMO AND ME* (EXCERPTS)

Excerpts transcribed from Satchmo and Me, *Riverside RLP 12-120*

Lillian Hardin (1898–1971), the second of Armstrong's four wives—he married her on February 5, 1924—was a decisive influence on the diamond-in-the-rough Armstrong. Very much the urban sophisticate, willful and assertive, she lay down the law when it came to matters of wardrobe, weight loss, and most important, persuading him to leave King Oliver to strike out on his own. A literate rather than purely "ear" musician, Lil had already made a name for herself in Chicago by the time Louis came to town on August 8, 1922. She had graduated from demonstrating sheet music, anything and everything from J. S. Bach to W. C. Handy, at Jones's Music Store on South State Street, to being a valued pianist in King Oliver's Creole Jazz Band.

The excerpts transcribed from her reminiscences, Satchmo and

Me *(Riverside RLP 12-120), detail her first meeting with Louis at the Dreamland Café, where she was working at the time, and describes the events that ensued once Armstrong had left King Oliver and was hired away by Fletcher Henderson in New York, only to be summoned back to Chicago by Lil herself. Of special interest is her passing reference to legendary cornetist Bix Beiderbecke (1903–31)—Armstrong and Beiderbecke had great regard for each other—however, contrary to what Hardin suggests, Beiderbecke was not in Paul Whiteman's band as early as 1922–23. —JB*

When [King Oliver] sent for Louis to join him at the Royal Garden—I'm at Dreamland, and the second night that he's there he brings Louis over to the Dreamland to meet me, and I met him while I was playing. I was a little disappointed because all the musicians called him "Little Louis," and he weighed 226 lbs., and I said "Little Louis"? I wonder why they call him "Little Louis" as fat as he is?

Well, I was disappointed all round 'cause I didn't like the way he was dressed, I didn't like his hairdo, he had bangs—that was the style in New Orleans he told me later.

[As for listening to Louis's cornet] I paid no attention to it. I must admit that from a musical standpoint jazz didn't mean anything too much to me. Maybe it's because I was as young as I was, and was interested in the money. . . . It was quite a change for me to be able to handle so much money to begin with . . . because as a rule girls, when they first start out working . . . don't make too much money. By the time I was with King Oliver I was making about $100 a week.

That's a lot of money then; no taxes, my mother didn't take any money, nothing. Just buy ice cream and clothes. I wasn't too interested in music, or musicians, or their ability. I paid no attention. I just liked the thing as a whole. I liked the numbers we were playing, but if you'd tell me he was good or that was good . . . it wouldn't make any difference. I wouldn't know the difference.

While we were playing at the Royal Garden a bunch of white musicians—10, 12, 15, sometimes 20, would come and they would all roll up in front of the bandstand to listen. I used to wonder to myself what they were listening [to] . . . what particular thing. That's how much I knew about what we were doing.

Louis and Joe said . . . that they were of some of Paul Whiteman's band and that Bix was in the bunch. They were in that bunch that used to come, but I didn't know their names. . . . You see, the boys never talked to me anyway. They used to talk to Louis and King Oliver and Johnny.

———

I probably would have never paid any attention to Louis's playing if King Oliver hadn't said to me one night that Louis could play better than he could. He says: "But as long as I keep him with me he won't be able to get ahead of me; I'll still be the King."

After he told me that I started listening. But, it was still very difficult to listen to somebody play who's always playing second to somebody else. . . .

Then I got the record date to make the Gennett Record. At the first session we recorded in the great big horn . . . and the band was around the horn. Louis was there, as he always was, next to Joe. Didn't work out; couldn't hear no Joe's playing. So they moved Louis way over in the corner, away from the band. And Louis was standing over there looking so lonesome. He thought it was bad for him to be away from the band. He was looking so sad and I'd look back at him, smile, you know. . . . Louis was at least 12–15 feet from us the whole session. So then I was convinced. H'm yes, he really can play better because if his tone overshadows Joe that much he's got to be better . . . I comes to feeling sorry for him . . . that's a bad sign when you begin to feel sorry for a man.

Louis and I started going to dances and . . . things together. Then we started getting to be sweethearts. In the meantime Oliver was keeping Louis's money; he was saving part of his salary for him. So, after I started going out with Louis I said, "No, no . . . you don't look right . . . you've got to change your clothes." So he said: "What's the matter with my clothes?" Everything he had on was second-hand. So I said: "Where's your money?" He said: "Joe keeps my money." I said: "Well, Joe doesn't need to keep your money; you keep your own money . . . go to Joe and get your money." He said: "What . . . I'm working for Mr. Joe . . . he sent for me, he looks after me."

I said: "No, I'm going to look after you from now on. I'm going to get you some clothes [and] you're going to give me my money back." So I went downtown and bought him a . . . grey overcoat and a $20 velour hat, and brought it back. So he tried the coat on and it fit perfectly, and he tried the hat on . . . the hat I measured with a tape measure and it fit as it should fit. But, in New Orleans they were used to wearing the hat sitting right on top . . . so he told me the hat was too big. . . . [W]e had a big argument on that. So I said: "Well, you go back down there now . . . wear your coat, and you try the hat on. So he came back with the same size hat in another color!

When he came to work that night the manager and all of them said: "Ooh, look at Louis, look at Louis, isn't he sharp! . . ."

But, Joe, he didn't say a word. He was very angry and told Louis that I was nothing but a spoiled kid, that I didn't have to give any money to home, that I could buy ice cream and clothes with all my money, and that I would make him spend all of his money like I did; he would have nothing. . . .

King Oliver's Creole Jazz Band, c. 1922, in Chicago. Left to right: Johnny Dodds (clarinet), Baby Dodds (drums), Honoré Dutrey (trombone), L. Armstrong (second trumpet), King Oliver (lead trumpet), Lil Hardin (piano), and Bill Johnson (banjo). Photo: Corbis-Bettmann.

I'm a Ding Dong Daddy

But, Louis kind of liked the way he looked himself. He liked looking good and he kind of liked me too. After Joe told him that I said: "Now you just get all your money from Joe and keep it yourself." So he did. . . .

Johnny Dodds found out that Joe had been collecting $95 for each member of the band while he had been paying us $75. So naturally he had been making $20 a week apiece off us for how long! So Johnny Dodds and Baby Dodds, they threatened to beat Joe up. Joe brought his pistol every night to work in his trumpet case. Everybody gave him their notice, except Louis. Louis always was so crazy about Joe; he was his idol. He wouldn't quit, so naturally I didn't quit. That's why you don't find Dutrey, Johnny Dodds, and Baby Dodds on this eastern tour with us; he had to replace everybody except Louis and myself. . . .

At first when he was working with King Oliver he wanted to play [like] the King. Because when we made the "Dippermouth Blues" and that solo became very popular . . . naturally Louis wanted to play the solo too. So we used to practice it at home—Louis on the trumpet and me on the piano; and Louis never could play that solo like Joe. I think it kind of discouraged him because Joe was his idol and he wanted to play like Joe.

Deep down . . . I got the idea that he should play by himself . . . so long as he is with Joe he would never bring himself out. I could hear Louis coming home whistling much more than a block away. He had the most beautiful shrill whistle; and all those riffs that he later made in his music he used to whistle 'em—such beautiful riffs and runs, and trills and things. I told him: "You can't be married to Joe and to me."

. . . Louis quit. Then he said: "What am I going to do?" So I said: "Just go out . . . go hang around musicians, find out who needs a trumpet player." The first band he went to was Sammy Stewart's orchestra; he had quite a society band . . . Sammy just slightly turned around and snapped at him: " No, I don't need anybody."

. . . Louis came back so disheartened. Then he hears that Ollie Powers is getting a band together. So he went to see Ollie Powers and, sure enough, Ollie Powers hired him . . . he had to be first [trumpet] because he was the only trumpet player they had. . . . That's when Louis started playing and showing what he had in himself, because as long as he was with King Oliver he was playing second to Joe and trying to play Joe's solos, which he couldn't play, because it wasn't his style at all. . . .

While he was playing with Ollie Powers, Fletcher Henderson heard about him and sent for him to come to New York and to play with him at the Roseland [Ballroom]. . . . Fletcher paid $55 a week. Louis came alone and I joined him after a couple of weeks. I noticed in Fletcher's billing there was nothing but "Fletcher Henderson's Orchestra"—nobody else's name.

I went back home [to Chicago] and bands were always changing. So I went to the Dreamland and I said: "I want to put a band in, I want to bring my husband back from New York, and I want him to be featured, I want $75 a week for him, and I want his name out there in front. . . ." I had him make a sign—"Louis Armstrong, the World's Greatest Trumpet Player."

I wrote and told Louis: "Give Fletcher your two weeks' notice and come on back home. I've got a job for you at $75 a week. . . ."

Louis didn't believe me . . . he didn't want to leave . . . he wasn't anxious to be a star . . . so he said he wasn't coming back.

So I said: "Well, I've already got the job, and if you're not here by whatever the date was . . . if you're not here by this date, then don't come at all." The next day I got a wire: "I will be there. . . ."

While he was at the Vendome [Theater] he made a high F. . . . People

Louis Armstrong, Chicago, 1925. Courtesy Frank Driggs Collection.

would come to two or three shows just to see if he was ever going to miss that high F; he never missed it. During the time that he had been playing . . . at the Vendome Theater and the Dreamland, Tommy Rockwell had heard him. It was he who suggested that he form a recording outfit, and as a result it was called Louis Armstrong's Hot Five. Now what we would do is have a date and they would tell you how many records you were going to make or how many numbers, and we would write the required numbers.

. . . Word was getting around that Louis was a good trumpet player. One night Freddie Keppard came in to hear us. . . . Freddie stood there by the bandstand, and he listened a while. Then he said to Louis: "Boy, let me have your trumpet." So Louis looked at me and I bowed my head, so Louis gave him the trumpet. So Freddie, he blew—oh, he blew and he blew and he blew. And then the people gave him a nice hand. Then he handed the trumpet back to Louis. And I said: "Now get him, get him!"

Ooh, never in my life have I heard such trumpet playing. If you want to hear Louis play, just hear him play when he's angry. Boy, he blew and people started standing up on top of tables and chairs, screaming. And Freddie eased out real slow. Nobody ever asked Louis for his trumpet again!

MAX JONES

LIL ARMSTRONG, ROYALTIES, AND THE OLD SONGS (1967)

The Melody Maker, 1967

This 1967 Melody Maker *interview with Max Jones gives her an opportunity to talk about her latest work and to give her version of a long-standing copyright feud. Lillian Hardin was given the rights to a number of compositions such as "Struttin' with Some Barbecue"—one of the 1927 signature pieces of Louis Armstrong and His Hot Five (she was the group's pianist), a work that is pure Armstrong in virtually every detail. Yet, when Armstrong's manager wanted to countersue he was told to cease and desist because Louis felt that his former wife needed the royalties more than he did. It is worth noting that Lillian Hardin never remarried, continued living to the end in the house that she and Louis had bought in Chicago at 421 East 44th Street, and—the ultimate irony—suf-*

fered a fatal heart attack on August 28, 1971, while playing a memorial concert for Louis at Chicago's Civic Center Plaza. —JB

Back in London for a few days' holiday over Easter, Lil Armstrong—one-time wife of Louis—enthused about her first visit in fourteen years.

"Do you remember that last time, the concert at Kilburn?" she asked me. "When the mike wouldn't work? That was real funny, eh? But I'm enjoying myself this time. I and a few friends are on a holiday. We're going to Paris, Rome, Barcelona, and Lisbon, then home to Chicago."

Is there any business in the air for the pianist-singer who, as Lillian Hardin, joined King Oliver in 1920?

"Business? I'm talking business. I had an offer for Copenhagen, but I can't make it now as I'm on a 21-day trip. But I'd like to come back, say in late September.

"I could do two weeks in Copenhagen, and a month in Paris if I want to take it. Maybe I could do a few concerts over there at the same time. I know Keith Smith would like to fix up something for me. I was out to his record shop at Richmond over the holiday."

On her previous visit, Lil Armstrong told me she was working as a single, doubling as a tailor and writing a book, *Decie,* on the side. How are these projects progressing?

"So far as music goes, I'm not doing too much now. But when I feel like working I go up to Canada and work by myself. I've been to Toronto, Montreal, Winnipeg. I've worked in Canada with the Scottish bass player, Jimmy McHarg.

"At home I play sometimes at jazz clubs, and do a few TV shows, but not often. Usually I do a set by myself and then the last half with the band.

"But the fact is, I can pick my time to work now because of my royalties. They don't come to an awful lot, but enough to provide the necessities.

"The tailoring, that's really just for myself—a hobby, you know. And the book's still in the making. Two or three publishers have had it and kept it, but they've all wanted to change so many things, and I don't want that.

"It's not quite finished, but the chapters they have they say need altering. It's stories about the early days and so on. It seems if you don't write about dope or something similar, they find it dull."

Getting back to song royalties, I asked Lil which numbers were bringing in the money still.

"Of course, 'Just for a Thrill' is one of my best-known numbers, and

Louis Armstrong's Hot Five, c. 1925. Left to right: L. Armstrong (trumpet), Johnny St. Cyr (banjo), Johnny Dodds (clarinet), Edward "Kid" Ory (trombone), and Lil Hardin-Armstrong (piano). Photo: Corbis-Bettmann.

they brought that back. Ray Charles, Nancy Wilson and many more singers have recorded that.

"As for the old ones from the Louis days: oh there's a gang of them. 'Struttin' with Some Barbecue,' 'Got No Blues,' 'Hotter Than That,' 'I'm Not Rough,' 'Perdido Street Blues,' 'Pencil Papa.'

"When we wrote those tunes, forty years ago and so forth, we didn't think it important to get our songs copyrighted or anything like that. We just put our names on them and thought about the immediate cash. Now I live off them, but it only happened after years.

"There was a big law suit, you know, over 'Barbecue.' It had Lillian Armstrong's name on it, though, so I got that straight."

Does Lil still see Louis these days?

"Yes, about a month ago, when he gave a concert in Chicago." [Lil laughed vigorously.] "'Course, he's not quite so friendly since that law suit. But you know Louis . . . he's all right."

ROBERT DONALDSON DARRELL

A BLACK EULENSPIEGEL FROM NEW ORLEANS (1927–1932)

Phonograph Review, *November 1929, April 1930;* Disques, *September 1932*

Robert Donaldson Darrell (1903–1988) was one of the pioneer discographers in the United States, and his 1936 compilation, The Gramophone Shop Encyclopedia of Recorded Music, *is something of a landmark—most likely the very first reference work of its kind to include selections of dance and popular music along with the classics by European and Russian masters. Born in Newton, Massachusetts, Darrell attended the New England Conservatory of Music and early on developed a taste for the repertoire staples by Beethoven, Wagner, Richard Strauss, Rimsky-Korsakov, and others. But it is to his everlasting credit that he also regularly reviewed recordings of jazz "almost exclusively in instinctive reaction to what I heard . . . I had no real jazz knowledge or background . . . when I began." —JB*

In the September 1932 issue of *Disques* Darrell wrote: ". . . in the fantastic trumpet rhapsodies, sky-scraping glissandos and perfervid pyrotechnics of a black Eulenspiegel from New Orleans, hot jazz redeems a lively art from decay, foreshadows the more fluent, weightless music of the future. Louis Armstrong . . . has brought a barbaric glee and humor to music that it has never known before. His insanely virtuoso playing emancipates the trumpet from the limits set by Berlioz, Rimsky and Strauss. His singing— if that untranslatable vocalization can be called singing—is an exuberant outburst at once primitive and subtle. . . . As a singing actor even Chaliapin must take second rank. Hearing Louis, one realizes that Lady Jazz is still articulate, still unregenerate and fecundly expressive."

However, perhaps more influential was Darrell's column "Dance Records," written under the byline "Rufus," which appeared between 1927 and 1931 in the Boston-based Phonograph Monthly Review. *It was there that he reviewed the latest recordings by Louis Armstrong, Paul Whiteman, King Oliver, Miff Mole, Duke Ellington, Clarence Williams, and many others. The following excerpts, from November 1929 and April 1930 respectively, deal with Armstrong's latest releases on the Okeh label.*

Louis Armstrong maintains his invariably high standard with worthy versions, sweet as well as hot, of "Some of These Days" (don't miss the beginning!) and "When You're Smiling"; the pianist shares honors with Louis himself. . . .

Okeh's star is the astonishing Louis Armstrong, whose orchestra goes from one brilliant success to another with absolutely no let down in the ingenuity or individuality of their playing. This month he does the "Song of the Islands" (Na Lei Hawaii) in ultra-smooth fashion, with marvelous wa-was to a hummed accompaniment, coupled with "Blue Turning Grey Over You," giving free play to Louis's own superb singing—a record not to be missed!

JOSHUA BERRETT

HOT FROM NEW YORK TO LONDON (1999)

The Harlem Renaissance was at its height. In its October 18, 1929 issue *The New York Herald Tribune* editorialized: "Negro dancing and music are, with the exception of Christian Science, the only American *articles d'export* which have really swept the world." It went on: ". . . [W]hen Broadway sets its sign and seal upon a movement it is made . . . the Negro, not merely as a vaudeville joke, and not merely as a highbrow cult, has arrived."

Much of the excitement had been aroused by the show, *Connie's Hot Chocolates,* that had opened on Broadway at the Hudson Theater on June 20, 1929 and was still going strong. This all-black revue written by Thomas "Fats" Waller, Andy Razaf, and Harry Brooks, which had moved from Connie's Inn in Harlem, was noted for two hit songs: "Ain't Misbehavin'" and "What Did I Do to Be So Black and Blue?" Even though Armstrong entered the show after the premiere and was therefore not mentioned in reviews covering the opening, his renditions of these songs were recorded almost immediately—on July 19 and 22, 1929—and took on lives of their own. This was especially true of "Black and Blue," which was elevated by the power of Armstrong's horn and vocal into a poignant, profoundly moving statement about the brutality of racism—a message that was to later inspire Ralph Ellison in his 1952 novel, *Invisible Man*. The following words are perhaps the most compelling:

> I'm white inside,
> It don't help my case,
> 'Cause I can't hide what is on my face.
> How will it end?
> Ain't got a friend,
> My only sin is in my skin.
> What did I do to be so black and blue?

The heat of hot jazz was soon to spread to England and the Continent; and the buzz surrounding Armstrong's tour of Great Britain was considerable. Shortly after his opening at the London Palladium on July 18, 1932 the magazine *Rhythm* ran an article in its August 1932 issue entitled "Greetings to Britain!" by Armstrong himself. In it he reflects on the timing of his coming to England and offers a succinct self-assessment of his style. The following excerpts are illustrative:

> When I boarded the steamer, I thought of another journey I made exactly ten years ago this month. I was a young man, and I packed my precious cornet in New Orleans, along with my other belongings, which didn't make more than a trunkful. I was leaving the city in which I had spent my entire life and where I had all my friends. I was leaving the city for lands I did not know and for people who did not know me. Fortunately, I had the supreme self-confidence of youth. I had evolved what I believed to be a unique style of playing, and I thought it would "catch on."
>
> Some people are tempted to perform certain "stunts" or novelties just because they are novel. But the real test is entertainment. Does it interest your audience? Of course, you can gradually teach them to appreciate new style and absorb new ideas, but it must be gradual and they must have no idea that you are "teaching."
>
> Style is, perhaps, the most important factor in the success of a musician.

You will find that the famous musicians and bands all have a style of their own. I determined from the start to cultivate an original style, and while I tried hard not to force it, I tried out all sorts of ideas, discarding some, practicing others, until I reached, not perfection, since that is unattainable for the true musician, but the best that was in me.

LOUIS ARMSTRONG SPECIAL (1932)

Rhythm, *October 1932*

Armstrong's first tour of Great Britain also provided a golden marketing opportunity for the firm of Henri Selmer, which announced with great fanfare the appearance of both its new Selmer "Challenger" Trumpet and the "Louis Armstrong Special." The October 1932 issue of Rhythm *carried the following ad. —JB*

Louis Armstrong "Special"

Louis "Satchel-mouth" Armstrong is going strong with his new Selmer "Challenger" Trumpet which he acquired on his arrival in London, and with which he was so delighted that he was constrained to pay it an entirely spontaneous tribute during his performances at the London Palladium.

He found the high notes came easier and more bell-like; that the general action was so lively and the response so ready, that he could make greater demands on it than on any other instrument he had ever used before.

This trumpet, engraved "Louis Armstrong Special," is an entirely new model to the original "Challenger," and is supplied, if desired, with a replica of the mouthpiece used by Louis himself.

It is in no sense a freak instrument, but a perfect example of the orchestral trumpet capable of giving you better results than you ever felt yourself capable of producing.

Armstrong as an English gentleman; first London tour, 1932. Courtesy Frank Driggs Collection.

DAN S. INGMAN

ENGLAND'S WELCOME TO LOUIS ARMSTRONG (1932)

The Melody Maker, *August 1932*

The mention of "Satchel-mouth" in the advertising copy prompts a comment or two about the legend surrounding the origins of Armstrong's familiar nickname—the contraction "Satchmo" as applied to the man himself. It seems that it was first used by Armstrong to address his actual trumpet—as in the 1930 recording "You're Driving Me Crazy," where he is heard to say "Watch it, Satchelmouth!" In similar fashion, Selmer's ad for August 1932 speaks of "Satch-mo as a Selmer Challenger Trumpet." And in his piece, "England's Welcome to Louis Armstrong," Dan S. Ingman, "technical editor" of The Melody Maker, *briefly touches on this point while also conveying something of the excitement and moments of panic associated with Armstrong's first visit to London. Yet amid this critical frenzy the reception of Armstrong could at times take on a blatantly racist tone that was anything but welcoming. A week after his debut at the London Palladium on July 18, 1932, a columnist in* The Daily Herald *spewed these words of venom: "Armstrong is the ugliest man I have seen on the music-hall stage. He looks, and behaves, like an untrained gorilla. He might have come straight from some African jungle and then, after being taken to a slop tailor's for a ready-made dress-suit, been put straight on the stage and told to sing."—JB*

Well, he's here! And has been for a fortnight by the time this appears. And has another week to go in London on holiday. After that, probably the Continent, as big offers have already been received from Berlin, Paris and Monte Carlo.

The News

When we first heard the news, some weeks ago, we were rather inclined to discount it. So many times have we heard rumours of dance-band celebrities coming to England, only to find, upon investigation, that Dame Rumour has been lying again.

As usual, however, we investigated the story, to find that this time it was true!

Details at first were vague—if you read the news story in the last issue of *The Melody Maker* you knew very nearly as much as we did at that time.

The little extra we did know at the time was that it had been suggested to Jack Hylton that he provide a supporting band for the Great Man. That J. H. had expressed willingness to help in any way he could, but that he would be out of town.

Still, with characteristic hustle Jack got things on the move. At first it was suggested that a coloured band, formed of English Negroes, would be the most suitable support. And for this purpose, Rudolph Dunbar, the famous *Melody Maker* clarinet authority, was approached and asked if he could form the required band.

Rudolph hustled around, but discovered that there were so few coloured musicians in this country that it would be impossible to form a worth-while band. He suggested going across the Channel to fetch one or two first-class English Negro players whom he knew in Paris.

But this was vetoed on the score of expense, and it was decided to have a white band. Spike Hughes was then approached.

While all this was going on, Harry Foster (the agent who booked Armstrong) had been in cable communication with Armstrong's manager John Collins, and had fixed a complete band of coloured musicians from Paris. (Incidentally, they were two short when they did arrive, and were completed by two players resident in this country.)

The Message

By this time Louis was on the *Majestic,* in the middle of the Atlantic.

Dave Toff, manager for Billy Cotton, had a brainwave, and 'phoned us up on the spur of the moment.

"Why not," he said, "give a reception and dinner to Armstrong from a few West End leaders?"

Great idea! we thought. So we hustled around and made some inquiries. Nearly everyone we spoke to thought it a great idea.

On the strength of this promising beginning we sent a radiogram to Louis on the *Majestic,* welcoming him to England and telling him of the dinner that was being organized in his honour.

On the Wednesday, not having heard from Louis and getting a little anxious, we put through a radio-telephone call to the *Majestic* whilst it was still in mid-ocean.

The line was not very clear (or maybe it was Louis's queer voice!), and we couldn't gather much beyond the fact that the boat was expected to dock at Southampton about mid-day on Friday; that he was O.K. for the dinner; that something was wrong with his trumpet, and that he was worried as to whether he could get it repaired.

Having reassured him about that we went ahead with the dinner arrangements.

On the Thursday we had a radiogram from Manager John Collins thanking us for our welcome and saying that as the *Majestic* was calling at Plymouth he was going to disembark there and would arrive in London about midnight!

Consternation! Frantic telephonings all over the place revealed:

a) That this was the first time the *Majestic* had ever stopped at Plymouth.

b) And that, in consequence, no one knew much about times or station of arrival of the boat train or trains.

c) And, most important of all, that the landing permits of the entire party had been posted to Southampton!

So everyone left it at that, deciding on a right royal reception at the station on the following afternoon.

By dint of almost continuous telephoning we discovered the time and station of the boat train from Plymouth—12:25 A.M. (midnight) at Paddington. Accordingly it was decided that I should go along, in case.

Eventually, the train drew in, and I scanned the compartments in an unexpectant sort of way.

When suddenly!

Good lord! Surely not! Was it? No, it couldn't be!

I jumped on the step as the train was still moving, and thrust my head into the compartment of startled people—three white and two coloured.

"Is this Mr. Armstrong's party?" I asked as casually as possible, with half-a-dozen porters trying to pull me off.

A large man with a small moustache blotted out my view of the compartment.

"Yes!" he said. Which was not much in the way of gossip, but which meant a lot to me.

Then out of the train stepped a young coloured boy and girl. The latter, chic, fashionably dressed and entirely charming, and the former a small, slight fellow with an enormous white cap and a long biscuit-coloured blanket coat. Where was Louis?

"This," said Mr. Collins, "is Mr. and Mrs. Armstrong."

I nearly collapsed! From his photograph I had been expecting a six-footer, broad in proportion, with a moustache, and at least thirty-five years of age.

And this boy. . . . I hardly believed it. That is, not until he spoke. There was absolutely no chance of mistaking that voice!

As a matter of fact, I was partly deceived by the miserable, far-away lighting of Paddington Station. When I saw Louis in daylight the following day, I saw that he was much older than I had thought at first, also that his flowing coat concealed his broadness to a great extent.

The absence of the moustache he explained by saying that he kept on trimmin' it and trimmin' it until one day he trimmed it right out of existence!

I asked Mr. Collins how he got ashore without his permits.

"Oh," he said genially, "I just talked."

Next I asked him if he had fixed up an hotel anywhere. No he hadn't.

So off I went to do a spot of 'phoning.

Fortunately I had a pocketful of coppers. I needed them! I 'phoned up eight famous hotels. Carefully explaining the circumstances.

"Sorry sir, we're full up."

However, I eventually found an hotel just off the Strand, opposite Bush House, which was courteously obliging. So we all piled into taxis, and off we went.

Before they went up in the lift I promised Louis that I would have an expert trumpet repairer round first thing in the morning. At which he seemed rather relieved, although slightly doubtful. I went to bed at 5 A.M.!

Later this same morning, bright and early, we were round at the hotel, together with the trumpet repairer, who looked over the instrument with an expert eye and promised to have it back within an hour.

The Dinner

During that day Louis and his manager had a lot to attend to, so we didn't see much of him, until we called at the hotel at 5:30 P.M. to take him to dinner.

More trouble! Louis had sent his suit to be pressed. It was the only one he had with him, and he travelled in it all the previous day. The rest of his clothes were still in the trunks at Paddington.

Eventually they turned up, so off we all went to the Ambassadors, there to find the following wire from Jack Hylton:

I AM TELEPHONING THIS MESSAGE FROM IRELAND. LET ME OFFER YOU A HEARTY WELCOME TO ENGLAND AND ALL BEST WISHES FOR A TERRIFIC SUCCESS AT THE PALLADIUM ON MONDAY. MY OFFICE IS AT YOUR DISPOSAL FOR ANYTHING YOU MAY WANT. KINDEST REGARDS. JACK HYLTON.

which is what I call real handsome!

The dinner was a great success. Here is a list of those present (it reads like a Musicians' Debrett!):—Garry Alligham (*Evening Standard*); Frank Barnard (Hylton's manager); P. M. Brooks and Peter Burnup (*Era* and *Sunday Referee*); Phil Cardew, Billy Cotton, Lew Davis, Tom Driberg (*Daily Express*); Buddy Featherstonhaugh, Vic Filmer, Roy Fox, Hugh Francis (Director of Parlophone), Nat Gonella, Bruts Gonella, C. Hadley (*The People*), Henry Hall, Harry Hayes, Spike Hughes, Dan Ingman, Edgar Jackson, Freddy Mann, Billy Mason, W. MacQueen-Pope, Ray Noble, Harry Perritt, Arthur Rosebery, Ray Starita, Lew Stone, Dave Toff, Maurice Winnick, Peter Yorke, and, of course, Louis and his manager.

The band arrived from Paris on Saturday afternoon, and Louis spent all the rest of Saturday, all Sunday and most of Monday rehearsing intensively.

During Sunday afternoon more than one musician was seen hanging round the doors of the Palladium. By placing one's ear to the cracks quite a lot could be heard of what was going on inside!

The First Performance

It is needless to say that my excitement was intense at the first house of the Palladium, Monday, July 18th. Louis closed the first half.

When his number went up on the indicator board there was a terrific burst of applause.

Robert Chisholm, who had appeared earlier in the programme singing straight ballads, introduced Louis, paying him tribute in a most sincere and charming manner.

Louis popped out in front of the curtain and took his bow. And what applause there was!

His first number was "Them There Eyes," his second "When You're Smiling," his third ("dedicated to the musicians") "Chinatown, My Chinatown," and his last "You Rascal You!"

Each one was received with tumult. The packed house absolutely rose to it. There is no doubt, of course, that musicians preponderated in the house—familiar faces were everywhere—but members of the lay public, once they had got over their astonishment, were equally enthusiastic.

The first *Melody Maker* "musicians' matinee"—for which the Palladium issued special privilege tickets to our readers—was packed to the doors and the reception beggars description. Robert Chisholm, in introducing Louis, hugged him in front of the curtain! I think he must be a fan!

At this performance Louis changed his programme, substituting "Confessin'" and "Tiger Rag." Of the latter he said, "This tiger runs very fast, so I expect I'll have to play five choruses to catch him up!"

He played *eight*—all different!

His technique, tone and mastery over his instrument (which he calls "Satchmo," a contraction, I am told, of "Satchel Mouth") is uncanny. Top *F*'s bubble about all over the place, and never once does he miss one. He is enormously fond of the lip-trill, which he accomplishes by shaking the instrument wildly with his right hand.

His singing is—well, words just fail me. It's like it is on the records, only a thousand times more so! He works with a microphone and loud-speakers—except for his trumpet playing, which varies from a veritable whisper to roof-raising strength—mostly the latter. His style is peculiarly his own, mostly long, high notes—there is no one else playing anything like it—they couldn't!

But the most amazing thing is his personality. He positively sparkles with showmanship and good humour the whole time. He talks to the microphone, acts with it, makes love to it, curses it ("You Rascal") and is on the move the whole time.

All the time he is singing he carries a handkerchief in his hand and mops his face—perspiration positively drops off him. He puts enough energy in his half-hour's performance to last the average man several years. He is, in short, a unique phenomenon, an electric personality—easily the greatest America has sent us so far.

The band—well, to tell you the truth, beyond noticing that it was painfully under-rehearsed (naturally) and had very little of anything, I didn't notice it. He should have had—and could have had—much better support.

Hail Louis, King of the Trumpet!

ROBERT GOFFIN

HOT JAZZ (1934)

No writers have better captured the role of Armstrong in the jazz milieu on the Continent in the early 1930s than Robert Goffin and Hugues Panassié.

Robert Goffin (1898–1984), a prominent Belgian criminal lawyer who was once dubbed "the world's most versatile jitterbug," authored books on topics ranging from finance, to spiders and rats, to jazz and history. His Aux Frontières du Jazz, *published in 1932, is a provocative period piece, as is the following essay: "Hot Jazz." Though at times overly simplistic in his thinking, Goffin gives a rich sense of context, drawing attention to other jazz musicians, prominent critics, composers, surrealist poets and painters of the day, not to mention the now-obscure James W. Ford, who in 1932 was nominated vice-president of the American Communist Party. Translated from the French by the then virtually unknown Irish playwright Samuel Beckett, the essay originally appeared in 1934 in a limited edition of a monumental compendium, Nancy Cunard's* Negro, An Anthology, *alongside essays by Langston Hughes, W. E. B. Du Bois, Zora Neale Hurston, and many others. —JB*

Not long ago André Coeuroy wrote: "improvised jazz is the most potent force in music at the present time; long may it remain so."

What then exactly is this force that has received the sanction of some of our greatest modern musicians and yet is so little known to others, such as Henry Malherbe, the critic of the *Temps,* that they cannot distinguish it from a counterpoint out of the *Tales of Hoffmann,* and assume in their simplicity that Maurice Yvain, Yves Alix, and Christine are the masters of jazz in France? And how is it possible to associate the discernment of the one with the flounderings of the other?

It is scarcely necessary to repeat that jazz is Afro-American music, developed in the U.S.A. during the war, and attaining its maximum of expression during the period 1920–1930. In my book *On the Frontiers of Jazz* I have dealt at sufficient length with the various musical, technical, and sentimental elements of jazz to make any recapitulation of them here unnecessary. They are common knowledge by now.

Let us therefore confine ourselves to hot jazz, otherwise known as improvised jazz, a type of music that was in existence long before it was formally tabulated. The epithet "hot" is applied to any passage "in which the executant or executants abandon the melodic theme and develop an imaginative structure on the basis of that theme and incorporated with it."

To write the history of this "hot" it would be necessary to trace the whole evolution of jazz in general. For we find its formulae, common enough today, present at every stage of the development of syncopated music. It may be said that jazz would have died a natural death long ago but for this "hot" which has always been its unfailing stimulation, its purest mode of utterance, and to all intents and purposes its *raison d'être.*

The Negro slaves, transplanted from their scorching Africa to the marvelous but inhospitable countries of North America, treasured as their last possession that prodigious sense of rhythm which their traditional dances and their tom-toms beating in the equatorial night had made so ineradicably part of them.

Instinctive and unhappy, highly endowed with the most complete, because the most simple, poetical faculties, they soon began to express their emotions in song; laborers in the cotton plantations, dockers slaving in New Orleans, young Negresses herded together in the markets, fugitives hounded down by mastiffs, they all sang their abominable captivity and the brutal domination of their masters.

The African rhythm had not been lost; they clothed it with simple sentiment, moving expressions of love, biblical cries of celestial yearning, pastoral laments; and thus the Negroes came quite naturally to improvise upon a given rhythmic theme with changes of tone, combinations of voices, and unexpected counterpoints—an improvisation that was to culminate in the incomparable harmonies that have bewitched the whole of Europe.

Little by little this habit of improvisation was extended to the brasses and it became customary for groups of musicians to meet and improvise on the themes of spirituals or simply on a given rhythm, each performer weaving his own melody.

Through the cake-walk, ragtime, and blues Negro music proceeded towards that jazz which was soon to assume such important dimensions and absorb the forms which had gone before it.

At this time jazz still belonged to the black musicians with their ancient traditions of invention and their unique faculty for improvisation and embellishment according to the dictates of their ingenuous hearts. They were the first teachers of the genuine lovers of jazz, while others in whom the commercial instinct was more highly developed ignored this necessary contact and transposed jazz airs in a way quite foreign to the Negro tradition.

This explains the upgrowth of a school of melodic jazz, exploited for a time with great success by Paul Whiteman, Jack Hylton, and other famous leaders, who industrialized jazz to such an extent that nothing remained but a weak dilution devoid of all real musical character.

Melodic jazz has contributed nothing to music and will only be remembered for its unspeakable insipidness; whereas hot jazz is a creative principle which can scarcely fail to affect the music of the future in the most original and unexpected directions.

Hot jazz has already exploded the automatism of musical composition as practiced before the war, when the composer wrote a melody, or a score, on the understanding that its realization should only vary in accordance with the interpretative ability of successive executants, who generally showed but little initiative in their reading of the work and could only express their own personality in their treatment of detail. It is obvious that the music of Beethoven and Debussy is played today exactly as it was when composed, and as it still will be a century hence.

The most extraordinary achievement of hot jazz has been the dissociation of interpretation from the stenographical execution of the work, resulting in a finished musical creation which is as much the work of the performer as of the composer. Up to the time of jazz it is safe to say that the performer was no more than the faithful representative of the composer, an actor whose function was to transmit the least phrase and stimulus of his text. But hot jazz has no patience with stimuli by proxy and requires more of its executants, insisting that each should have ample scope for independence and spontaneity of expression. The task of the performer is to realize, in whatever terms he sees fit, the possibilities of syncopation latent in the generally simple theme written by the composer. He is no longer a conscientious actor reciting his part, but one improvising on the idea or impression of the moment in the Italian *commedia dell'arte* tradition.

The admirable achievement of the first orchestras was an unconscious one, ignored at the time and not fully appreciated till twenty years later. We must turn back to these primitive orchestras and listen humbly to the musical inventions of these untrained Negroes before we can realize the brilliant audacity of these musicians who devoted themselves with enthusiasm and in the face of the most fatuous opposition to this new field, later to become the monopoly of the intelligent and cultivated section of the new generation. From this moment every black orchestra played "hot," with occasional discordant abuse of wa-was, washboards, and drums, which soon calmed down.

At that time only very few whites were able to appreciate the sublime grandeur of this music of the heart. We must not forget the first white orchestras to play "hot" in an America rotten with color prejudice; they laid the foundations of a solidarity and a mutual esteem whose benefits came too late for the majority of those most apt to enjoy them. The Cotton Pickers, New Orleans Rhythm Kings, California Ramblers and Original Dixieland Band will all have an honored place in the eventual pantheon of syncopated music.

Already a definite tradition is taking form in the domain of hot jazz and a codification is being gradually developed; such discerning critics as Panassié, Prunières, Coeuroy, and Sordet concern themselves with the manifestations of hot jazz and keep its development under the strictest observation and control. We are now so familiar with hot jazz, thanks to the countless records made of different orchestras, that we can distinguish the unmistakable note of its lyricism even in the most florid of its vulgarizations.

The talent and genius of certain composers and performers have received their proper recognition. A number of jazz orchestras have conquered the unanimous approval of the public. Finally, certain individuals have enriched jazz with contributions of so personal a nature as cannot fail to delight all those who take an interest in the subject, and it is to them that we owe all that is best in modern jazz.

There are many orchestras in both Europe and America whose musical perfection has elicited the admiration of such competent judges as Ravel, Darius Milhaud, and Stravinsky, and in these orchestras [are] some exponents of "hot" whose style, to my mind, has had an enormous influence on the development of jazz in general. Special reference must be made to Louis Armstrong, whom I consider as the supreme genius of jazz. This extraordinary man has not only revolutionized the treatment of brass instruments but also modified almost every branch of musical technique as practiced today. Nor should we forget that colossus of jazz, the late Bix Beiderbecke, pianist Earl Hines, or tenor saxophonist Coleman Hawkins. There are hundreds of others hardly less important than these four and no less deserving of honor for not being mentioned by name.

Before I conclude this essay I would like to draw attention to the analogy between the acceptance of "hot" and the favor enjoyed throughout Europe by the *Surréaliste* movement. Is it not remarkable that new modes both of sentiment and its exteriorization should have been discovered independently? What Breton and Aragon did for poetry in 1920, Chirico and Ernst for painting, had been instinctively accomplished as early as 1910 by humble Negro musicians, unaided by the control of that critical intelligence that was to prove such an asset to the later initiators.

Finally, it may be mentioned that hot jazz is regarded today by all the intelligent and cultivated youth of Europe as its staple musical nourishment. As Dominique Sordet says, many young men have derived an almost religious enthusiasm from the contact of this superabundant source of lyricism. For them hot jazz is almost the only form of music that has any meaning for their disrupted generation, and it is my fervent hope that America will not disregard this extraordinary element in its sentimental life and one which is surely of more importance than sky-scrapers and Fordism.

HUGUES PANASSIÉ

LOUIS ARMSTRONG AT THE SALLE PLEYEL (1946)

From Douze Années de Jazz

Hugues Panassié (1912–1974) was one of the founders of the Hot Club of France in 1932 as well as Quintette du Hot Club de France two years later—an ensemble identified with Stephane Grappelli and Django Reinhardt. He became a lifelong friend of Armstrong, writing a notable biography and discography of him, producing records, and more. Armstrong himself was honorary president of the Club from 1936 until his death.

The chapter "Louis Armstrong at the Salle Pleyel," from Panassié's Douze Années de Jazz, *a book that covers the years 1927–38, is presented here for the first time in English, in my own translation. His essay is a product of a time when French passions for hot jazz had been aroused by the earlier appearances of Sidney Bechet and Josephine Baker in such musicals as* La Revue Negrè, *not to mention the concerts of Duke Ellington. This was a world in which conditions were markedly more hospitable for blacks than in the United States, shrouded as France was in a certain myth of primitive African innocence. Among the notables in Armstrong's audience on opening night at Salle Pleyel was Darius Milhaud, composer in 1923 of the celebrated jazz-inflected, Afrocentric ballet score* La création du monde. *—JB*

"He sang songs which meant for him alone all the tenderness of his character."

—*Pierre Reverdy,* Risks and Perils

After Duke Ellington's concerts I spent more than a year without setting foot in Paris, despite the appearance of several groups of black musicians, notably the band of Cab Calloway, which was famous but which I did not like very much.

During this year in the country I worked a great deal on my book, *Le Jazz Hot.* Dissatisfied with the initial version, I decided to start it again and shape it very differently because I had come a long way since 1930 in understanding jazz. It is thus that a modest manuscript of about 150 pages became a volume of almost 400 pages.

Thanks to the help of several friends, I managed to find, after many rejections, an editor, Robert Correa, under the condition that a certain number of subscriptions would be guaranteed with the help of the "Hot-Club." The publication of the book was set for early November 1934. If I spent this long a time without returning to Paris, it was because I was awaiting the imminent, long-delayed appearance of Louis Armstrong.

For Louis was again in Europe since July 1933. He had gone to England where Jack Hylton—he had become his manager more or less—had organized some tours for him throughout the whole country. Unfortunately, Louis had come alone from America and the bands that accompanied him [in England] were not up to his level. He played with various English groups, but fortunately also in the end with a band of various black musicians in England; or "on the Continent," as the English say. This last group, though not transcendent, had at least several good members and, above all, an excellent musical director in the person of saxophonist Fletcher Allen; at any rate black musicians were better suited than the English ones to understand Louis and play with him.

It was announced every month that Louis would make an appearance in France, but these announcements did not have any effect. Meanwhile Louis was to be heard in Holland and the Scandinavian countries where he had considerable success, much greater, it would seem, than what he had had in England. He won over to real jazz both amateurs and classical music professionals who had not up to that point shown themselves to be truly rebels. It is thus that A. Ysaÿe, the son of the celebrated violinist, after hearing him in Holland, wrote about him in an enthusiastic article from which I have excerpted these few lines:

> I thought that Goffin exaggerated when he spoke of the "genius" of Armstrong. I have gone by the evidence. One witnesses new manifestations of human genius which taps at the purest root source of a primitive people.
>
> One understands the overwhelming importance of this statement coming from a man raised in the tradition of classical and romantic music, and who, I confess, has not appreciated the true significance of jazz. . . .
>
> Armstrong undoubtedly brings a new element to music. It is true inspiration. . . . It is the purely primitive, a new point of departure, and art, our art, beautiful but stale, will have to bend to the force of this naturalness.[1]

Meanwhile Louis seemed to be settled in England, and there were rumors to the effect that he would never return to the United States. While this was going on at the start of 1934, Jack Hylton and the English jazz review *The Melody Maker* began preparing for a big concert in London with Louis and the greatest of black tenor saxophonists, Coleman Hawkins, who, with Armstrong, was considered the most important jazz figure. In the United States during this period Hawkins played with the orchestra of Fletcher Henderson in which, after ten years, he found himself to be the star attraction.

In drawing Hawkins away from Fletcher Henderson, Jack Hylton scored a major coup against this wonderful orchestra; this did not concern him very much.

Once Hawkins arrived in England the date of the concert was set, and *The Melody Maker* began a major promotion of this evening "which would reunite the two jazz greats"; Louis Armstrong's orchestra was to accompany the two stars.

A few days before the concert, a theatrical coup: Louis Armstrong refuses to play. This at least is what is announced in *The Melody Maker,* which starts publishing article after article to drag Louis in the mud.

Mathison Brooks, the unlikeable manager of this publication, claims that he had tried in vain to let Louis give the reasons for his change of attitude, and that what he got from the great trumpeter was puerile and incomprehensible sulking.

The editors of *The Melody Maker* thought their readers would swallow the stupid story that Louis refused point blank, without any reason, to play this concert. They did nevertheless succeed in somewhat hurting his reputation.

Being absent from these events, I don't expect to solve the question or determine which side was wrong. But I believe it is useful to report here the testimony of a musician who was able to see things with his own eyes; I want to talk about Fletcher Allen, the arranger of Louis's orchestra, who was supposed to participate in this concert. A few months after this incident Fletcher Allen told me that one of the main reasons for Louis's attitude was that Hawkins was not present at the rehearsals that had been organized, or that he had shown up too late to make any serious work possible. And later I had occasion more than once to ascertain how difficult it was to get Hawkins to be present at rehearsals, even the most important ones, which led me to put even more faith in the testimony of Fletcher Allen.

At last Louis set out for France and rented a furnished apartment in Paris on rue de la Tour d'Auvergne, which indicated his intention of remaining some time in our country. Unfortunately, hardly had he arrived than Canetti got him in his clutches, offering himself as manager and succeeding in having him sign a contract on his terms. It was therefore Canetti who became involved in organizing Louis's Paris concerts, and I did not foresee any good coming of it.

Meanwhile the relationship between Canetti and me was slightly poisoned after various incidents, notably the following: Towards the end of 1933 Milton Mesirow (Mezz Mezzrow) had recorded some discs leading a band assembled for his Brunswick Company sessions in New York. Canetti decided to have these discs issued on French Brunswick. He wrote me at the beginning of 1934 that he would be releasing them to the public, but under the name of "Benny Carter and his Orchestra" instead of that of Mesirow. Benny Carter had in fact participated in this recording session, but it was not at all his orchestra; nevertheless Canetti considered the name of Benny Carter more commercial than that of Mesirow because it was much better known.

Before this unacceptable fabrication, I very hastily wrote to Milton in

America to warn him of what was happening. Mesirow went immediately to seek out Jack Kapp (who then directed the Brunswick Company in New York) and demanded that he intervene. Jack Kapp made the Brunswick Company in Paris write saying that Mesirow's name was the only one authorized by signature on the discs in question, and Canetti was obliged to cave in. But, he could not help but understand whence the attack came.

I regretted that I had not thought about informing Louis Armstrong, protecting him against Canetti; but nothing led me to suppose, to foretell, that the latter would aspire to be Louis's manager. Besides, he succeeded in having him sign the contract so quickly that I did not have time to intervene. Yet, there is nothing to prove that Louis would have listened to me for, as far as he was concerned, there was no reason to distrust the person.

The concerts were set for November 9 and 10 at Salle Pleyel. Louis was to be accompanied by the same black band that had backed him in London, with some changes, the chief of which being the departure of Fletcher Allen, who had preferred to rejoin the excellent band of Freddie Taylor at the Villa d'Este, and the inclusion of pianist Herman Chitison. The group consisted, among others, of Alfred Pratt on saxophone and Oliver Times on drums; in the ensemble he was not first-rate.

I hoped to have my book ready in time for sale on the evening of the concert in Salle Pleyel, which would have been all the more opportune because Louis had agreed to write an amusing preface. But I managed only to correct the second proofs, and time was running out despite the good intentions of the editor.

The day before the opening concert I went to the Salle Pleyel where Louis was supposed to rehearse one last time. It was the first time I had come, at last, to hear him other than on disc, and one can imagine my emotion. The first piece tried was "Them There Eyes." After the first chorus by the band Louis opened in the low register of his trumpet—a majestic solo with a melodic line so supple and so delicate that one could believe it to have been created rather for the clarinet. I enjoyed hearing that magnificent sonority, naturally even more beautiful than on disc.

It should be said that I was somewhat concerned because Louis's recent discs were less good than before because of the shrill virtuoso effects to which Louis had a tendency to resort at this point in his career; and John Hammond asserted that his inspiration had declined. I looked with some anxiety for the signs of this so-called decline. But when Louis, after playing the first chorus of "On the Sunny Side of the Street" attacked the second one with grand élan, my concerns were dispelled in one fell swoop. All [the rumors] that I had heard evaporated before this; more than ever, he surpassed all the other jazz musicians by 100 percent and it seemed to me that it would have been crazy not to recognize it.

Besides, when I entered Salle Pleyel the evening of November 9 I had promised myself a wonderful evening. The entrance of Louis on stage was something unforgettable: as the first measures of his band resounded he made his appearance running, like a brilliant meteor flourishing his trumpet, saying some words covered by the sound of the music. He paused, laughing in the middle of the stage. He gave the impression of approaching the room as one approaches a person, as if he did credit to a host and wanted to share as quickly as possible the extraordinary life force that animated him. Contact was immediately established, one was irresistibly captured by the incredible dynamism that was released by his entire being.

When Louis sang, he seemed to address himself to the microphone, to caress it or contrarily to attack it; his eyes gleaming, he gave himself up to series of mimicries that were stupefying in their mobility. A strange thing, watching Louis sing I had the very clear impression of déja vu; but where could I have seen these grimaces, these eyes, in turn fierce and imploring? Suddenly I recalled various black singers, Louis Cole, for example, and I understood: jazz singers had copied not only Louis's vocal style, but also even his facial expressions, all his mimicry. I had not known this last point because records could not have revealed it to me. Needless to say, these imitators were pygmies compared to Louis, both as actors and as singers.

When Louis played the trumpet it was completely different. In general, he planted himself in the front of the stage, closed his eyes, and seemed to improvise, completely enraptured. Meanwhile, his body posture would change little by little in time to his playing; when Louis reached the second chorus with an increased passion, his body bent over more, his trumpet defiantly raised in the air, the music was underlined by the same brief but dynamic movements. And all those who saw Louis know well his gesture when getting ready to hit a very high and difficult note from his instrument: he opens one eye, sometimes both, as if he is contemplating the note before playing it, then gives a slap to his thigh or suddenly lifts a leg, and a low F or G would come out of his instrument with a round, full, admirably pure sonority.

He also had a wonderful way of directing his band when he was not playing. One saw him surveying the stage to and fro, and watching it as if in a daze; he strolled at full speed, knees bent! From time to time he stopped in front of one of his musicians, and with the arm he would make a gesture of pumping him up as one would do with an automobile tire; then he would turn and face the public, grinning as if to call them to witness. And in doing all of this he would not stop humming, as if to better enjoy the playing of the band. Nothing could give an idea of the intense vitality that set off this spectacle.

The concert began with the performance of "Them There Eyes," with a chorus more or less the same as the one I heard the day before at the rehearsal. Louis continued with "I've Got the World on a String," "Dinah," "Hustlin' and Bustlin' for Baby," and plunged into "On the Sunny Side of the Street." It was here that a deplorable incident occurred that greatly undermined Louis's success with the Parisian public.

Louis is not able to sing, in a large hall at least, without the help of a microphone because, contrary to what one would be led to believe from records, his voice is very feeble in spite of the beauty of its timbre. The microphone installed under the supervision of Canetti at Salle Pleyel was poorly adjusted and detracted from it unexpectedly. I don't know how, but from the first numbers it was evident that it was most defective: at times Louis's voice was amplified in monstrous fashion, at others it was not amplified at all in a way where one can perceive no more than a murmur. The situation got worse the moment that Louis began his chorus singing "On the Sunny Side of the Street"; there was a veritable rumble coming out of the amplifiers. The hall lost patience and protested; but a certain number of listeners, showing a gross boorishness, hissed and booed Louis loudly, as if he had been responsible for the poor functioning of the equipment. In the first rows, I was able to see, with a shrinking of the heart, the pained and disturbed expression of Louis, who did not properly understand what was happening.

After this piece the microphone was dispensed with pure and simple. What is inconceivable is that no one set up another one after the intermission, nor for the concert the day after! Louis had to sing without a microphone, in such a way that, except for the listeners in the first rows, his vocal choruses, which were as admirable as his choruses on trumpet, could not be heard. Thus Louis had been able to sing in the United States, in England, in Sweden, wherever, in a word, with a microphone, and he had come to Paris where he had been deprived of this indispensable piece of equipment! Indeed, I had not been wrong in deploring the fact that Canetti had become Louis's manager.[2]

Louis delivered effects of pure virtuosity in only four or five pieces, above all in "St. Louis Blues" and "Tiger Rag," of which the last chorus included one or two shrill notes on the trumpet that were endlessly repeated. These were clearly the least good moments in the concert; still you have to acknowledge that Louis played these notes with such swing and fullness of sound that it was irresistible. In contrast, there were some pieces where he improvised in wonderful fashion, "Ain't Misbehavin'" among others, in which he played a chorus entirely differently than on disc, with the exception of one "break." Nor will I ever forget his sublime vocal chorus on "Rockin' Chair," and I can't console myself to this day that three-quarters of the spectators were not able to hear it because of Canetti and his accursed microphone.

The public was not sparing in its applause of Louis and this evening was, in sum, a fine success. However, most of the listeners lacked discernment, as was proven by the particularly warm reception of a performance by the band of "Rhapsody in Blue," which Louis was content to direct in the most vivid manner, thereby resting for some time from his hard work on trumpet.

During the intermission I met several renowned composers and was curious to know their impressions. Unfortunately, most of them seemed incapable of responding to this beautiful music. Darius Milhaud walked around repeating to whomever would listen: "Very 1920, very 1920." It is an affectation which has become a cliché in the milieu of Milhaud—I think, for example, of the pianist Jean Wiéner—to claim that jazz could entertain and be of interest in 1920, and then to say that it has lost all spice because its novelty has become passé.[3] For those people, having known jazz during that period through second-class bands, should have felt their interest perk up again hearing the bands of Louis Armstrong and Duke Ellington. This proves very simply that they had seen only the superficial side, the outward originality of this music, totally ignoring its essence. It is enough to hear two minutes of Wiéner trying to create jazz on the piano in order to realize that he has never understood anything about this music.

Sauguet disappointed me less because he criticized mostly the band, and it was undeniable that it was really bad. But this should not have prevented him from being moved by Louis's playing.

As soon as the concert was over, I rushed behind the scenes and found Louis seated in a nook flanked by Canetti who was in the process of proposing some changes to the concert program the following day. Above all, he tried hard to get Louis to omit "Rhapsody in Blue," saying that it had been poorly received by part of the public. To tell the truth, I believe that some ten people had hissed this piece, but the vast majority of the public had applauded it more than anything else. It is for this reason that Louis resisted. Just as Canetti was insisting, Louis cut him off sharply: "No, I am keeping this piece because it is really very good."

When Canetti was gone Louis invited me to come spend the rest of the night with him and Alpha at some nightclubs in Montmartre. One can imagine with what pleasure I accepted this invitation. After a few minutes we rode in a taxi in the company of two of Louis's black friends, one of whom was the journalist Edgar Wiggins, Paris correspondent of *The Chicago Defender*, the most popular black-American newspaper. During this short ride Louis expressed his satisfaction with the success of the concert, and added these words: "Canetti does not understand. He wants to suppress 'Rhapsody in Blue.' As far as I am concerned, I don't like this 'Rhapsody in Blue' at all, but since the public received it so well, it might as well be repeated tomorrow."[4]

We went down to the Cabane Cubaine, on rue Fontaine, where a small mediocre band was playing, but where one found several of Louis's friends. At one point I recognized Georges Auric at one of the tables. I pointed him out to Alpha, saying: "Here is a well-known musician and critic. I will go tell him about Louis; I hope he will say many good things in his articles." Alpha looked at me defiantly and said to me in a lightly teasing tone: "And if you don't talk to him, he won't have anything good to say about Louis?" From this moment I suspected that Alpha had a peevish attitude and the future only made me more certain; her influence over Louis would reveal itself repeatedly in a troubling way.

I talked with Georges Auric for a few minutes. I was pleasantly surprised to discover his enthusiasm: "Of course, he is formidable, overwhelming," he told me animatedly, and as I recall, he wrote an excellent article on Louis.

We then went to another cabaret where a white band was playing, including notably Alix Combelle on tenor saxophone. I had the pleasure of hearing Louis say that he considered him an excellent musician.

The night ended at Bourdon, a cafe restaurant at the intersection of Fontaine, Mansart, de Douai, and Duperré. It was there that one could find most of the black musicians in Paris in the wee hours, once their night's work was over. Around four in the morning one could eat sauerkraut with sausages or steak and fries of questionable quality. This did not stop Louis from eating heartily. One had to see the curious way in which he pulled apart his sauerkraut; meticulously he spread at various places on his plate different pieces of ham, sausages, potatoes, of which the dish was composed, carefully cutting a small bit of each, then simultaneously eating little bits together in order to mix the different flavors in his mouth. This was done with such systematic care that you could think he was completely absorbed in this activity. But, at the same time, he talked with blacks seated at adjoining tables, laughed, and told the funniest stories.

At one point I caught sight of Stephane Grappelli at the other end of Boudon. I went up to him and he introduced me to his companion, who was none other than the incomparable gypsy guitarist Django Reinhardt, who had been talked about a great deal for a year in Paris but whom I had not yet had occasion to hear.

Django immediately shared with me his enthusiasm for Louis Armstrong. Grappelli went one better; I remember that he said something like this: "My friend, there is nothing more to say; there is only one musician; it is Louis Armstrong. The others may be wonderful. Next to him they don't stack up. Let it be understood. The orchestra of Duke Ellington is formidable. But after Armstrong one forgets."

Django and Grappelli ate up Louis with their eyes. I felt that they both were very aware of the dynamism of his personality. "Go ask him some questions," they told me, "so we can hear him talk." I returned to Louis's table; just then he was in the process of telling a story to one of his neighbors. Approaching the table, Django and Grappelli—who did not know a word of English—listened to him eagerly; the sound of his voice was enough to fascinate them. "Formidable, he is formidable," Grappelli repeated with a beatific smile.

Around five in the morning Louis and Alpha insisted on dropping me off in their cab before returning to their apartment.

The second concert was even more successful than the one of the previous evening. Louis interpreted some new pieces and he was wonderfully inspired in his improvisations on "Confessin'" and "Dinah." He played, accompanied only on piano, "Dear Old Southland" in a way that more or less resembled the one on his famous recording. The applause, which was especially sustained for this interpretation, allowed me to assess all the harm that the band did to Louis by accompanying him badly and too loudly in the other pieces.

Louis let go even more than the evening before. His activity on stage was such that he sweated profusely and constantly had to wipe his face with innumerable handkerchiefs that he took out of all his pockets.

I savored, even more than the evening before, every one of his notes, the smallest of his gestures. The manner in which he announced each piece left me gasping. Coming to the front of the stage, he leaned towards the audience and said: "Now we're going to swing for you that good old favorite 'Rockin' Chair,' 'Rockin' Chair.'" He always repeated the title twice, the first time announcing it in a normal way, the second time always with a tone and gesture that were in some way unusual; for example, opening his eyes very wide as if he were astonished by what he had just said and was listening to himself repeat it in order to take account of what he had said; or, the second time, the title might be announced in a foreboding way and the final syllables would be lost in a light laugh, as if to say: "Ha, do you understand what I mean?"

The concert over, Louis invited me to accompany him, as he had the night before. The famous black boxer, Al Brown, joined us. We went to the Villa d'Este, a dance club very close to the Arc de Triomphe, where Freddie Taylor's small black combo played—certainly the best band in Paris at this time.

Louis was determined to go back there because two of his best musicians, Fletcher Allen and Charlie Johnson, had left him to rejoin Taylor's band, and he wanted to show all of them that he didn't hold any grudge against them.

When we made our entrance the room was absolutely packed. There wasn't a single free table, a single empty chair. But for people as important as Louis Armstrong or Al Brown what wouldn't they do? Immediately they brought, from who knows where, a table and chairs that were set in front of the band in a corner of the tiny dance floor where the dancers were already squashed.

Freddie Taylor's band played superbly. It was composed of eight musicians, almost all excellent: two trumpets (Freddie Taylor and Charlie Johnson); two saxophonists (Fletcher Allen and Chester Lanier), a pianist (John Ferrier), a guitarist (Sterling Connaway), a classy drummer (William Diemer), and a bass player of extraordinary virtuosity named José Riestra. Fletcher Allen had written some arrangements of remarkable quality for the band. Stimulated by Louis's presence, the musicians strove to give of their best, and the hot solos of tenor saxophone Fletcher Allen, supported by the powerful drumming of Diemer, made a strong impression on me. As for Freddie Taylor himself, he played or sang only rarely. His true métier was dance, and he had worked on the trumpet a relatively short time. He amused himself from time to time by reproducing some of Louis's choruses recorded on disc, casting a sly wink in our direction. Louis smiled politely, like a child who asks only to be amused.

About an hour after our arrival Freddie Taylor gave us an amazing exhibition of tap dancing, what in France is strangely called "clapper dance." Since then I have seen and heard the best tap dancers in the world and I am sure that there are very few who can surpass Freddie when he is in top form. That evening, galvanized by Louis's presence, he really took off, taking chorus after chorus, inventing hot, swinging breaks here and there. When you see and, above all, hear a man like Freddie dance, then you realize to what extent tap dance is a natural part of the music of jazz, just like a good drum solo. Some of Freddie's bits were so beautiful that Louis roared with pleasure and Al Brown lost his blasé attitude and was one big smile.

That night I spoke with Louis about Milton Mesirow who was . . . one of his best friends. Some Americans, notably John Hammond, have tried to make me believe that Milton was very poorly regarded by the majority of black musicians. I questioned Louis on this subject: "That's not true," he told me, "Milton is, above all, poorly regarded by whites because he lives in the black quarter of New York, in Harlem. But in Harlem there is nobody more popular; almost everybody knows him, and when he strolls around Seventh Avenue or Lenox Avenue every minute somebody is calling out to him: Hello Mezz!—or stops to talk to him for a few minutes. If you think I am exaggerating, ask all the black musicians who come from New York and you'll see." And Louis, to bolster his statement, called over some of the musicians who were present, who came over to us one by one, and who asked about Milton, spoke of him with enthusiasm, beginning with Freddie Taylor. I was very surprised because I did not know that Milton was so popular with black musicians.

We left the Villa d'Este around three in the morning for the Cabane Cubaine. And a little later Louis left me home in his taxi.

The following days Louis went to give some concerts in Belgium, then returned to Paris, where he gave about a forty-minute broadcast on Paris radio. I was present at this broadcast, in a small radio studio where a hundred or so people were packed in. There Louis could be heard far better than at Salle Pleyel; one did not lose a note of his vocal choruses and, as I was only two or three meters away from him, it was easy for me to see the slightest nuance of his trumpet playing, even when the band loudly accompanied him.

After that Louis Armstrong left with his band for a tour of major French towns, a tour that Canetti had organized. He was also scheduled to play in Italy, Switzerland, and some other countries, always under the control of Canetti, who pompously styled himself on his letterhead as "Louis Armstrong's All-World Manager."

The articles in the press about his Paris concerts were as wretched as those for Duke Ellington. One of the critics surpassed all the others in nonsense; that was Lucien Rebatet, who wrote the following lines in *l'Action Française* (November 16, 1934):

> One has to hear and watch him [Louis Armstrong] for two hours. It soon becomes childishly monotonous.
>
> The famous hot improvisation consists of endlessly spinning out a fragment of three or four notes at the most on a trumpet or saxophone. This exercise requires only some blowing and the knowledge of some rudimentary harmonic progressions that the players pass back and forth like brothers.
>
> It could be rather curious to see negroes roll their wild eyes, gyrate, and shake with the pulsations of the drum, like the ancestral beat. One was caught by it two or three times. But one discovered afterwards that, beneath the appearances of scary trances, it is all blatant fakery, bad acting, pretty much unchanging, which Armstrong himself did not escape. His final high note has the same emphasis as that of a bel canto tenor. . . . We were very bored. The hot players have themselves agreed with this.

Thus, for Mr. Rebatet, the rich solos of Louis Armstrong were reduced to a "fragment of three or four notes." Strictly speaking, if you think about it, the finales of "Tiger Rag" and "St. Louis Blues"—for which Louis repeatedly lingers on one or two shrill notes—this remark makes sense. But those were exceptional moments in the course of two concerts. The rest of the time Louis created such varied and complex phrases that Mr. Rebatet would sweat for hours if he had to transcribe the music. But this is how history is written: one speaks to the reader about the exception and he is led to believe that the exception is the rule.

As for accusing an actor as spontaneous, as "good a boy" as Louis Armstrong, of quackery, indicates evil intentions or absolute lack of knowledge about musicians and actors of the black race, whom Mr. Rebatet seems, above all, to reproach for not conforming to the conventions of white actors. This "blatant fakery" has not prevented Louis from being used in Hollywood in five films in which he appears not only as a musician, but also as an actor, sometimes in a fairly extended role, as in *Goin' Places*.

Moreover, for anyone who personally knows Louis Armstrong this accusation does not hold up. It is not unusual to see Louis in his daily life behave exactly as he does on the stage: the same exuberance, the same facial expressions. For example, on stage Louis often seems to hear with an ecstatic air a mediocre chorus from one of the musicians in his band or a poorly executed ensemble; one hears him hum or sing along with them enthusiastically, and certain people naively say: "How can the great Armstrong gyrate to music like this?" They do not understand that they can't judge Louis's reactions in the same light as theirs; they don't have any idea what music is for him. One cannot say that music has a great place in his life because the truth is that music is his life blood, that he lives it every single moment. One day I was with him in his apartment on rue de la Tour d'Auvergne; he walked up and down while talking with some people. Suddenly somebody in the courtyard below began to sing an atrocious sentimental song. Immediately Louis went to the window, absorbed in what he was hearing, and began to sing, his mouth closed, the last notes that he had just heard. You felt that the value of the song did not mean very much to him; his ear had heard notes, and that was enough to arouse from deep inside of him a whole world of music that was never completely dormant.

But to grasp all that, to understand a genius as exceptional as Louis Armstrong, one has to abandon all preconceived ideas, the prejudices learned in the course of a musical education that has its good aspects certainly, but which cannot be much help when it comes to judging musicians of another race whose art is entirely developed on the fringes of such an education.

NOTES

1. *Jazz-Tango-Dancing*. March 1934.

2. The poor functioning of the microphone, followed by its suppression, was very prejudicial to Louis, as was attested by various reviews of the concert, notably the following: "Louis Armstrong, not content to play the God-given trumpet, sings. His voice, which comes across to us as sweet on records, is nothing but naked, feeble, and somewhat raw, more appropriate for comic effects than for exuding charm." (*Intransigeant*, 18 November 1934)

3. Let's be fair and recognize that Darius Milhaud had written these complimentary lines four years earlier on a disc of Louis Armstrong: "We find on Odeon a veritable masterpiece which the whole world ought to experience. It is 'Exactly Like You' by jazzman Louis Armstrong. The impression is heart-rending. One is overwhelmed at the pain and the despair. It is a sublime disc." (*Art and Decoration*, 1930)

4. This was, one can see, the real significance of Louis's decision; but Canetti, too stupid to understand it, spread the news that Louis loved ghastly pieces like "Rhapsody in Blue."

Part Three

YOU RASCAL YOU

MANAGEMENT, MARIJUANA, AND THE MOB

With an absentee father and a motley succession of surrogates and stepfa-
thers, Louis Armstrong learned early the necessity of depending for his
survival on the power and protection of men in whom he could place his
trust. Most revealing is an anecdote that New Orleans trombonist Kid Ory
tells about the young Louis and muscleman, drummer, and protector
Black Benny Williams:

"One evening, Benny brought Louis, who had just been released from
the Waif's Home, to National Park, where I was playing a picnic. Benny
asked me if I would let Louis sit in with my band. I remembered the kid
from the street parade and I gladly agreed.

"Louis came up and played 'Ole' Miss' and the blues, and everyone
in the park went wild over this boy in knee trousers who could play so
great. I liked Louis's playing so much that I asked him to come and sit in
with my band any time he could.

"Louis came several times to different places where I worked and we
really got to know each other. He always came accompanied by Benny, the
drummer. In crowded places, Benny would handcuff Louis to himself with
a handkerchief so Louis wouldn't get lost."

The larger lesson was not lost on Louis himself. In a letter to Joe Glaser (August 2, 1955), Armstrong recalls some advice that Black Benny had given him in those early years: "Dipper, as long as you live, no matter where you may be, always have a white man [who] can and will put his hand on your shoulder and say 'This is my nigger,' and can't anybody harm ya." —JB

LOUIS ARMSTRONG
TOMMY ROCKWELL (1943–1944)

Excerpted from the "Goffin notebooks"

Before Joe Glaser became Louis Armstrong's manager in 1935, Armstrong's career was handled by a number of other men. The first to be mentioned is Tommy Rockwell, an executive with the Okeh Record Company; a hard-drinking Irishman who reportedly "couldn't carry two notes of a melody—completely tone deaf." It was he who redirected Armstrong's career, positioning him for his success on Broadway—most notably in Hot Chocolates—*and helping him diversify his playing with more pop-song material. Armstrong became involved with Rockwell in the spring of 1929 at a point where his career in Chicago was in a downturn. He had just completed a most unusual stint at the Savoy Ballroom— "[T]hey'd always have a basketball game first, then the dance would start." Stripped down to his bathing suit, the 230-pound Armstrong and his teammates would drive the crowd into hysterics. "I put it [the ball] under my arm and started running like mad with it. And the people laughed an' roared thunderously. I ran almost to the basket, took a good aim at the basket, threw it up there. Then I missed it. Both of our teams were so weak from laughing at me. Oh, what fun we had." But the good times did not last, and what follow are some pertinent comments by Armstrong as found in the so-called "Goffin notebooks," a series of reminiscences sketched out by him between 1943 and 1944 for the Belgian jazz writer-lawyer-polymath Robert Goffin. —JB*

Business began to get slow, just like any other big amusement that opened up in Chicago—go real big for a while then, ka-blip, the bottom would drop out. So Mr. Fagan the owner [of the Savoy Ballroom] would come to us every week; and the way he would lay this story on us, we just couldn't leave him, that's all—but looked like Mr. Fagan was laying that hard luck story on us a little too often. I was still signed up with the Okeh Record Company. But Mr. Fern turned my contract over to Mr. Tommy Rockwell, who was stationed in New York. And at the same time Mr. Fagan was coming up short with our money. Mr. Rockwell sent for me to come to New York immediately and make some records, and also book me into a show called *Great Day* produced by Vincent Youmans. When I received Mr. Rockwell's telegram in Chicago I showed it to Carroll Dickerson, Zutty [Singleton], and the rest of the band boys. They as well as myself were so attached to each other until we hated like hell to break up our band. Mr. Rockwell wires me again. Right away myself and the band held a private meeting. I told them—what say if we have our cars fixed up, and Mr. Rockwell has just sent me enough money, and I can give each man in the band $20 to eat off of and help buy gas, and we'll all go to New York together? They all jumped up into the air with joy.

We all finally arrived in Harlem—I immediately went downtown to Mr. Rockwell's office. He certainly was glad to see me. He said: "Louie, I've just arranged to put you in the *Great Day* show." I said, "Oh fine, Mr. Rockwell. But I brought my band with me and you'll have to book us some place." Mr. Rockwell hit the ceiling saying, "Band? I did not send for your band. I sent for you only." I said, very calmly, "Just the same, Mr. Rockwell, we're here now. I just couldn't leave my boys, that's all. I know you can book us some place." Finally Mr. Rockwell gave in and gave me all the money I wanted. And inside of two weeks we had a job down in Connie's Inn in Harlem, at 131st and Seventh Avenue. That club and the Cotton Club were the hottest clubs in Harlem at that time. And Harlem was really jumping.

All the white people would think it was a real treat to spend a night up in Harlem. After my band was set at Connie's I started doubling in *Connie's Hot Chocolates* show downtown.

LOUIS ARMSTRONG

GROOVIN' HIGH ON GAGE

Excerpted from "The Satchmo Story," an unpublished sequel to Satchmo: My Life in New Orleans

After some six months at Connie's Inn—Armstrong and his band had started their gig there on June 24, 1929—things went sour. Some of the "band boys abused the job"; that is, they began show-ing up late. Before they knew it, Connie Immerman gave the whole band two weeks' notice and sent the band members on their way. Amidst all of this the country as a whole had been shaken by the Depression—Black Friday, October 29, 1929, had come and gone—and Prohibition continued in full swing. But Armstrong was undaunted and Tommy Rockwell got him some bookings as a single act. By May 1930 he was aboard a train bound for Los Angeles, even though no gigs had apparently been lined up either by him or Tommy Rockwell.

This phase of his career proved eventful in ways he could never possibly have imagined. It was not so much that Armstrong was chosen to front the resident band at Frank Sebastian's Cotton Club in Culver City, or that "these boys had something on the ball musically that I had not witnessed." Nor was it that "in the band were such fine players as Lawrence Brown on trombone and Lionel Hampton on drums," two youngsters whose greatness he admitted discovering "the very first day I went to rehearsal." It wasn't even his landing his first role in a full-length feature movie, Ex-Flame (1931), produced by the MGM studio next door. The real event for Louis centered on his regular use of marijuana.

The young Buck Clayton, eager to learn the secret of creating a glissando on his horn, remembers seeking out his hero backstage at the Cotton Club. Armstrong, in a mellow mood after sharing a reefer with his young admirer, proceeded to show him how to create the special effect by pushing the valves way down and tightening the lips. Unfortunately, Armstrong's relaxed attitude toward marijuana use brought him into conflict with the law, when in late March 1931 out in the parking lot of the Cotton Club, Armstrong and drummer Vic Berton got busted for smoking marijuana by "two big healthy dicks [who] came from behind a car." The details of Armstrong's brush with the law are as interesting as his views on marijuana. In the manuscript "The Satchmo Story" (part of an unpublished sequel to Satchmo: My Life in New Orleans*), Armstrong expresses his puzzlement about the linking of marijuana with narcotics, a position that would be readily applauded by those seeking the legalization of the drug. —JB*

The first time that I smoked marijuana (or gage) as they so beautifully calls it some time, was a couple of years after I had left Fletcher Henderson's Orchestra, playing at the Roseland in New York. And I returned to Chicago. It was actually in Chicago when I picked up my first stick of gage. And I'm telling you, I had myself a ball. That's why it really puzzles me to see marijuana connected with narcotics, dope, and all that kind of crap. It is actually a shame. I was twenty-six years old then. And it never

Armstrong (holding record) with Les Hite (seated) and His Orchestra, Sebastian's Cotton Club, Culver City, California, October 1930. Courtesy Frank Driggs Collection.

did impress me as dope. Because my mother and her church sisters used to go out by the railroad track and pick baskets full of pepper grass, dandelions, and lots of weeds similar to gage, and they would bring it to their homes, get a big fat slice of meat, and make one most deelicious [*sic*] pot of greens anyone would want to smack their lips on—physics you too.

I am different. I smoked it a long time. And I found out something. First place, it's a thousand times better than whiskey. It's an assistant, a friend, a nice cheap drink if you want to call it that. Good (very good) for asthma, relaxes your nerves, great for cleanliness. Much different than a dope fiend. A dope addict, from what I noticed by watching a lot of different cats, who I used to light up with but got so carried away, they felt that they could get a much bigger kick by jabbing themselves in the ass with a needle—heroin, cocaine, etc. or some other ungodly shit, which would not ever faze a man like myself, who's always had a sane mind from the day he was born. As I said before, I've always been a great observer from a baby. Mayann, my mother, told me when I was very young. She said, "Son, always keep your bowels open, and nothing can harm you." And she never said truer words than those.

It's funny how Vic and I got busted. It was right in front of the California Cotton Club during my intermission, and Vic came over for a few drags. We'd pick a stick alternately. Then too, the law wasn't so strict on gage, even out at that time . . . I did not know why we were busted until after the arrest and was talking to the two detectives who took me down to the station from the club. Now dig this. That's why I still say there's actually no written law against gage; but the person with the evil mind or thought, and with a little money to spend for his own personal evil spirit, or I could even say jealousy, with a little money, the no-good person, set up a trap (if it means anything to them) or out of a clear sky. Because they know that you don't have a leg to stand on. That's what happened to Vic and me. You see, I've always been a happy-go-lucky sort of fellow.

~

In a retrospective letter written to Max Jones around 1970, Armstrong fleshes out some of the details of the bust:

When we reached the police headquarters there were several officers, including the man at the desk, sitting around. And the minute we came through the door they all recognized me right away. They too had been diggin' my music nightly over the radio. Oh boy, were those guys glad to see me. They gave me one look (with glee) and said, "What'ta hell are you doing here this time of night away from the club?" So we yakity yakity while I was being booked. That's one reason why we appreciated pot, as y'all calls it now. The warmth it always brought forth from the other person—especially the ones that lit up a good stick of that "shuzzit" or gage, nice names. I spent nine days in the Downtown Los Angeles City jail, in a cell with two guys who were already sentenced to forty or forty-five years for something else. Robbery, pickpocket, or whatever they were in for, didn't make any difference to me, and they cared less as to what I was in for. The most important thing was we were so very glad to see each other. Because it was a week ago I was blowing some good shuzzit with both of those characters.

On the way to court we stopped at the clothes room to pick up the suit I went in there with. The man handed me my suit, which was torned [*sic*] all through the lining, looking for some stuff I guess, stronger than pot. Referring to me, he said, "Why, this man is no Heeb" (their word when talking about dope fiends).

So I go to trial. Everybody was there—which takes in my boss, manager, and a whole gang of lawyers—and I said to myself that I was straight. Meantime the Chicago papers were all on the stands, with big headlines saying Louis Armstrong will have to spend six months for marijuana. The judge gave me a suspended sentence and I went to work that night—wailed just like nothing happened.

LOUIS ARMSTRONG

JOHNNY COLLINS (1943–1944)

Excerpted from the "Goffin notebooks"

Enter Johnny Collins, a fixer and manager who had apparently been sent by Tommy Rockwell to get Louis out of jail—hence the suspended sentence. If anything, all the notoriety surrounding Armstrong's arrest, imprisonment, and trial had boosted his popularity a few notches. But now, at the end of March 1931, things were winding down at Sebastian's Cotton Club, and he was off to Chicago accompanied by Collins. After a brief stay at the Regal Theater, Armstrong began a residency that April at the Show Boat, which, it turns out, was a nightclub doubling as a bookie joint. It was there that Louis was threatened at gunpoint by a thug most likely sent by Rockwell—an allegation Rockwell denied. Writing in the "Goffin notebooks," Armstrong put it as follows. —JB

Mr. Johnny Collins, who was my manager in California through some deal he made with Mr. Tommy Rockwell, my other manager—damn, come to think of it, I sure had a manager's fit. Anyway, Mr. Collins booked me in a little night club downtown in Chicago called the Show Boat. This place used to be where Wingy Manone once held sway and used to rock the joint. But funny thing, I did not know that Johnny Collins and Rockwell were having a feud over my contract. Why and for what, I've never figured out until this day. All I know is, whoever was the gang in New York sent gangsters to Chicago where I was working and tried to frighten me into quitting the job and coming back to New York to open up back at Connie's Inn again. And I felt that, as dirty as Connie fired me and my band, I did not want any part of those people ever again. I am just that way. If you kick my ass once, you can bet I won't come back, if I can help it, so you can kick it again. And Connie's Inn was going down by degrees, and at that time I was the rage of the nation.

One night the gangsters started a fight in the Show Boat—right in front of where I was standing, playing my trumpet. I usually stood, playing with my eyes closed, leaned against a post that was made into the bandstand—was built down on the dance floor. I mean they were really fighting worse than a bunch of spades. One of the gangsters took a chair and hit a woman over the head with it. And the chair crumbled up—in a lot of little pieces. Some of the pieces hit my horn. But even that could not make me leave the bandstand, you know. The captain must go down with the ship. Then too, things like that never frighten me. I've seen so much of that bullshit.

Ain't but one incident at the Show Boat that kind of got me. And it happened one night as we were justa playing and the people were all dancing. I felt someone touching me—speaking in a whisper. It was a big burly looking gangster saying, "Somebody wants you in the dressing room." After the set was over I ran lickety split to my dressing room to see who it was, and there, bless my lamb, who did I see [but] a white guy with a beard—thicker than one of those boys from the house of David. So he spoke first—"hello" kind of sarcastically. I still ain't hep to the jive. He said, "Do you know who I am?" I said, "Why, er no, I don't."

In fact, it didn't really matter as long as he talked about music. I really knew he and I were going to really run our mouths a while musically. Then this guy said, "I am Frankie Foster." At first I still didn't pay any attention—then it dawned on me what he said. And I turned in cold sweats—mugged, and took a double look as I said to him, "What you say your name was?" By this time he had his big pistol, pulling it out as he said, "My name is Frankie Foster." And he said he was sent over to my place to see that I catch the first train out to New York.

I still try to make it appear that he ain't frightening me. I said, "New York? That's news to me. Mr. Collins didn't tell me anything about it." Frankie Foster said, "Ah, bad sonbitch. Oh yes. You're going to New York to work at Connie's Inn, an' you're leaving tomorrow morning." He flashed his big ol' pistol and aimed it straight at me with my eyes as big as saucers an' frightened too. I said, "Well maybe I am going to New York. Ooh God." Then Frankie Foster said, "Okay—now you and me are going to the telephone booth an' you'll talk." By this time anything he ordered of me was alright because it's no trouble at all for a gangster to pull the trigger, especially when they have you cornered an' you disobey them. Sooo, we went to the phone with a gun in my side, an' sure enough, someone said "Hello," a familiar voice, too [mobster Dutch Schultz or one of his henchmen]. The first words he said to me were, "When you gonna open here?" I turned and looked direct into Frankie Foster's face and said "tomorrow."

ED SULLIVAN

BACKFIRING AFFIDAVITS (1931)

Evening Graphic, *October 9, 1931*

Collins stepped right in to defuse the crisis, sending Louis and the band on the road. There were exhausting one-night stands and occasional engagements lasting a week, with the troupers crisscrossing the country, from Milwaukee to New Orleans, to Boston and New York. Once he was back in New York, however, Armstrong was fair game for Tommy Rockwell and Connie Immerman, who sued him for breach of contract. But things then took an ironic twist as plaintiff Rockwell sought to establish by a series of affidavits from the likes of Paul Whiteman and others that Armstrong's services were of a unique order. In the Evening Graphic *for October 9, 1931, the young Ed Sullivan, working as a reporter in his pre-TV incarnation, wrote as follows about "the affidavits that backfired." —JB*

Paul Whiteman was one of the first to make out an affidavit to that effect. I believe the Columbia Broadcasting System, through a high official, also swore this to be a fact. And at least one phonograph company did likewise. The affidavits from these experts were extravagant in their praise of Louis Armstrong. Rockwell's lawyers presented them to the court, confident that this expert testimony would settle the case in Rockwell's favor and serve as a setback to Armstrong and Collins. The court decided otherwise, however, and denied Rockwell's petition. The big laugh is that Armstrong will use the affidavits filed against him to advertise the band.

CONTENTION WITH COLLINS (1953)

Interview, November 11, 1953

Armstrong's relationship with Johnny Collins over the next two years or so was far from ideal. And his handling of Armstrong's first visit to England in July 1932 left much to be desired. In fact, the following summer, aboard the Homeric *in late July bound for England and the Continent—he opened at London's Holborn Empire on July 31—Armstrong and his contentious manager came very close to blows. What follows is a transcript of part of a rap session that took place on November 11, 1953, between Louis Armstrong and George Avakian. Most striking is not Armstrong's use of profanity, but his ability to contain his justifiable rage in the face of racist behavior. —JB*

Called me a nigger in the middle of the ocean. When that motherfucker called me a nigger for no reason at all, he's my manager and he's never done it before. But, you can see that "nigger" brings out your fucking thoughts sometimes. He waited till he got drunk to talk with me about my program. I said, "You know, Mr. Collins, I have been in show business for a long time. I'm an old hustler [from] way back. I know that horn better than I know my wife" [at the time, Alpha Smith].

Anyway, when I said that's why I'm going to play these numbers, he said, "Are you mad?" I said, "Listen, cocksucker, you might be my manager and you might be the biggest shit, booking the biggest business in the world. But, when I get on that fucking stage with that horn and get in trouble, you can't save me." He said, "Take that thing off the boat."

I was the coolest thing on the boat. Everyone sided with me. Why don't you club him? They wanted to put him in irons. People were giving him dirty looks and everything. Then I said this [to] Alpha, "You know, I'm a Southern boy. Everybody on this boat is against Johnny Collins— acting an asshole, you know." They're mad at him. Okay, and I'm mad at him too. Now, I could bash his fucking brains out. See what I mean. But, it's a different story. It's a white man. So I don't fuck with Johnny. Then he got up and walked right into a bucket of water.

Went downstairs. John Hammond played some records. And then he wandered down there. Looked right at John Hammond. John Hammond said, "What the—get out of here!" He swung at John Hammond. Missed—[Hammond] gave him a short, hard jab in his fucking chops. Zoom! And I'm standing right behind him, seeing he's falling. All I can do is just catch him with a finger. But I said, "I'll get this motherfucker myself." But, I still let him fall and bash his fucking brains out. Boom! Let him make an ass of himself. And he did. All I did was step aside. And then it was the same as though I had hit him with a fucking right myself.

JOSHUA BERRETT

JOE GLASER (1999)

Joe Glaser, who became Armstrong's manager in 1935, remained an enigma to the end of his life. In its obituary of June 8, 1969, *The New York Times* quoted Glaser as saying, "You don't know me, but you know two things about me: I have a terrible temper and I always keep my word." In fact, the full details of just how he conducted the business of Associated Booking Corporation, which he founded in 1940 and of which he was president throughout his life, remain elusive to this day. In any event, Armstrong first got to know Glaser in 1926 when he was managing the Sunset Café, a black and tan at 35th Street and Calumet, on Chicago's South Side.

As Armstrong recalls the time in the "Goffin notebooks":

I finally left the Vendome and settled down to the one at the Sunset. I liked the setup there better, with Earl Hines at the piano, Tubby Hall on drums, Darnell Howard, sax and clarinet, and down the line of the good ol' times. Joe Glaser was the boss of the place. I always admired Mr. Glaser from the first day I started working for him. He just impressed me different than the other bosses I've worked for. He seemed to understand colored people so much. And he was wonderful to his whole show and band, would give us nice presents, etc. And don't you think for once that Mr. Glaser didn't pitch a bitch when things aren't jumping right. I did not know about managers, etc. like they have nowadays. I don't think Mr. Glaser was thinking about it either, or else he would've signed me up then."

By the time Armstrong returned from Europe to the United States at the end of January 1935, his financial situation was a mess. His former managers Tommy Rockwell and Johnny Collins were hounding him. N. J. Canetti, the French promoter, was suing him for breach of contract. Lil Hardin was insisting that Louis provide her with a "maintenance" of six thousand dollars. But by May he was on the rebound, after shaking hands in Chicago with Joe Glaser on what was to prove a lifelong business arrangement—an arrangement with a man who "seemed to understand colored people so much." There are two basic versions of how the alliance came about. Max Jones and John Chilton quote Glaser's side of the story as follows:

> [When] Louis came back from England, he was broke and very sick. He said, "I don't want to be with anybody but you. Please, Mr. Glaser, just you and I. You understand me. I understand you." And I said, "Louis, you're me, and I'm you." I insured his life and mine for $100,000 apiece. Louis didn't even know it. I gave up all my other business, and we went on the road together.

To hear Louis telling it to jazz buff and publicist Ernie Anderson:

> When I found him I could see he was down and out. He had always been a sharp cat, but now he was raggedy ass. I told him, "I want you to be my manager." He said, "Oh, I couldn't do that. I'm stone broke." "That don't make no difference," Louis explained. "You get me the jobs," Louis went on, "You collect the money. You pay me $1,000 every week free and clear. You pay off the band, the travel and hotel expenses, my income tax, and you take everything that's left."

To quote Laurence Bergreen, what is clear about Joe Glaser is that "to the extent that he could ever redeem his own sins, he would do so through the vehicle of Louis Armstrong." Certainly Glaser was the defendant in a number of paternity suits, had a record as a rapist, pedophile, bootlegger, racketeer, and more. At the same time, one cannot fail to be impressed by how swiftly he set Armstrong's house in order. Debts were promptly settled. Louis was paired with the orchestra of Luis Russell. A contract was negotiated with Jack Kapp and Decca—the legal basis for recording with Bing Crosby—and there were movie deals, beginning with *Pennies from Heaven* and *Artists & Models;* not to mention a contract to host a radio series sponsored by Fleischmann's Yeast on the CBS Network. It was also largely thanks to Glaser's initiative that Armstrong became the topic of

Manager Joe Glaser, Armstrong, and Cork O'Keefe, 1937. O'Keefe, partner with Tommy Rockwell, and a band-booker, was mentor to Joe Glaser at the time. Armstrong was signing papers to mark his appearance on the Fleischmann's Yeast radio show. Courtesy Frank Driggs Collection.

articles in the mainstream white press as well as in periodicals like *Down Beat, Esquire,* and *Vanity Fair.*

Perhaps most interesting of all is how very early in their relationship Glaser came to epitomize for Armstrong the memories of two powerful influences from his New Orleans years—the toughness of muscleman-drummer Black Benny Williams and the protectiveness of the Russian-Jewish Karnofsky family. Armstrong's account of life on the road with Joe Glaser in the South of 1936 is revealing:

> Lots of times we wouldn't get a place to sleep. So we'd cross the tracks, pull over to the side of the road and spend the night there. We couldn't get into hotels. Our money wasn't even good. We'd play nightclubs and spots which didn't have a bathroom for Negroes. When we'd get hungry,

my manager, Joe Glaser, who's also my friend, Jewish and white, would buy food along the way in paper bags and bring it to us boys in the bus who couldn't be served.

At times to Armstrong Glaser was "daddy," "my manager and pal—the best friend that I've ever had." Yet, in the course of their thirty-four years together there were times when tempers would flare and obscenities fly. Stanley Crouch has mentioned a dressing room incident when Armstrong put a knife to Glaser's throat, threatening: "I can't prove it, but if I find out you've stolen one dime from me, I'll cut your goddam throat." Then there was Glaser's ongoing objection to the way Louis and the band would smoke marijuana in public—something likely to be met with a "fuck you!"

But musically speaking, it appears that Glaser did not always feel the pulse of change. The publicity manual on Louis Armstrong produced by Associated Booking Corporation specifies:

> Louis Armstrong is always billed as the trumpet king of swing, and particular care should be used at all times to assure use of the phrase "The Trumpet King of Swing" in all advertising copy. There are, in addition, such catch lines as "Gabriel in Swingtime," "The Toscanini of Swing," and "The Real and Original King of Swing."

What is significant in all of this is that the critical decision to form the All Stars in 1947, which so regenerated Armstrong's career during the final twenty-three years of his life, apparently had little to do with any initiative on Glaser's part—he was still of the big band mind set. Instead it seems to have resulted either from prodding on the part of Leonard Feather, who organized the Carnegie Hall concert of February 8, 1947 with Edmond Hall, or from a daring move that Ernie Anderson claims to have engineered. According to Anderson:

"Privately I had learned the true facts. Confidentially, A[ssociated] B[ooking] C[orporation]'s booker Bert Block had whispered to me that the fee for the sixteen-piece band had fallen to $350 for a week night or $600 for a Saturday. Moreover, bookings were so scant that the band bus, now a bit broken down, often had to make six-hundred-mile jumps. Bobby Hackett and I decided we'd have something to do about this. Our idea was to present Louis playing with his peers in a program of his classics.

"We presented the idea to Louis in his dressing room at the Earle

Theater in Philadelphia where he was playing his annual engagement. Louis was wonderful. He obviously loved the idea.

"I got a cashier's check at my bank made out to Joe Glaser for $1,000. Then I went up to Joe's luxurious office on Fifth Avenue and Fifty-seventh Street. He had one of the upper floors of a white marble skyscraper. The next obstacle was his waiting room—on the wall there was also a sliding glass window behind which sat the telephone operator. I slid open the window and handed the check to the operator. 'Could you please give this to Mr. Glaser?' I asked. She looked at the check, saw that it must be important, then she disappeared.

"Then the door out of the waiting room opened to reveal Joe, holding the check. He seemed to be in a purple rage. He threw a hostile glare at me and shouted, 'What are you trying to do, you jerk?' I was deeply offended by this, but I remained calm and said, 'That's for Louis for one night without the band.' After all I knew Joe Glaser well enough to know that he was never going to give up that check. Still snarling, he waved me through the door and into his office.

"He continued to glare at me as I quickly outlined my plan for a midnight concert at Town Hall on May 17, the year was 1947, with an assortment of Louis's peers. I said, 'You've been accepting dates for the whole band for $350 on weekdays and $600 on Saturdays when you can get it.' 'Who told you that?' he roared. I didn't answer. He examined the check very carefully. Then reluctantly he muttered 'Okay.' I could hardly leave it at that. I said, 'If this works as I think it will, instead of $350 a night for Louis, you'll be getting $2,500 a night.' He threw me an intense look, but said nothing more."

The Price Tag

What kind of price tag did Armstrong's trust in Glaser carry? Upon his death on June 6, 1969 Joe Glaser left an estate valued at over $3,000,000. By comparison, Armstrong's Last Will and Testament—it is available for inspection at the Surrogate Court, Queens County, New York—indicates a total worth of only $530,775. This kind of information has prompted rumors that Glaser robbed Armstrong blind. However, the fact is that at the time of Glaser's death his Associated Booking Corporation also represented Duke Ellington, Barbra Streisand, Pearl Bailey, Dave Brubeck, the Kingston Trio, Benny Goodman, Stan Kenton, Creedence Clearwater Revival, the Rascals, Josh White, and Miriam Makeba. What is more, on Glaser's death, according to David Gold, vice-president and treasurer of

ABC, "because of the unique nature between Glaser and the Armstrongs we felt that rather than create any question of propriety, we felt it best that they handle their own funds." Independent accountants reportedly then took charge and gave Lucille Armstrong the power to make major financial decisions.

Furthermore, Gold has maintained that Glaser took no more than the standard 15 percent agent's fee. What was left was put into an account out of which was paid general travel expenses, taxes, the mortgage on the Corona house, living expenses, and such. But the financial details of the early Glaser-Armstrong years will forever remain murky. There was minimal record keeping and nobody paid taxes. It has therefore been speculated that during the early years Glaser probably gave Armstrong just enough to keep him happy and kept for himself whatever was left after paying expenses.

Part Four

MEMORIES OF YOU

LIFE WITH LUCILLE

In August 1954 *Ebony* ran a feature by Armstrong entitled "Why I Like Dark Women"—a tell-all story about his four wives. In it he elaborates on his attraction to dark-skinned women, quoting the phrase, "the blacker the berry, the sweeter the juice." But it was Lucille Wilson, whom he married on October 12, 1942, who was singled out for special praise. It was his fourth marriage, her first; this time, however, he did it right. The darkest girl in the line of the Cotton Club, she exuded a glow and "her deep-brown skin got me deep down." More important, she was "the only one who ever understood me completely and gave me real happiness—a woman of poise and patience, good sense and understanding." When she was interviewed in 1983, Lucille spoke of maneuvering her man into spots. While recognizing that he was always his own man, she knew that he "needed someone to stabilize him" so that he could do his life's job with the horn that much better. —JB

LOUIS ARMSTRONG

EARLY YEARS WITH LUCILLE (EXCERPTS)

Louis Armstrong Archives Series, Manuscript, No. 1/4

In an undated autobiographical statement that he penned, Armstrong writes about his early years with Lucille in his charac- teristic stream-of-consciousness, elliptical style. The following excerpts describe various incidents in their life together: the trem- bling excitement of their first real conversation; the atmosphere in the courtroom at the time of his divorce from Alpha Smith; his feelings at the time of his marriage to Lucille; and the purchase of the property at 34–56 107th Street in Corona, New York, which in March 1943 became their home and is now known as the Louis Armstrong House. —JB

[I]f you want to know what kind of eyes that I am talking about, I am talk- ing about bedroom eyes. "You're just the gal for me. Now I know you're going to tell me that you might be a little too young for me since there is such a difference in our ages," [I said]. "I am only twenty-six years old," she said, "and you are around forty or forty-one, somewhere around there. After all, I'm just a little small chorus girl, lucky to come in contact with a bunch of lovely, well-hipped people." That's when I stopped her from talking by slowly reaching for her cute little beautifully manicured hand, and said to her, "Can you cook red beans and rice?" which amused her very much. Then it dawned on her that I was very serious. She being a northern girl born in New York City and me a Southern boy from New Orleans, she could see why I asked her that question. So she said, "I've never cooked that kind of food before, but just give me a little time and I think I can fix it for you." That's all I wanted to hear, and right away I said, "How about inviting me out to your house for dinner?" Two days later I was at her house on time with bells on, also my best suit.

When I went out on the road with Luis Russell's band and we played Chicago, I had to appear in court to get my divorce from my third wife, Alpha. It was 10 o'clock in the morning, and I had been out balling all night—meaning having one drink after another, no sleep and juiced

Armstrong and his wife Lucille on tour in England, September 12, 1960. Photo: UPI/Corbis-Bettmann.

(drunk) personified. Quite naturally, by the time I got to the court house I was very hoarse and could only be heard above a whisper, just happy to get the trial over with, one way or another.

Just before our trial started I happened to slowly look around [to see] if I could see anyone I knew outside of Daisy. And there, bless my Lord, I looked straight into those beautiful eyes of Lucille (Brown Sugar) Wilson. Wow—I lit right up. And sharpened up for the questions that the judge was going to ask me—Lucille had surprised me by taking the weekend off to come to Chicago to dig my trial and be with me. Just then the judge turned to me and commenced asking me a few questions. I was so hoarse and my voice sounded so bad until the judge immediately looked straight at me and said, "Look here, young man, have you caught a cold?" I said, "No judge, it's just this saw mill voice that all my fans said that I have." The judge gave a little chuckle of laughter and immediately said, "Divorce granted!"

Lucille came over to me, and we went home to my hotel. Played the gig in Chicago.

———

St. Louis was next. My vocalist Velma Middleton, who came from St. Louis, was with our band at the time—I mentioned to Velma privately that I planned to marry Lucille real soon. And I won't let her out of my sight by returning back to New York. And Velma, bless her, right away said, "Since we're here in my home town, why don't you and Lucille get married at my house?" So we all agreed and set October 12 [1942] as the wedding date. All set. Then a day before the wedding there was a real situation which raised its ugly head. Lucille is Catholic and I am a Baptist. We went to several priests and they all turned us down, and would not okay our marriage license—then all of a sudden it dawned on Lucille and me. After all, we both are deeply in love. Which priests or no human could understand or care less. So we decided to forsake all others, and go on with the wedding—I bought a beautiful orchid and pinned it on Lucille. That was the first orchid I'd ever bought in my life—I only went by how nice 'n' pretty mine looked on her. We made a very good-looking couple, with me —down to my fighting weight—and I had on a sharp, hard hitting gray suit as we cats expresses it. Luis Russell and his boys all looked nice and had a real good time—the next night we played at the Tune Town Ballroom, the place where Bix Beiderbecke and Frankie Trumbauer used to blow a lot of times during the old days.—

The Rev. who married Lucille and me—uhmm. His wife, who was also at our wedding, surprised us when two weeks later—she sued her husband, Ol' Rev., for a divorce. Well sir, she caught Reverend in a particular position with one of the young church sisters who sings in his church choir—I did not have any fear of something like that ever happening to Lucille and me. We had too much sincere love and devotion. In other words, never divorce each other. Our home must be our castle.

I commenced to calling ol' Lucille Moms. My Moms. She's so atten-
tive, and she reminds me and does a lot of things just like my mother
Mayann. And since she [Mayann] passed in 1927 it seems as if Lucille has
close features just like Mayann. Some of Lucille's ways and little gestures
are just like my mother's. Then I came to a conclusion that I must set
Lucille down. Not just to be a housewife or anything like that. I figured if
we want the comfortable happiness that I seek with the girl, she must stay
home and keep our citadel. . . .

The money that I could afford to send to her after paying expenses at
home she would save as much as she could, and when she saved enough
for a down payment on a house she came out here in Corona and was very
lucky to run into the same white family—their children were raised with
Lucille when she and her family lived in Corona in her young school days.
These white people were moving out, going to another neighborhood. The
house was, and still is, so high-powered and distinctive looking [and I had
never seen it] until the night I came home off of the road. Caught a cab
downtown after we unloaded our bus. I gave the cab driver the address
and told him to drive me to this address—and me, I've never been to this
house before. It was in the wee hours in the morning. And I was real beat
for my youth. Tired as old hell. Lucille and the family were all in bed
sound asleep, not knowing when our bus would get into the City of New
York. Anyway, I get up enough courage to get out of the cab and ring the
bell. And sure enough, the door opened and who stood in the doorway
with a real thin silk nightgown, hair in curlers. To me she looked just like
my favorite flower, a red rose. The more Lucille showed me around the
house, the more thrilled I got.

LUCILLE AND LOUIS ARMSTRONG

LOSE WEIGHT THE "SATCHMO" WAY

Over the years Lucille and Louis grew more and more attached to their house and the surrounding Corona community. There were specific physical features of the house that came to mean a great deal to him—"a whole lot of comfort and happiness": a garage with a remote-controlled "magic" gate, a wall-to-wall bed, and most important of all, a bathroom with mirrors everywhere, "since we are disciples to laxatives." Indeed, Louis's bathroom was the extension of a great anal fixation, a quality directly traceable to behavior instilled in him by Mayann early on. It was she who impressed upon him the need to cleanse and regulate the bowels by taking a "physic."

Later, influenced by the writings of Gayelord Hauser—whose Diet Does It *was among the books in Louis's collection— Armstrong became obsessed with an herbal laxative called "Swiss Kriss," often taking it three times a day. He even had thousands of cards printed with a photograph of himself, pants down, seated on his toilet, with the accompanying legend: "Satchmo says, 'Leave it all behind ya!'" Because his weight fluctuated, he combined the Swiss Kriss routine with a diet co-authored by Lucille and himself that is best described as idiosyncratic. —JB*

Louis Armstrong
    featuring:
    Swiss Kriss—herbal laxative
    Bisma Rex—it cuts gas. You can buy it in any drug store. . . . Rexall Drug Store.
    Fresh orange juice—it's delicious, softens fat.
Directions

At Bedtime

P.S. Your first dose will be real heavy, in order to start blasting right away, and get the ball to rolling. After you get over your surprises and whatnots, you'll be very happy. The first week, take a tablespoonful of Swiss Kriss. Put it into your mouth and rinse it down with a glass of water. Fifteen minutes later, drink a large glass of orange juice. Don't eat no food before going to bed. After the first week, cut Swiss Kriss down to a teaspoonful every night.

At Breakfast Time

Large glass of orange juice and black coffee or tea, etc.

At Lunch Time

Eat whatever you want, as much as you want. Just have slices of tomatoes with lemon juice over it—mm. It's good. In fact, you may choose any salad that you like—just see that you have some kind, any kind. Coffee, tea, or, etc. Twenty minutes later take a tablespoonful of Bisma Rex. Stir it in a glass of water—stir real good—and drink it right on down. Chase it down with a half glass of water.

Between Meals

If you should get a little hungry between meals, just drink a large glass of orange juice, two glasses if you should desire.

Supper Time

You can eat from soup to nuts, eat as much as you want to. Please see that you have, at least, either sliced tomatoes (with lemon juice) or your favorite salad. All kinds of greens are good for the stomach. So, eat to your satisfaction. Of course, the less you eat is in your favor. . . . Hmm?? Twenty minutes later, after you have eaten your supper, take a table-spoonful of Bisma Rex in a glass of water. Don't eat before bedtime.

Comments 'n' Stuff

It's a known fact, while eating your meals, if you feel yourself getting full it's in your favor to leave the table with a satisfactory stomach. It's better to have a satisfied, full stomach than to have an over-stuffed stomach. . . . Aye?? P.S. That's where Bisma Rex steps in—it's really great for over-stuffed stomachs, or people who suffer with gas, etc., etc. Yes—it's a "Gassuh"!

In case you do get gas, Ol' Bisma Rex will straighten you. That's why she's on the Mound—to cut gas, grease, and a lot of discomforts from a lot of foods and liquors that won't act right in your stomach, lots of times. When you eat and go right to bed, it sort of makes it tough for Bisma Rex and Swiss Kriss to take over and do its stuff, the right way. . . . Savvy?

Orange juice is so delicious—you should never get tired of drinking it. P.S. It's a sure thing—if you dig this set-up here in this chart, you will automatically lose all the weight that you don't need. And no one should want a lot of excess weight when here's an easy way to get rid of it. Just like I've said before—it takes time, but not as long as an old strenuous diet would drag you, trying to cope with (meaning, to dig). This is not just a diet chart—nay, nay—it's a ticket to a long long healthy life. Make this routine a part of you and there won't be any need of even getting sick, let alone staying fat. Those 'erbs is an old remedy from way back. It's known to clean your whole system out the same time that it's reducing you. This is what I have lived by—especially the laxatives. From a child, my mother always kept me an' my sister Beatrice physic-minded. She'd always say, "You children probly [sic] won't ever get rich, but you'll always be healthy." She's right. All of my days are the same—healthy and happy. I can put on weight and take it off just as easy. Even when I was ninety-five pounds overweight—which I have just lost within a few months and never stopped blowing my trumpet, etc.—I continued to take my Swiss Kriss and Bisma Rex real religiously.

I always could see the wonderful things that orange juice did, and it tastes so good. . . . yum, yum. P.S. When you buy your Bisma Rex, inquire about those Bisma Rex tablets. Always carry a package in your pocket, pocket-book, or your purse so in case you're out some place away from home—having dinner, or eat something that didn't agree with you, etc.— you can still keep up your routine that you have at home by puttin' one Bisma Rex tablet into your mouth twenty minutes after you finished. Or two tablets if you should feel it necessary. Don't get frantic because you have to trot to the bathroom several times when you first get up (awakened). P.S. You won't need an alarm clock to awaken you. . . . No-o-o-o. Relax if you feel a little tired from the Swinging Actions of dear old Swiss Kriss. . . . Ha Ha. You'll have to expect being a little tired after you've finished with S- K- for the day. Orange juice softens it, Bisma Rex cuts it, Swiss Kriss swishes it—tee hee. Everyone should have an orange juice day—give your stomach a good rest for one day a week. Or skip breakfast and lunch and just eat supper.

It really isn't necessary—your main routine will straighten you, and that's for sure.

Orange juice is famously known to kill that hungry desire for food at the wrong time. In moments such as those, drink all the juice (orange juice, that is) that you want to drink. One glass isn't enough, drink two glasses—it's so delicious. When dieting or taking physics, it would be a good idea to choose some kind of vitamin that meets your approval. Take at least one, four times per day. Take before breakfast, lunch, dinner or supper, and last but not least, before Swiss Kriss time.

So, that's about it—I have explained to the very best of my knowledge. So I'll be like the little boy who sat on a block of ice—my tale is told. . . . tee hee. Have a good time.

P.S. In case you're wondering as to how much Swiss Kriss I take—well, even though I've always taken a heaping tablespoonful every time I go to bed to rest my body, I shall do the same every night for the rest of my life. Because, when you and Swiss Kriss get well acquainted, then you'll dig—he's your friend.

Swiss Krissly,

Louis Armstrong.

P.S. When the Swiss Kriss Company gives me a radio show, my slogan will be—"Hello Everybody, this is Satchmo speaking for Swiss Kriss. Are you loosening???????"

JOSHUA BERRETT

DESSERT: FOOD FOR THOUGHT (1999)

Armstrong's home in Corona, the citadel that Lucille helped build for her man, was an immense depository of memorabilia, notably reel-to-reel tapes and scrapbooks. He loved to have the tape recorder on whenever friends or colleagues were around, whether at home or backstage. These recordings he would store in boxes decorated with collages created from news clippings, photographs, and such. But his home also housed a library of books covering such topics as diet, poetry, biography, history, and race relations. Among them were biographies of Adolf Hitler and Paul Robeson; and special presentation copies from Langston Hughes (*Famous American Negroes*), Richard Avedon, Truman Capote, and others, including a physicist who had been inspired by Louis's trumpet. The methodical way in which Armstrong proceeded to read the literature on his shelves reveals something of his commitment to expanding his knowledge. A case in point is a rather obscure two-volume work from 1946–47 by J. A. Rogers: *World's Great Men of Color: 3000 B.C. to 1940 A.D.* Armstrong selected twenty-two names, beginning with Samuel Taylor Coleridge, Toussaint L'Ouverture, and Frederick Douglass, each name being checked off the list as he worked his way through.

Part Five

RED BEANS AND RICELY YOURS

LOUIS, THE LETTERWRITER

"Ever since I was a small kid I have always been a great observer," writes Louis Armstrong in his memoir, *Satchmo: My Life in New Orleans*. Almost invariably, when he put words to paper, whether in the form of reminiscences, anecdotes, gossipy tidbits, outrageous puns, ribald humor, witticisms, or confessions, Armstrong's powers of observation are unmistakable. Perhaps no body of writing captures his range of style better over a long span of time than his letters. They are filled with distinctive quirks—oddball and inconsistent spellings, the interjected chuckle, "tee hee," the frequent sign-off "Am Red Beans and Ricely Yours," and much more. Most remarkable of all—and we need to be reminded of this— they are the boldly unadulterated products of a man with little more than a fourth-grade education.

Already in August 1922, when he first arrived in Chicago, Armstrong was using his own typewriter to correspond with friends. Rather telling is that one of the earliest surviving letters, from September 1, 1922, complains that three previous letters (one to the recipient, two to other friends) have gone unanswered. Over the following four or five decades Armstrong was the prolific correspondent, pouring out letters in torrents of elliptical phrases, somewhat like swinging riffs—"reeling an' arockin' and justa enjoying that fine music"—almost never proofreading (although he did come to edit some of them in later years), writing or typing missives in his dressing room between sets, in his hotel room while on the road, and at home in Corona, Queens. The letters included here have been edited only minimally so as to preserve the flavor of the originals as much as possible. —JB

TO LEONARD FEATHER (1941)

The first letter reproduced here was written shortly after an appearance in late September 1941 at Fort Barrancas, near Panama City, Florida at a time when GI's were largely segregated. It is remarkably rich in intimate detail, describing Armstrong's performance at the military base before the white soldiers, his receiving a medal from the commanding officer, his visit to the post hospital, his playing for the colored dance that night, and much more, including matters of hair styling and diet. The original letter, on fourteen single-spaced typewritten pages, is addressed to Leonard Feather, the British-born music critic, arranger, and producer who became an American citizen in 1943. Feather, who was a major promoter of jazz in the United States from the 1940s to the 1980s, was associated with such periodicals as Esquire, Metronome, *and* Down Beat, *and towards the end of his life taught at California State University, Northridge, and UCLA. —JB*

Panama City, Florida.
October 1, 1941.

Planes fly,
The birds flew,
Dig this Jive
I'm writing you.

Dear Feather:

Now don't bawl me out for taking so long to write to you this time—after all I am a very busy man making these fine one nighters. When we arrive into town there isn't very much writing that you can do [before] getting ready (you know?)—primping up, etc. for the dance. After all, we have to look nice to the public every night as well as playing well every night. And Feather, if I have to say it myself, these are the cleanest musicians I've played with for a long time. Not mentioning their very fine playing abilities. Another thing that I admire about my present band is they're not Konk conscious. They don't visit those gas stations to get their hair dressed like a lot of lazy musicians and acts that I know do. They dress it and keep it looking nice and natural themselves like they're supposed to do. In slang gas station means the barbershop. Konkoline is that hair stuff we colored folks (meaning the ones that like that kind of stuff) apply to our hair (when in the mood for straight hair); it straightens it straighter than Canal Street in New Orleans my home town. I merrily mentioned about the hair to you (although you'll probably won't dig what I'm laying on you anyway about this hair jive. But it's very interesting to me because I am a colored boy myself (at least, I think I am) and I can see the difference to the looks which one makes, you look the youngest—Konk has a tendency to make one look much older than himself.

While I am on the subject, that reminds me of an incident that happened in Chicago the time when we played the Regal Theatre there. A few "us" boys from my band (P.S. you get the "us" boys? . . . tee hee). Anyway, [a] few of us boys were invited out to a very nice party after the last show. We certainly did have a swell time. The conversation came up about the show we had at the Regal, etc. Different ones passing their little comments, etc. What really did knock me out was when this girl, who was sitting there with us in the party around a great big dining room table, said, "Well there's one thing that I admire about your band Sachem (meaning me)—I noticed that didn't any of your boys have their hair Konk'd—and they certainly did look nice." Well sir, it took me off of my big feet.

Speaking of hair reminds me of the time when I used to didn't wear a hat. You know—??? way back in the good old days when me and Zootie [sic] Singleton (that drummer man from my home town of "Knor"leans (meaning New Orleans) were beating it out in Connie's Inn. Lawd today. Those were the days if there wuz ones. Me and old Zootie used to run together. We went everywhere together and had some real righteous kicks. Ole Ted Kohler that great creator of songs will knock one out telling them about the good ole days around Chicago and Zootie and I took him out one night showing him our South Side. Ole Ted and I sure were glad to see each other in California when I made the flicker *Artists'N'Models*. He's a fine cat. I hope he writes a hit every time he breathes—.

You know Leonard, although I am writing this letter to you personally, I do think that it would be very nice to let our dear public in on the inside situations and things about "our" bunch and our tours and our playings of our music for these wonderful publics. Oh it's so interesting until I don't think that I can hardly explain it. Especially the Sunday afternoon we play an hour's concert in Pensacola, Florida for the Soldiers there at Fort Barrancas Barracks. The concert started at six o'clock that afternoon, and over five thousand soldiers attended. And was it thrilling when we started "The Star Spangled Banner" and every one of those soldiers stood up and every one of them gave the same right-hand salute as they stood to attention. Good gracious, was I thrilled. Man, I couldn't help but keep one eye on my trumpet, one eye on the soldiers and concentrate on "The Star Spangled Banner"; and man by diggin' all of that I really did blow some "Star Spangled Banner." Ump.

After "The Star Spangled Banner" was played—we took our program on down from the top. From "Swing That Music" clean on down to the medley. And pardner, I'm telling you it was really in there. Then we played "The Star Spangled Banner" again and me diggin' the same kicks. The funny thing—the Colonel came up on the bandstand where we were playing. We were playing our concert out into an open field where all of the soldiers could sit around and get a good load of things—plenty went on I'm tellin' you. I guess you call it a grandstand that we were playing in. It's built round like the ones we find in our hometowns directly in the center of the city. And when we were kids we used to go there every Saturday night and listen to the hometown brass band beat out a couple of six eights, etc. And we (meaning me and the chick I was with) find ourselves staring at each other so very serious with the stuff in our eyes (as Nicodemus says)—and canoeing and carrying on. Well, that's the way this bandstand was built. And the way it was situated it made everything look swell and the view and the music also sounded oh so swell to me.

Speaking of the colonel at Fort Barrancas, the evening we gave them a concert, he came up on the bandstand where we were playing right in the middle of our concert and said to me, "Satchmo, I've tried my best to not to disturb your fine concert, but over half of the soldiers appointed me to come up here and ask you if you'd be so kind as to tell all the rest of the soldiers the same joke about the colored boy who wanted to join the Royal Air Force the same way you told it to Private (lst class private) George Grow and the other members of the camp when they were bringing you out here from the city and you all were telling lies from way way back. And you told them this one and they told it to most of the other soldiers that they could get to. But since you're here with us we would really like to hear it again and let the other soldiers that didn't hear it, hear it."

So gradually I pulled myself to pieces (I mean together) and went on to tell them about the colored boy who went up to Mr. Winston Churchill and said, "Look heah, Mista Churchill, I wants to fly with this Royal Air Force." So Mr. Churchill said to him: "Well, if that's the way you feel about it, report here on this field at eight o'clock. I'm sending fifty planes over Berlin Germany to drop some pamphlets then return to England." The colored boy said , "Okey dokey—I'll be right here and on time." Sure 'nuff—this colored boy was on time and Mr. Churchill gave the command takeoff, and away they went to drop these pamphlets over Berlin. Well sir, all of the planes returned but this colored boy's. So quite naturally the British pilots would give him up as shot down, etc., feeling sorry for the poor lad. So, three days passed and still no sign of the colored boy. Six days passed and now by this time all of the R.A.F. Pilots just knew that the colored boy was gone bye bye. All of a sudden they looked and heard a plane justa roaring over England, and they could tell from the insignia that it was one of their planes. Everybody went running out into the field to see who it was, and blow me down if it wasn't this colored boy returning. So Mr. Churchill said to him, "Where have you been? I sent those planes alongside of yours to drop those pamphlets over Berlin. What happened?" And the colored boy said, "Awa, I was putting them under their doors." And Leonard those soldiers laughed so loud they scared me—no foolin'. Nice huh?

The chaplain is a very nice gentleman also. He right along with all the other soldiers came up and congratulated us all for everything. I have written him and some of the other boys letters already. And I've received answers from every one of them—they really did write me some knockout letters. The chaplain killed me in his letter when he told me that the cannon that went off so loud the Sunday that I was out there with them wasn't nothing. I should have been there that following Wednesday. I had to changes clothes immediately after I'd finished our concert out there that Sunday before I went out to town to play for the colored dance that night I was so wringing wet. Perspiration's the cause of it from the strategy I suppose. Oh, I couldn't never finish telling you all the nice things they said about me and my gang. It's some of them though I just can't forget. The night of the dance right after we finished the concert for the soldiers, Private George Grow, who's a very popular guy around the whole Fort Barrancas Camp—and he is as groovie as a two dollar movie, and I mean that—George and I went home from camp. The colonel, the chaplain and several of their very fine friends drove us into town at my house, the place where I was staying while there, and they dropped me and George at home and they went on [to] some other place saying they would dig me at the colored dance that night. So George and I went on into the house where Alpha (my little gatemouth wife and hip'd as she can be) had a big fine dinner ready for us. And I'm tellin' you, we ate so much until we had to say "forgive us" as we rose from the table.

Now this will kill ya. After we finished dinner we went directly to the dance. And the dance hall where this dance was—really too small for the crowd they had. "Ahem." And the bandstand (there wasn't none) was on the floor. The best we could do was to have Mutt, the "Valaa" (valet to you) of the band—put our music trunks up in front as best he could—kinda a barricade—so that made George Grow sit right down there with us near Ann Baker. And they would run their mouths as the night (that hot one) would roll on. And he's enjoying everything. He didn't have to report back to camp before the next morning. And child, he had a ball. Funny thing—the first number on down was knockin' Ol' George Grow completely out, although we had just finished playing a very swell concert for his company that afternoon. By the way, I think George Grow was responsible for us meeting such a fine bunch of people as those soldiers.

What I'm really trying to make clear was how thrilling this dance was for him. The next day when Ann Baker and I would be talking about George Grow, Ann said he would say to her the night at the dance as I would play one tune to another—he asks Ann, "Doesn't he ever run outa riffs??" Kinda cute, eh? Along about the third set of dance tunes—we usually play half-hour sets at all of our dance dates, and rest a few minutes—take one half hour intermission. And by doing that the public can't squawk, and it keeps a dance much livelier (sometimes too lively) ha-ha. I should have some of the boys in my band tell you about this particular incident. Especially when those spades commenced to fighting like cats and dogs. Ooooweee! I ain't never seen the like in all of my born days, honestly. The fight started so quick and everybody started towards the bandstand and the cop, to quiet it all down, pulled out his pistol as if he was really going to shoot and didn't look like he cared where he was going to shoot. And Dat Did Settle It.

Those colored folks were running in the direction of the band so fast, and George Grow (the white boy) who was sitting up in front of the band alongside Ann Baker. And when the party got rougher and rougher, and as rough as he thought he would take it, I looked around and George was standing way back there by Smoothie (Frank Galbreath my get-off trumpet man who took Red Allen's place), justa running his mouth with Smoothie and watching the Battle Royale. As long as he was "allreet" I was sausagefried (meaning satisfied). I'm telling you, between watching those bottles flying up into the air, the policeman with his gun in the air, and every time he went to put it back into his satchel—look like the gun would be pointing directly at me. Ump. Between all of that and watching and see that nothing happens to my guest and figuring out the maneuverings of that heat and those notes from my trumpet, I'm telling you I was a very busy man indeed. But it all ended up all in fun. Then too, no one gotten hurt, that is, none of our group.

After the dance let out, which was around two in the morning, Grow and I went home where Alpha was waiting for those wet clothes that I changed at the dance so she could pack them some place until our bus reaches the next town. Then she usually puts them in a laundry. She has that routine down to the last frazzle. She even taught [me] my routine of how to keep plenty handkerchiefs (one of the smiley main things), and also took good care of these fine vines. Savvy? Anyway Grow and I went home, and I lay across the bed and relaxed as he told me about so many wonderful things the Army has, and how he's really enjoying them and still enjoying every moment with me and Alpha. He stayed with us until six the next morning, for he had to report for duty the following morning at seven.

That is just some incidents Leonard. You know what a very fine white trumpet player said to me in one of these towns? He said, "Satchmo, you're one trumpet player that every trumpet player in the universe is so happy and glad just to know—you are still—playing as fine as ever." He also said, "I'm not saying this from an angle that we want to fight you with a trumpet or anything bringdownish as that, but we all feel (maybe we don't have a chance to—express it) but we feel that every time a solo is played there's an essence of Satchmo Armstrong around somewheres. That goes for the great—the marvelous, the very good, the superb, the legit to the hottest trumpet player—the minute he stands, or sits, to take a solo on his horn, there's, an essence of Satchmo standing right behind him saying to him just as he gets ready to take off, 'Go on Gate, Ol' Satch is right with ya; let's lay that soul in there together. And, sure enough, here comes a very beautiful solo." It was nice of him to say such as that, huh? But that's a person's feeling. Of course, you know I nearly blushed all over the place . . . tee hee.

Oh yes, you remember me writing to Mr. Glaser (my personal manager) concerning the "Ten Days Diet Chart" Alpha dug out of a *Vogue* Magazine? Well Feather, that chart is the last word. No fooling. Ever since Alpha put me on this diet, which is the one that she'd gotten streamlined 'n' everything, the whole band (my band) is now on the same diet. Honest they are. And they're doing okay with it too. You should see these cats streaming up. Well this diet chart is so easy to get along with, especially when it lets you have steaks, chops, and chicken. What more could one ask? Shucks, I've seen times when I wasn't on no diet and I didn't have steaks, chops, nor chicken . . . ha-ha. So I'm doing all reet now. By the time you see me though I should be rather streamlined myself because I sure am coming down, getting rid of that excess weight. And boy, if I ever get back down to my normal weight, which is around a hundred and seventy five the most, or I might say a hundred and seventy two pounds, that would strike me very pretty.

When I returned from Europe in 1935 I wasn't weighing over a hundred and sixty five pounds, and Alpha, who picks up weight the same time I do, was only weighing a hundred and twelve pounds, and were we two cute little people. My, my, my. Of course, you can verify my statement on this because you were in England (your home) the same time we were over there, and everybody treated us so swell. You know it's a funny thing how things in life strike you as you go from one end of the world to another. Looking at George Washington, my first trombone man and the comedian in the band, reminds me of that fellow who used to do the comedy on the bandstand in Jack Hylton's Orchestra. Whenever they were on the stage or any place Mr. Hylton would appear with his orchestra. What's that boy's name again? I'm sure you should remember him. He was one of the alto sax men, and he would be always doing something while someone was singing—just like George Washington does a lot of times when he's in one of those jovial moods. Ump, dat woid. Oh yes, this alto man that I'm speaking of was a German musician. Quite a coincidence isn't it, or wasn't it. . . .

Speaking of weight, as I said before, everybody in my band is weight conscious, that is the fat ones, us fat ones, I should say. All the boys are not quite so fat. When I speak of the fat ones, I'm talking about Scad (Shelton Hemphill, my first trumpet man), Lawrence Lucy, my guitarist, Carl Fry (who has picked up considerably just since he joined the band), Tapley Lewis (who has been in Rupert Coles's place ever since he's been sick) holding down that first sax, Hayes Alvis (who was formerly with the Duke and now with the Juke), holding down that dog house (the bass), Mr. George Crow (our road manager), and of course myself. I gave them all a copy of the diet chart that Alpha dug from a *Vogue* Magazine. And you should see them getting their grapefruit juice together when we hit these towns nowadays. And they're eating more sensibly too, instead of all of these heavy meals that's facing us up and down this road 'cause [of] all these "bread baskets." And all they had to do was to cut out all of their starches and stop eating at night.

You take the rest of the cats, like Sonny Woods, Luis Russell, Smoothie, Jean Prince, Norman Green, Prince Roberson, Joe Garland—those guys all are holding their weight pretty good. I forgot to tell you of the instruments these boys play. Sonny is the vocalist that you know, Russell is the pianist, Smoothie (Frank Galbreath) trumpet man, Jean Prince another trumpet man, Norman Green one of the trombones, Prince Roberson is one of the tenor sax men, and Joe Garland is the other tenor sax man and musical director. Now there's my other trombone man Henderson Chambers (who replaced Higginbotham and [is] doing a very fine job indeed. He's another one that's doing okay with keeping his weight where it belongs. Of course, there's Smiley (my right-hand man). He never has a worry about his weight. He's kept the same weight ever since he and I were working for Mr. Glaser (my manager) when he had the Sunset Cafe on the South Side of Chicago—way back there in the days when men were men and everybody had money. Smiley's weight has been around one hundred and seventy six pounds all of the time and still is. And he's still looking fine. I know he feels fine. The way that Cat can eat. . . .

Mutt (Benjamin Harris), our band valet, is a small cat also. I guess those heavy music trunks, etc. keep him in perfect trim. He's so small and wears pants that he works in—so big until one day I had to help him keep them up on him. And can he eat! My my. Just for fun I asked Mutt one day would he like to join us in our dietings, and honest, he immediately jumped up and started running as hard as he could away from my direction. He really thought that I meant it. He said, "Nay nay. Never will I do without my rice, potatoes, etc., before I go to bed." Ump, how he does it! And here I am—whenever I eat a heavy meal and go to bed I usually have to stand directly up in bed after I have gone to sleep to avoid indigestion, nightmare, bad dreams, etc. No foolin'. So you can quote me as saying I ain't ever gonna' eat at nights before I go to bed. Now wait a minute. No wisecracks—ha-ha.

Ann Baker (our vocalist) is just the opposite when it comes to the weight question. She says she wants to gain weight instead of losing it. She claims that she's tall and can take it. Well, I do agree with her to a great extent. She was only weighing a hundred and fourteen pounds when she joined our band. And now she's gained fifteen pounds, which makes her weigh around a hundred and twenty nine pounds. She looks real fine right now as she is. She explained she's picked up these pounds directly in the places where she said she needs them most . . . I hope she won't try to overdo it and gain too many more pounds, because I'm afraid that they won't be as becoming to her as the few pounds that she has already picked up. She sure looks good though. She was a little ol' skinny gal when she joined us. One thing it shows—that she's at least been eating; we've been doing the same. Now I'm not casting any insinuations about Ann . . . I do know she looks better now than—ever.

Now you take Shanghai, our bus driver. His real name is Joe Schavoni. He's a real small fellow also. So he can stand aside with Woods and the rest of the tribe. But you just wait until me and my fat gang come through. We're gonna show everybody something. Yessuh.

Speaking of Pensacola. The time we were there I stayed with a man and his wife by the name of Singleton. This man also had a wonderful business there. He had a restaurant and he made some of the very best ice cream that anyone would want to taste. Ooh, that ice cream was good. You know he must be mighty good at making cream—used to be the head man downtown at some great big ice cream company. Now he's in the business for himself and the white folks from downtown and everywheres come to his place and get a load of his cream. . . . He has a place in the rear of his restaurant about the size of a good size room. Big enough for what he needs anyway. That's where he makes that fine ice cream . . . yum yum.

Mr. Singleton also has an alligator farm in the backyard of his establishment. Ooh, you oughta see those great big alligators he has. And he calls them all by name—feeds them only once a week. Now that's something that I didn't know before. I thought that alligators ate more than only once a week. Well, in that case, a camel hasn't anything on an alligator at all huh? Although the camel has that water situation sewed up . . . tee hee. Mr. Singleton feeds his alligators fish, and fresh fish at that. Had a whole box of fish the day I was there, feeding them; and that big one, Horace I think his name was, would just open his big ol' mouth real wide while Mr. Singleton would wait for his mouth to open [to] stick the fish down his throat on a long handle fork. Mr. Singleton wasn't afraid of them at all. In fact, he's raised them, especially Horace the big one since he or she was a little bitsy baby. And it's around twenty eight years of age right now. He'd stick that fork into this 'gator's mouth so fast until one time this big alligator grabbed fish, fork, an' all, and was just about to cut out into the water when Mr. Singleton had to hand it another fish on another fork so he would open his big mouth to grab at that one, and quick like a flash he would grab the other one out of his mouth. Ooh such patience! He can have it. Mr. Singleton also showed me how he feeds his little baby alligators. He had them in the other section of the yard in a box. Little bits of things. He feeds them calves' liver. It's really cute watching their little mouths, looking so innocent 'n' everything as they open them to receive the liver he's feeding them [in] little tiny pieces with a tooth pick. Honest you wouldn't think that they can do so much harm with their chops after they grow up. It was very—interesting though. . . .

Speaking of Mr. Singleton, I wonder if he's related to Zutty Singleton, the drummer in New York? After all, I think I did hear Mr. Singleton say that he was from somewheres down South around our (me and Zutty's) way, around New Orleans. Gee wiz, wouldn't that be swell if Mr. Singleton was related to ol' Zutty, and Zutty's my boy. He and I could go down there and eat all the ice cream that we wanted. Mmm, that sure would be something. Tell ol' Zoot about this when you see him. I'll bet that that cat will crack his side from laughter. . . .

While I was looking at Mr. Singleton's alligators while he was feeding them, I told him the one that George Williams, the blackface comedian who works with the great Bill Robinson shows, [tells] . . . That cat kills me—just to look at him on the street with his makeup off. So I told this one to Mr. Singleton since we were around alligators and also on the subject. He (George Williams) said when he was a little boy living way out in the country one day his mother sent him down to the pond to get a pail of water. She said, "Boy, run down to the pond and fetch me a pail of water right away." So he went running down to this pond to get this water, and the minute he went to dip his pail into this water he looked over there and spied an alligator lying in this water. George said he'd gotten so terribly frightened until he clear forget to get the water and immediately started to running home. And no sooner had he gotten to the porch of his home, his mother said to him: "Boy, where's that water that I told you to get?" And George said, "Mother, there's an alligator in that water." And his mother said, "Aw boy, go and get me that pail of water. Don't you know that that alligator was as afraid of you as you were of him." Sez George, "Well mother, if that alligator was as afraid of me as I was of him, that water isn't fit to drink."

I guess he told her something, eh? . . .

Mr. Singleton's wife isn't afraid of his alligators either. I noticed her making them go back into the water by just shoving a little broom into their faces—or something like that . . . tch tch . . . The only way that I'd be an alligator tamer is that they'll give me a crow bar or something like that into my hands. I wonder what kind of bait they use to catch alligators . . . Hmm?

Ann Baker and I received a couple of Gold Cross cannons from the Colonel Lloyd B. Magruder, Commanding Officer at Fort Barrancas. Ann announced that she was going to have all her fall costumes shaded and tailored so as to set off her cannons with the proper military sprig. And they asked me what I was going to do with my cannons. I laid that fine thankful smile of mine on him and said, "Man, them's gold. I'm going to put 'em away in my safe deposit box. I shall never part with them. No suhree." The cannons are emblematic of the coast artillery branch and these were the only pure gold ones the colonel possessed. They were a token of his own appreciation of the enjoyment the entertainers gave his troops and the ones in the hospital wards.

When they pinned that Official Coast Artillery Insignia on my lapel, I was almost in tears. It was really a touching moment. Lt. William P. Maxwell, post chaplain George Grow, and some doctors took me over to the post hospital to visit the sick soldiers. And Feathers, you've never seen anything like it—the way those soldiers, colored and white, all brightened up just at the sight of me. Gee, what a wonderful feeling that was to know that I cheered them all so. Before I left there I led off one of those good ol' spirituals, "When the Saints Go Marchin' In." And George Grow and the rest of them joined in on the chorus. And it was real touching. They appreciated it so. They had a big pail of fresh lemonade and some sandwiches freshly made. I joined them in that session. One of the colored patients wanted a few bars of "Whatcha Know Joe." So I laid it on him lightly before I departed. . . .

The doctors and nurses told me that some of those patients, [who] hadn't been on their feet in weeks, were up this day and smiling when they found out that I was coming to visit them. You could tell from their hand clapping that they [were] really enjoying things that were going on. Then I signed a whole gang of autographs, including one on the cast of one of my fans confined to his bunk with a broken back. This young feller said that he's never gonna part with that cast, even after he's well and out of the army. He expects to send it home to his parents when he comes out of it. I inscribed Louis Satchmo Armstrong on it for him. In case you don't know it Leonard, Fort Barrancas is one of the country's oldest army posts, and I was escorted on an inspection tour of the barracks. And boy, I marveled at the modern conveniences, and beamed as soldiers, candid cameradicts snapped my pitture (meaning picture). Ann and I both had our pictures taken while sporting officer campaign hats. From an official release of the camp's newspaper there was an article in there about that wonderful—day out there, and it said, "The sepian bandleader, whose music is as familiar on the Nile as it is on the Mississippi, left a big joke book he had recently typed so the men could enjoy a few chuckles between duties. When his life story, soon to be filmed by Orson Welles, come to the Fort Barrancas Theatre, there should be little worry about attendance." Now isn't that just grand of them? And just think, by the time we get to the coast to make this film I should be kinda trimmed up a bit (losing weightly speaking). Heh-heh. Now don't expect too much, Leonard, when you see me. After all, I've been forty pounds overweight for almost five years now. How 'bout that?

I picked up all of this excess weight when I was playing downtown at the New Connie's Inn on Broadway. When I would get off from work we (me and my gang) would go uptown in Harlem to a little restaurant that used to run all night at that time, and they have at that time in the mornings (four to five o'clock) red beans and rice, pig ears, hog maws, pig tails—and all that sort of real honest-to-goodness home cooking. And, quite naturally, me being a down-home boy, I'd latch on real heavily each a.m. to my regret, because I went right away to bed soon as I ate; that's why my weight increased so rapidly. And before I knew it, I was as big as a house. And when I did try to get rid of it, there was no soap because I had let the fat harden. But—I certainly have learned some sense since then, especially when it comes to eating sensibly. I find that it's just imagination to want to eat at night after you've had a very good supper the evening before. I know you're glad you're small, ain't cha? You're not much smaller than our new drummer man, Spencer O'Neal or O'Neal Spencer. He's the smallest little cat to play so much drums. And where he puts so much food is beyond me.

While writing this letter I've received a letter from the chaplain down in Fort Barrancas, Florida. He still insists that I haven't heard a gun go off until I hear that big one that he was tellin' me about some time ago. He still insists that the one I heard is just like a firecracker compared to the one he's talking about. That goes to show you Gate Ol' Uncle Sam is getting groovy. Ha-ha. The chaplain said (while speaking of this great big cannon going off), he said that he knew I would have enjoyed hearing it. I wonder?? He also said that he came down to the dance the night we played in Pensacola, but was unable to get near the place. 'S too bad too. Because I wanted him to get a load of us beating out a dance date which is something very fine. P.S. A light pat on our backs. You can stand it, I'm sure. I wrote and told him about the way those bottles were flying and he said that had he known it he would had the army there to help watch those bottles while I was blowing that trumpet . . . ha-ha. Ol' Chapie kills me; indeed he does. What a sense of humor he has. He said then I wouldn't have had to strain my eyes keeping one eye on the bottles and the other on my trumpet, and not have to get eye strain from trying to see two things at once. He also said, if you ask me, "I think your eye strain comes from trying to keep an eye on the trumpet and Ann Baker, and not the pop bottles, you rascal you." Now isn't that just too cute for words? Tee hee. I tellya Rev., I mean chap for chaplain, ain't nothing but a bone tickler. He closes his letter by saying, "Well fella, when you are down this way again be sure and stop, and I will try to save you some lemonade and sandwiches. Keep your chin up and your nose clean, and I will see you again." Now that's what I call a real letter.

George Grow kills me too when he writes. He has been down in New Orleans since we were last in each other's company. He was tellin' me about those real good and deelicious [sic] pralines they serve down there. He said they were full of those good ol' pecans. Speaking of pecans reminds me of the time when I was in San Antonio Texas playing a white dance, and after the dance was over I was talking to some of the musicians of the town. Amos Ayala was one of the musicians. I was telling Amos about the time we played at New Iberia, La. That's where Bunk Johnson lives. We went out to Bunks's House for dinner, me and a couple of the boys in my band. And as I was tellin' Amos about those great big pecan trees Bunk had in his backyard, Amos looked me right square in my eye and said, "What kind of trees?" And I said, "Aw, pucahns trees." We both laughed.

I tell ya Leonard I really do meet some funny cats out on this road. Very seldom [is] there ever a dull moment. Especially when you run into fine guys like Amos, Emilio Caceres—who can really play a whole gang of fiddle. Oooo but he's good. And don't leave out Jimmy Gomez on that guitar. All of San Antonio, yessir. When Amos looked at me when I was justa runnin' my mouth about the pecans and he dug me and I had to change to pucahns. That really was a funny moment for me. It's the way it happened, I guess—was the cause of it being so doggone funny. Then he killed me when he said to me, "Since you've been up north running round with Zutty and those northern hep musicians, you're getting awful proper on our hands." God, that man had me holding my sides. And when I get that tickled I gets weak all over.

Ran into Don Albert the ex band leader who had a very fine band a few years back. Don's not doing anything too much nowadays. I am talking about the music game. Of course, he's working for the government. Some of his men are still around San Antonio, gigging and doing little odd jobs, etc. His fine trumpet man by the name of Alcone, [a] little Creole boy, is now in New Orleans playing with Sidney Desvigne's band. And they tell me that Sidney has the hottest band down there. I know this kid Alcone really has lots of power. With the least [bit] of experience with a big name band, he's really going places. That is, if he'll just reserve his chops and don't abuse them. He seems to be a very sensible little chap though.

Oh yes, I saw Paul Barbarin our ex drummer while we were down in New Orleans. Him and young Robichaux have a band together. That's what they tells me. And they say that it's really coming on. All the boys in my band didn't get a chance to dig ol' Paul while were there, because the first time we passed through New Orleans it was about six o'clock in the evening and our road manager told us that he's only stopping over then just to give Shanghai, our driver, about five or six hours' rest, as he was driving all the night and day before. Tough cat, that Shanghai guy. I don't know who's the toughest, he or Tex our old driver. They both can really endure a whole lot of road. So while Shanghai was taking his beauty nap we went to a Creole place and had some good ol' gumbo fleecy [sic] [as] they call it down there. Mmm, it's so very delicious. After we had our gumbo we had some raw oysters on half shell—a light dinner, but so delicious and everything . . . Those Creoles down there downtown certainly did treat us swell. Gee, they came runnin' from every direction when they heard that Louiee [sic] Armstrong's bus was parked at Dumaine and Claiborne Avenues, two popular streets. I remember way back in the days when the Odd Fellows and the Labor Day parades used to pass that corner—I was quite a youngster then—but I still can remember that I had to do a lot of runnin' [and] second lining behind those parades—just to hear Joe King Oliver or Bunk Johnson or Emanuel Perez blow those trumpets. Those Creoles were certainly bad in those days. The downtown boys would not let the uptown boys pass Dumaine and Claiborne without putting up a fight or getting sapped up. Of course, ever since I was a youngster my mother always told me that a good run is better than a bad stand any time. Therefore when the selling out (meaning the runnin') was in session I would be right up there in the lead, outrunnin' a striped (?) ape. There's a little lunch stand that opens up on Dumaine and Claiborne every night and he's famous. I'd say he's very very famous all over the world for the fine sandwiches he has been making for years and years. You get your sandwiches, as many as you can eat, and you'll never stop at just one of any one of them you should get. His stuffed crabs, stuffed peppers, boiled shrimps—there's lots of other sandwiches he makes—His name is Joe Sheep. Just ask any Creole cat that's from New Orleans about Joe Sheep's sandwiches, and they'll verify my statement.

When we returned to New Orleans to play the dance uptown at the Rhythm Club every cat from my old neighborhood were up there. And the place was packed and jammed. My old boss of years ago, Mr. Morris Karnofsky and his wife were also there and enjoyed themselves and our music to the highest. He and I talked about the good ol' days when I was just a kid working on his coal wagon with him selling coal to the sporting class of people down in the red light district, which were running full bloom at that time . . . I was so small until I had to put on long pants whenever Mr. Karnofsky would go down in the district to sell his stone coal (as we called it then); five cents a water bucket. Oh, I really thought I was somebody down there amongst those pimps, gamblers, etc. Oh Leonard, it was a picture within itself. Just think, you weren't even due here when all that was going on. . . . What really amused me so when I went down in New Orleans this time was, when I went sight-seeing I passed through these places where the red light district used to be, and they have built some of the most beautiful homes there one would ever want to see. Why you'd hardly recognize the ol' landmarks.

Another cute moment in New Orleans nowadays when we play there is my grandma, Mrs. Josephine Armstrong. She'll dig me no matter when I come to town. And the night of the dance you can see her sitting right up on the bandstand with me and the rest of my crew, reeling an' arockin' and justa enjoying that fine music we usually lay under her belt. Everybody in town knows her. She's the grandma whom I lived with for a long time when I was real young. When I used to get unruly grandma would send me out into the backyard and dig that great big willow tree and have me pull the switch off of there—I'm to be whipped with. And man, I'd try to find the smallest switch that I could, ha-ha. She and I laugh about those days right now. I always lay a little scratch (money) on grandma, alongside of the long line of cousins and step-brothers and sisters I have down there. And there's my real sister, Beatrice (Mama Lucy) Armstrong. I greases her mitts real heavy.

My sister and I are the only two what's left of the Satchmo family. She and I get together every time I'm down there and just talks about old times and almost crack our sides from laughing. I'll never forget the time when I was about seventeen years old and I used to hustle quite a bit around the older musicians—playing for them until they take a few minutes out, etc. And if their tips were good they would give me as much as they could spare me. Then too, me being a youngster, I was doing all right. But this particular night business was very dull and at the end of the night I only received fifteen cents. Anyway I went home and divvied up with mother just the same. I told mamma that business was kinda bad last night and this fifteen cents was all that I had. And immediately my sister Mama Lucy awakened out of a sound sleep and said, "Ump. Blow all night for 15 cents. Ump, ha-ha." Of course, it's funny now, but sis made me so dog-gone mad. I have a fine sister and she is just wild about her big Anklemouth Brother Satchmo. And Satchmo is crazy about her too.

Oh yes, I received a very fine letter from England today. It was from the Secretary-Founder of the Dewsbury Rhythm Club. He really did knock me out when he said the Rhythm Clubs over there have never stopped runnin' regardless. And that they are stronger and more enthusiastic than before. Yes, indeed. They also said over there during a Hot Club Meeting they are looking forward to me and my little Satchmo Trumpet crossing again and beating out some more riffs over there. Now isn't that just too cute for words? . . . I MEAN . . .

Well Feather, I guess I've about beat up my chops enough now. So you must take 'em slow and answer my letter or my newspaper, whatever you might call it. When I writes, I writes, that's all. Tell all the cats up in Harlem way that I, Ol' Satchmo is now reducing, believe it or not, and I want all of these fat boys who used to admire each other's bread basket to LOOKOUT. I am on my way to the streamline department, and I don't mean perhaps either. Nightie night Feathers ol' deah. I'll a'be aseein' you's. Tell my daddy, Father Glaser, howdy.

Am dietingly yours,
Louis Armstrong.

TO BEATRICE ARMSTRONG

Louis Armstrong Archives Series, Letters 3, No. 1/7

Towards the end of his letter to Leonard Feather, Armstrong refers to his sister Beatrice (Mama Lucy), his only full sibling, saying, "I greased her mitts real heavy." She apparently spent almost all of her life in relative poverty and obscurity, most of it in New Orleans. For a time in the early 1920s she worked in a Florida saw mill and ran a "little gambling joint" with her common-law husband. The following undated and very cryptic telegram to Mama Lucy reveals a stern, anxious side of Armstrong. It was handwritten on seven Western Union sending blanks and presumably originated from Hollywood Knickerbocker Hotel in Hollywood, California. —JB

Mrs. Beatrice Collins
1926 Lassepp Street
New Orleans, LA.

Dear Sis:

I am giving my wife, Lucille, the same amount of money each week to send to [you] which will have to stop the month of December. Then I can't send any more money. I am going to have a long layoff. And there will not be any work or money coming in. Sis, that is a lot of money which will take care of your troubles completely. Lucille and myself both have troubles also where bills and money is concerned. So please govern yourself accordingly and realize that we are doing the very best we can to make you happy. From now until December you will have received a lot of money by that time if you just don't waste it. We love you.

Our love to the family.

God bless you all.
Brother Louis Armstrong.

TO FRANCES CHURCH (1946)

From an uncataloged collection in the Library of Congress

Armstrong's letter to Frances Church—she was Joe Glaser's personal secretary for many years—is interesting for several reasons. While it bubbles over with typical good spirits, it captures some of the frustrations and humiliations that were very much part of life for a black musician working in the backwaters of Louisiana, and indicates how Armstrong was able to outsmart the authorities when push came to shove.

In addition, he does not hesitate to speak his mind about wasting his time signing autographs in record shops that do not bother to stock his records. And there is a vivid account of Mardi Gras in New Orleans, a preview by almost three years of Armstrong's own appearance there as King of the Zulus. For it was in its issue of February 21, 1949 that Time *magazine featured Louis Armstrong on its cover and ran the story "Louis the First." In that article the reporter commented: "Among Negro intellectuals, the Zulus and all their doings are considered offensive vestiges of the minstrel-show, Sambo-type Negro. To Armstrong such touchiness seems absurd, and no one who knows easygoing, nonintellectual Louis will doubt his sincerity. To Jazz King Armstrong, lording it over the Zulu Parade (a broad, dark satire on the expensive white goings-on in another part of town) will be the sentimental culmination of his spectacular career, and a bang-up good time besides." —JB*

Opelousas, La.
March 10, 1946.

Said one strawberry to another—
If we hadn't been in the same bed together
We wouldn't be in this jam—
Tee Hee.

Dear Mrs. Church:

How are you today? Am sure you and the rest of the tribe at the office are all well and enjoying the finer things in life. As for myself, you know

I'm a happy cat—Tee Hee. The wife has just cut out for the Apple (New York) and girl, we really balled a while. Mrs. Church, I just had to write and give you a big laugh over that awful "drag" we ran into in Shreveport, La.—ump ump ump. A bunch of jerks (as the high priest, Mr. Glaser would say) sure thought they were smart by attaching all our music trunks, etc. I noticed when I went to work I saw the ofay promoter and two sheriffs kinda waiting for me to arrive—ahem—Immediately the promoter said to me: "Sorry, Pops. I hate like hell to do this to you, but I was given a raw deal." Bla bla bla, and that kind of B.S. So I told him: "That's all right, old man. I have nothing at all to do with it. When the office tells me to go some place and blow my horn, dat's all brother."

Just then two old cracker sheriffs came up to me and said (kinda roughly): "Are you Louis Armstrong?" I said: "Yassuh." Then one of them asked me: "Is that your band?" I hurriedly said: "No, suh. I only play in the band—(tee hee), and the other said: "Just the same, we are going to take your trumpet when you finish tonight." That's when I got real loud and said: "FOR WHAT?" And they (all three of them) said: "We have a case against you and when you finish playing tonight we want that trumpet. Is that clear?" I said: "It's clear as a whistle." Haw haw haw. And sho 'nuff, when we finish the dance and finished playing "The Star Spangled Banner" here they come right into me reaching for my trumpet. But I tricked them so pretty. When they asked me—"where's your trumpet?"— I pointed to a trumpet case and said: "There it is." The promoter was kind of hip'd to the jive and asked me: "Are you sure that is your trumpet?" I said: "Yassuh, boss. That's the one I blow every night." But it wasn't. I gave them Joe Jardan's (one of my trumpet men's trumpet instead of mine) and that was that—Tee hee. Cute? You see, Joe and I made the switch during our intermission, right under their noses. So they weren't so smart after all. We had to cut out the next morning and leave Frenchy [Pierre Tallerie, road manager] there to put up a bond, etc. In the next town we had to play all night by "head." That means we faked everything we played, but good. Made me real proud of my band. Everything's in order again. That's life.

I certainly did enjoy the carnival and Mardi Gras down in my hometown, New Orleans. Oh, it was simply grand. And the day of the Mardi Gras parade I was right in the middle of that mess. B'lieve that. On that day, you know, the Zulu King (which I'm a member of the Zulu's Club), they turns out on Mardi Gras day, and the Zulu King arrives in the New Basin Canal. This year they had around six or seven floats. The King rides in the first float. I was on the float with the King, and Mrs. Church, they really gas me to no end. You should have seen me bowing an'a waving to the folks and cats as they cheered at the sight of me (their home boy). Oh, it's only great. I had Velma [Middleton] (my vocalist) on the King's float with me. And she was thrilled. Yass she was.

The Zulus are very popular and known or heard of all over. The parade had several stops where people and friends waited for the Zulus to arrive, and they were serving the King nothing but champagne. No, no, no, the King wouldn't drink anything but champagne. And every time he raised his elbow, I raised mine right along with him. And—I gotten so full of champagne until I thought I was seeing two floats with a gang of Kings and Satchmo's on it. Haw haw haw. Honest to goodness, we were having so much fun until we almost forgot we had to go to Mobile and play that night—Tee hee. And we did miss the bus (our bus) at that. They just couldn't wait any longer, congested as the traffic was. Velma and I had to beg away from the King of the Zulus and his boys to let us cut out so's we could catch that 3:20 train to Mobile, Alabama. And we did just make it. While Pugh [Doc Pugh, Louis's valet] (who waited for me instead of going with the bus) and I were packing, Velma went some place and drummed up a couple of ham-and-egg sandwiches, one for me and one for her. And away we went to the L. & N. Station. I was so beat for my youth when we gotten on the train until the minute I ate that sandwich (like mad), laid my head back on the seat where I was sitting, [and] slept all the way to Mobile. We arrived in Mobile at 8:45, and we hit at nine. Now you can see, we were some maneuvering set of cats, huh!

It was really worth the sacrifice considering the sort time we had. Just think. If we didn't have to go to Mobile or any place to play that Mardi Gras night, I guess I would have about "annihilated" my foolself [sic] in my hometown. Haw haw haw. They want me to run to be the King in next year's Mardi Gras. So I'll have to check up on it and talk it over with the big Magaffy (Mr. Glaser). I imagine I'd have to have the whole week off during carnival. Lots of time for it, anyhoo—My band boys (the northern ones) have never seen anything like our Mardi Gras in their whole lives. And I know they're talking truth.

We're stopping here in Opelousas with a fine kinda middle-aged lady, and she knows life. Ump. I knocked her out this morning. At breakfast she did not feel so hot. So I gave her a great big glass of pluto water (tee hee). And I'm telling you. Between she and me, having a foot race for the bathroom, it was a great situation. Haw haw haw. Now she's happy again. You know I'm happy. I have a new pluto water customer. Doooo.

That reminds me of a guy going into a swell restaurant, and he could not order anything but a hamburger sandwich. The place would be crowded with all the swells and the elites, an' stuffs. And here comes this guy ordering a hamburger sandwich. So the waitresses, they all jumped real salty (got sore) with him. And the waitress who waited on him told the other waitresses "the next time that guy comes in here I'm gonna scratch hamburger off the menu." And sho 'nuff, here comes this guy in the place. And as soon as the waitress saw him coming to his table she scratched hamburger off the menu. When he sat down the waitress said to him (as she handed him the menu): "Sir, I've just scratched what you like." The guy said to her: "Oh, that's all right. Just wash your hands and bring me a hamburger sandwich." Ump.

Well Madam Church, I guess I'll eat my duck (meaning) I'll come to a close by saying thanks a million for going all out of your way to type for me the route sheet. Of course, you know I appreciate it. Everything went well in Texas. Other than those personal appearances at those record shops to sign or autograph records, etc. Don't get me wrong; it's kind of a good deal. But, what I'm driving at is. You consent for me to go to these places to (I guess) to sign my records. And when I get to the place I find out that they don't have any of my records at all. There I have to sit signing a lot of old crap they've bought that's recorded by someone else. Now does that make sense for me to break my good doing rest (as well as I like to sleep or lay around getting ready to go play my job)? And especially when Lucille's with me, nobody can get me out of the house. Nay nay nay. Only to blow that trumpet. Now you can imagine me sitting around some E-flat record shop waiting for some pimply faced boy come in and ask me a lot of silly questions just to impress me that he's so hep till it hurts. Ump. And then too, the way I see it, Mrs. Church, that's old time stuff. If they were my own recordings I wouldn't mind so much. But, just the same, keep me away from all that mess in the future if you can. Of course, if you can't, that's a horse of another change (I mean color)—Tee hee. Remember the old saying, "all work and no play makes Jack a dumb sommitch [*sic*]? It just don't have to be Jack. Anybody, ya dig. Well nightie night, Mrs. Church.

My regards to the staff and bless ya.

Am Pluto Waterly Yours,
Louis Armstrong.

TO MADELEINE BERARD (1946)

Louis Armstrong Archives Series, Letters 3, No. 1/6

Armstrong started writing his letter to Madeleine Berard in San Francisco on November 25, 1946, and resumed it at 2 A.M., December 4, in Tulsa, Oklahoma to complete it. Yet the five-and-a-half-page, single-spaced typewritten missive was mailed almost three weeks later—it carries a Miami, Florida postmark of December 21. Madeleine, a charming Swiss journalist and aspiring dancer, first made Armstrong's acquaintance when interviewing him at New York's Roxy Theater, and Armstrong's great affection for her comes across in almost every line. He talks about his efforts at reading and speaking French, the making of his latest movie— New Orleans—*his tour, his dog, and more. Incidentally, Madeleine was soon to become a member of Armstrong's extended family, marrying his bassist, Arvell Shaw. —JB*

Golden Gate Theatre.
San Francisco California.
November 25, 1946.

The Bee is such a busy soul
He has no time for birth control.
And that is why in times like these
We have so many Sons-of-B's.

Dear Madeleine:

No doubt you've wondered what has happened to ol' Satchmo Armstrong, huh? It has certainly been ages since I've had the opportunity to write you and thank you for the song you sent me; also the photograph in the Switzerland Magazine [sic]. I cut the photograph out and pasted it in our scrapbook. My wife, Lucille Armstrong and my vocalist, Velma Middleton—in fact, the whole band sends their best regards. We've been reading about your taking dancing lessons from the great Katherine Dunham. Isn't she marvelous? You tell her hello for me. And here's wishing you the best of luck. And you can't miss with her teaching you those fine dance routines.

As for myself, I'm well and doing just about the same. Here and there and everywhere. Playing one night stands in a different town every night. And we play a lot of army camps for the soldiers. Of course, we are playing here at the Golden Gate Theatre here in San Francisco for one week, which in our estimation is a real good deal. P.S. In case you don't understand what "good deal" means, just ask any one of your companions in your dancing school or Madam Dunham—Tee hee. That means I laughed. Kind of cute? I noticed in one of your letters where you asked the definitions of several little things I said, such as "tee hee," "savvy," "wee wee," and nightie. Of course, I've not paid any attention to the expressions to that extent. Using them all my life. But since you didn't dig them—ahem, I'll do my very best to make you latch on (I mean understand them). I've explained them—Tee hee—

Don't forget to say hello to the newspaper in your hometown. They are still talking about sending me and my band to Europe. And if they do, I'm sure they will send us to Switzerland also. I've played there several times. I gave concerts all over Europe. One of my biggest ovations were in Switzerland. I love the place.

The song you sent to me, "Hello Baby Mademoiselle" looks very promising. I've rehearsed it over and over on my trumpet. Now I'll give it to my arranger and soon we will be playing it, giving it everything we have. I hope you'll like the way we'll play it. Of course, I am a little rusty in my French (language) . . . It'll all come back to me as soon as I start rehearsing a song. It won't take me long to "latch on" C (I mean "catch on") . . . Ump.

Well I finally finished making the film called *New Orleans*. And let me tell you, I think it's going to be a pretty good lecture on this music called jazz. It starts way [down] there in Storyville in the good old days of 1917 in New Orleans, where this real jazz started. You'll witness a seven-piece band playing some of the finest old tunes you ever heard. Of course, there are the good old popular ones such as "West End Blues," "Mahogany Hall Stomp," "Tiger Rag," "Basin Street Blues," "Ballin' the Jack," "When the Saints Go Marching In," "Maryland, My Maryland," "Milneburg Joys," "Temptation Rag," "Farewell to Storyville." This tune was taken from the recording of "Good Time Flat Blues." Probably you've heard this recording by Maggie Jones. I played the accompaniment with my trumpet on this recording way back there in 1924. So they changed the name of this tune from "Good Time Flat Blues" to "Farewell to Storyville." Billy Holiday sings this tune, but oh my God, she sings it so beautifully. . . .

—Another tune Billy Holiday sings is called "Do You Know What It Means to Miss New Orleans?"—a very beautiful tune . . . There you have the line up of the tunes we're using . . . just a rough idea. So until you see the film, which I do hope you will, I'll leave the rest up to you. Of course, Billy and I are doing quite a bit of acting (ahem); she's also my sweetheart in the picture . . . Ump Ump Ump. Now isn't that something? The great Billy Holiday, my sweetheart? . . . The picture will have it's premiere in New Orleans during the Mardi Gras. And we're going down there for the event. Now isn't that nice? I always sez to myself. Good things come to those who wait. Just think—me in New Orleans during carnival time. My home town. All the old folks and the young folks too will be so glad to see and have me there—Yass Lawd.

Oh, yes. I almost forgot to tell ya. We, Lucille and I, have a cute little son. My manager, Mr. Joe Glaser, gave me the cutest little Boston bull dog you ever laid eyes on. His name is General. And already he looks like he wants to call me "Daddy Satchmo." Haw haw haw. He's traveling on the road with me. And eats more red beans and rice than I can. I'll introduce you to him when I return home (NY). The General sends his best regards, was intending telling you that I received all of your letters. Just didn't have the time to answer them before now. And right now I have a room full of people (my dressing room) and I'll have to write awhile and stop—talk awhile. Kind of please everybody. So everybody [is] happy. I shall send a photograph to Mr. Peter Wydler the first chance I get. Right now I have to close your letter until I get to Tulsa Oklahoma. And that will be Wednesday, December 4, 1946. Now it may seem funny to you for me to do this. But I have quite a few words yet to say to you and I'm determined to finish. Owing to the fact that I'm writing this letter on closing night here at the Golden Gate Theatre, and as I've said before, my dressing room is crowded with old friends, new ones, and my fans. So I'd rather wait until then and continue writing you. Okay?

November we leave San Francisco on tour.

Sacramento California (26th). Army camp. Concert and a dance.

Los Angeles, California (28th). Elks Ballroom. Was real groovie indeed.

Phoenix, Arizona (29th). Mixed dance.

El Paso, Texas (30th). White dance. Colored spectators. After the dance we went across the Border to Juarez, Mexico. I gotten real high off tequila. And tried to eat up all the Mexican food I could find. Haw Haw haw.

Denver, Colorado (December 2). Mixed dance, and how.

Tulsa, Oklahoma (December 4). All colored dance.

So you can see for yourself just how far we have been traveling since we left San Francisco. We're still traveling by bus, or should I have said charabank [*sic*]. Tee Hee. That's the way they call buses over in Europe. Aye?

December 4th, 1946. Well, Madeleine. Here I am, still in Tulsa. It is now two o'clock in the morning. We've just finished playing for the dance. We started at ten o'clock last night. Instead of me going to bed, I am just determined to finish this letter to you if it takes me until time to get on the bus and go to Tampa, Florida. We are leaving here at ten o'clock in the morning for Tampa. That is over thirteen hundred miles. Goodness. Have to be real troupers to get with those long jumps like those. But it's great fun, b'lieve that. Especially when you're making money. Haw haw. Cute? When we get to Florida we will have a good rest (I'm a thinking). We will be in Florida eight days. We will play some nightspot in Miami for a week. Sounds good to thine ears. My wife Lucille and our little son (our Boston bull dog) will soon be leaving me and my tribe to return home and sort of get things ready, just in case we get a chance to come home for Xmas. Ump. Well, she's had enough of this rough and tumble jive anyway. Of course, I hate like hell to see her leave, but there ain't no use laying too much on the kid. After all, she's only a woman. We old hard characters can take this, and some more.

Was just looking at your photographs in the newspapers you sent me, and I must say, you really photographs very well. You must keep up the good work. And I'll guarantee you, you will become a big star before you'll realize it. And of course you know—you have quite a few real admirers here in the United States already. I'm one of your biggest boosters. That is, alongside of Miss Dunham. So you finally found an apartment. Well I know you must be happy now. There's nothing like having a place of your own. You can go and come when you feel like it. Now when I come to the Big Apple (meaning New York), you'll have to explain to me these words "TAUTE MON ANITIE ET MES MEILLEURSS"[1]—something like that. Anyway, I sho [*sic*] would like to know what that means. It couldn't by any chance mean "No credit." Huh? . . . Tee Hee.

You must write me any time you feel like it. I receives all of your letters and clippings you send from the newspapers, etc. I probably won't answer them right away. That's because I just don't have the time. You can see from what I've been trying to explain to you concerning my tour that

I'll gladly write you when I get the chance. It's indeed a pleasure, Madeleine. But, I'm one person just don't like to force myself to do anything. That's why there's such a long delay in letters from me to you. But, as the old American saying goes, "it's better late than never." Didja ever hear that one before? We old timers remembers them all. Yass we do.

If you still have the French newspaper with the write-up about me, I wish you would keep it until we meet. And then you can kind of translate it for me . . . I can speak a little French. But I cannot read anything in the language. But, when I was in Paris and wanted something to eat, believe me girl, when I got through pointing for this and making faces for that, I had all I wanted to eat and more besides . . . Haw haw haw. And had enough left to give to some of the other American musicians who weren't working. And no matter how well they could speak the language, it didn't mean a thing. Because they did not have that "l'argent," meaning "money." So they would come "Scarf" with me. And after our meal we would wound up jamming like mad. Oh we had a real grand time in Paree, especially when the old bunch from Harlem were over there. Those days are gone now, I imagine. I'll see soon. We're slated to go over there some time next year, maybe after Don Redman, Count Basie, and those boys finish up over there. It's just like home over there for me. Of course, you already knows that. . . .

Gee, I do hope to see you before you return back to Switzerland next summer. You'll probably get over there and they won't let you return. We should be there in New York by the middle of February. I'm supposed to do a concert, so Mr. Glaser and Leonard Feather sez. They're the bosses. So don't leave at least until that happens. If it does jump off, you'll have quite lots to write back to the old country of Switzerland. If I do give a concert, I'll just about throw my everything into it. Oh yes, I noticed you had a card from Mr. Arnold Gingrich, the editor of *Esquire* magazine. Do you see much of him lately? He's certainly a fine fellow. I'd like to write him first chance. If you should happen to run across his address, send it to me willya? I'd like to surprise him with a fine letter. People like Mr. Gingrich are not easily forgotten, nay nay.

Last, but not least. Please say hello to Butterfly McQueen for me. She's one of my favorite actresses. We (she and I) worked in play called *Swinging the Dream*, a Shakespearean play. And every night I'd wait for her to come on the stage and do her act. And it would just knock me completely out. Yea, she's a great little actress. This gentleman, Mr. Berner— his name sounds very familiar to me, and I'm quite sure I met him when I toured all over there. Just the same, I'm happy to know he asked about me. Kindly remember me to him when you write over there again. It's been quite some time since I was over there doing my stuff. Hm, mmm.

Before I close this letter I want to tell you how I laughed at what you said, when you said you did not believe that I remembered you. Why Miss Madeleine, my memory isn't that short. Tee Hee. Why I have a memory of an elephant, b'lieve it or not. Sure I remember the visit you gave me at the Apollo Theatre, etc. Also the sending your train card. I remembers it all the same as it happened just yesterday. Are you kidding? How in the world could one forget a fine person like you?

I'm mailing this letter here from Tulsa, Oklahoma sos [*sic*] you can answer right back, that is, if you can. We will be in Florida by the time you get this letter. So if you care to answer, which I wish you would, then you can write me in care of the Mary Elizabeth Hotel, 642 NW 2nd Avenue, Miami Florida. A letter from you would be most "appreciateable." Ump. Did that come outa me? Well, Madam Berard, I guess I've about tired your eyes out long enough for now. I'd like very much to say more, and with just a little encouragement I'd carry on until tomorrow this time. There are such things as wearing your welcome out, even with a too long a letter. Savez? So I don't want to ever be a drag to you if I can help it. So until the next writing time, I'll say nightie night. Keep up the good works and may the Lord bless you forever.

Am Red Beans and Ricely Yours,
Louis Armstrong.

NOTES

1. Given Armstrong's fallible memory and imperfect French, we can presume that he was referring to the fairly standard envoi "Toute amitié et mes meilleurs voeux" (With great affection and best wishes). —JB

TO LUCILLE ARMSTRONG

Louis Armstrong Archive Series, Letters 3, No. 1/1

Road travel could at times be frustrating for Armstrong. Drivers could fail to show up, buses could have no toilets, and one could reach one's destination a little too late for comfort. The following undated letter written to Lucille in longhand on Howard Johnson's Motor Lodge letterhead from Bordentown, New Jersey, is a case in point. At the same time Armstrong is able to ride out with a chorus that is loving, even seductive, in tone. —JB

Dear Lou my darling:

I forgot to give you this address before I left the house. So busy waiting on Rupert the bus driver. At that, he didn't show up. Another driver came who was a worker around the garage with a bus just like the ones on Northern Boulevard, with a meter 'n' everything. No toilet or anything. Oh well, that's the shit we've been getting from Rupert and his company all the time. Only Ira and our office have been picking up on it until this time. This old driver did the best he could. We only had forty-five minutes to check in our hotel, grab a bite, and get back into the bus and haul ass to the job, which was twelve miles from where we lived. We were supposed to hit at 7:30. We arrived at the place at 7 o'clock, rushed and dressed, ready. So, we hit at 9:35—-wow, wow. Whatta gig. It seems that these cats that's running the place, which is a very nice place, just don't know what they are doing. So I see where we're just [going to] to go along with them for ten days. Myron Cohen is on the bill and sends his very best to you.

I will at least get a very good rest here anyway. The audience appreciated us very much. Now for the address:
Mr. Willem Langenberg
45 Bachlaan
Hilversum,
Holland
Netherlands.

That's it. Love you madly. Will dig you subsequently.

Ol Sackreface
Armstrong.

P.S. Hope and dot enjoy you all's freakiest outfits.
Tee Hee.

LOUIS ARMSTRONG

TO JOE GLASER (1955)

From an uncataloged collection in the Library of Congress

On August 2, 1955, Armstrong, this time at the Moulin Rouge in Las Vegas, wrote a sixteen-page rather rambling letter to Joe Glaser. The original, written in blue ballpoint pen and not the norm for Armstrong, is in the Library of Congress. It finds Armstrong on the defensive, eager to allay concerns about a possible paternity suit. At the same time, Armstrong is forthright about the details of his current extra-marital affair, his early life around pimps and such, and most critical, the importance of seeking the protection of white men. The following excerpts are most telling. —JB

Dear Mr. Glaser:

Am sorry that I have to write this letter with a pen, but, on arriving at the airport in Las Vegas yesterday, my typewriter fell from on top of all that luggage that was on the truck, and the jolt sprung everything. Tch tch, isn't it a drag? And I wanted so badly to swing a lot of typewriting tappings on ya—.

Lucille (my darling) is arriving here at 11:48 P.M., Las Vegas time. So I thought I'd get my seriousness over with before she gets here. First I want to make myself very clear. You know deep in your heart that I love my wife Lucille and she loves me. Or else we wouldn't [have] been together this long. Especially doing the crazy things that I usually do for kicks. That's why I love her, because she's smart. The average woman would have quit my ol' ass long long ago. The woman understands me and there's no "ifs" and "an's" about it. That's when I explained to her the reason why and when we first saw each other up in Montreal, Canada we had no intentions about sex. But after we had been together sitting in my room, talking about everything in general, somehow it dawned on us that we both hadn't had any ass in ages. With Lucille riding around in her big and beautiful Cadillac, and would only travel if persuaded by you, period. Which was O.K. I still enjoyed blowing my horn every night, cunt or no cunt—we both met after the show in Montreal. I'll never forget it. As much as she tried to talk me out of it, I just kept on laying those hot kisses up on her fine "chops." When two people are in a room by themselves, kissing will lead to fucking every time.

P.S. Of course—[we] didn't swing but once in Montreal. Sort of

My 'ol ass. "So Busy" until I only have to "Shhhh Shhave and Shower" Ha, Ha. But I just love it. When, one keep busy, They usually forget about, Old Age. Which Seems very lodgical to me. But what I am realy whriting you for Lucille (my darling) is Arriving here at 1148-P.M. Las Vegas time. So I thought I'd do my seriousme over with you before she gets here. First I want to make my self very Clear. You know deep down in your heart, that I love my wife Lucille + she love's me. or else we wouldn't been together this long. Especialy 'doing the Crazy things that I usually do for kricks. Thats why I love her, because she's smart. The average woman would have "Quit" my 'ol ass-long 'long Ago. The woman understands me and there's no, 'if's' and 'Bu's' About "it. That. When I explained to her, the reason why (SWEET) And when we first saw each other upin (MONTREAL) (Canada) we had no intentions About Sex. But →

Page 2 of a letter written to Joe Glaser from the Moulin Rouge, Las Vegas, August 2, 1955. Library of Congress.

"warm up" once in Toronto, Minneapolis, etc. But where we whaled and that cute little baby girl was made, was in Las Vegas, during the time when we were appearing at the Sands Hotel, and Robert Merrill and I did that fine finale together. Every night we whaled. I mean, I really grined [sic] in that cunt. I could feel it, just as good as when I struck oil, and planted that cute little baby. Oh, Mr. Glaser, you and Dr. Schiff have got to see that baby. You see? I don't like to do anything wrong. It's so much easier and more wonderful to do things right. I like to see people happy. All the money in the world couldn't make me happier than I am right now, this minute. Why? Because I've just come from the bathroom, taking a good shit. And what's any better than a good shit? Hm? A man just don't have to be with a woman all the time to feel good. But it's such a grand and glorious [feeling] to be with a woman—why fight it? As Billy Kyle expresses it. That's why I have several chicks that I enjoy whaling with the same as I do with Lucille. And she's always had the choicest ass of them all. But regardless of the genuineness of asses, I was taught when I was a teenager hanging around gamblers, pimps, people of all walks of life—they all loved the way I played my horn and they did everything within [their] powers for me, an innocent kid at that time—.

⸺

Black Benny said to me, when I was getting ready to go up north (Chicago). He said, "Dipper"—abbreviation for Dippermouth, which was my little pet name at the time. He said to me: "You're going out into this wide wide world. Always remember, no matter how many times you get married; always have another woman for a sweetheart on the outside.

"Because, mad day might come, or she could be the type of woman whose ego, after realizing that you care deeply, may, for no reason at all, try giving you a hard time."

⸺

All those bitches, whenever they'd start showing their asses, you can go to hell. Because I have my horn to keep me warm. Something else Black Benny said to me came true. He said: "Dipper, as long as you live, no matter where you may be, always have a white man (who like you) can and will put his hand on your shoulder and say 'This is my nigger.' And can't nobody harm ya."

TO LEONARD FEATHER (1969)

Louis Armstrong Archives Series, Letters 3, No. 1/9

Armstrong's strong work ethic was deeply embedded in his nature. Despite a recent brush with death in the intensive care unit of Beth Israel Hospital (March 1969), and the passing of Joe Glaser, Louis remained the seemingly tireless trouper until almost the very end. The following letter to Leonard Feather, written a few weeks after Glaser's funeral (he died June 6, 1969), captures some of Louis's old-time humor and spunk. —JB

June 28, 1969.

Dear Leonard:

Received your letters with the write-ups from the papers, and they were very interesting. In fact, everything you write is just fine. I am writing my letters on the back of my diet charts (if you'll notice) because I have so many of them. And with so many charts and my own personal writing papers, man that will really clutter up the joint. So, I am killing two stones with one bird, or vice versa. Man, that's talking backwards—feeling good I guess.

We are just about cooling down over the passing of our dear pal Mr. Glaser. Lucille and myself went to the church service where he was laid out. A real nice funeral. Everybody was there. The family, the members from the office (N.Y.C.) and the head men from all over the country, and all of his admirers and acts were there. Dr. Alexander Schiff managed all of the funeral arrangements. He was with Mr. Glaser the whole time he was sick, and when he passed. The family came from Chicago, and when the service was over they flew the body to Chicago for burial. There were quite a few people who were there. I could only wave at them.

I am sure that you personally know all of the New York folks who attended. I am just waiting, resting, blowing just enough to "ulagize" [*sic*] the chops, in other words, to keep my embouchure up, ya dig ? That's a beeg [*sic*] word that I very seldom use. Anyway, it all sums up that I'm about to feel like my old self again. I never squawk about anything. I feel like this—as long as a person is still breathing, he's got a chance, right?

Lucille's fine. Sends a big hello to you and your wife. Thanks again.

Here's swinging atcha.

"Satch" Louis Armstrong.

P.S. Write any time. Always glad.

Part Six

DO YOU KNOW WHAT IT MEANS TO MISS NEW ORLEANS?

THAT MODERN MALICE

"Moldy fig," a term applied to the jazz traditionalist, was reportedly first used in print in June 1945 when it was included in a letter to the editor of *Esquire*. It was soon seized upon by jazz journalists as a way of fanning the flames of dissent between the supporters of the older jazz and the modernists championing the boppers. (Arvell Shaw's comments—which appear in the chapter that follows this one—are most revealing on this point.) Certainly the jazz world of the mid-late 1940s had a schizoid quality. On the one hand there were the New Orleans revival, the highly publicized premiere of the movie *New Orleans,* and the launching of Armstrong's All Stars; and on the other, the burgeoning of bebop groups on 52nd Street featuring the likes of Charlie Parker, Dizzy Gillespie, Thelonious Monk, and J. J. Johnson.

Armstrong was caught in the middle of the fray. Long idolized by so many musicians, he was now accused of being an Uncle Tom and struck back by attacking bebop as "that modern malice." It was a time fraught with acrimony, hurt feelings, simplistic generalities, and a fair amount of hot air, with no apparent inclination or opportunity to savor the modernist subtleties of such 1945 Armstrong recordings as "Jodie Man" and "I Wonder"—both of which were praised by Dan Morgenstern for their "long-lined, harmonically complex trumpet playing." Few people seemed prepared to ponder some of the points made by Armstrong in his interviews.

The following pieces are fairly typical of the period. An excerpt from the February 21, 1949, issue of *Time,* the cover of which featured Armstrong's face, outlines the conflict in the most simplistic terms:

> Louis gives the back of his hand to the latest variety of jazz, bebop (or bop). The boppers, who know the way he feels, tend to speak of him in the past tense. "Nowadays," says Negro Bop Trumpeter Dizzy Gillespie, "we try to work out different rhythms and things that they didn't think about when Louis Armstrong blew. In his day all he did was play strictly from the soul—just strictly from his heart. You got to go forward and progress. We study."
>
> Louis likes playing from the soul. Says he: "That bop is nice to listen to for a while, but not all night. It's not jazz—all them variations—it's more an exercise. You've got to have that lead too."

However, there were those who struggled to give Armstrong the respect he was due, while recognizing and engaging bebop as a new force in jazz. [What is more, as the two final readings in this part of the book clearly show, by 1959 the relationship between Dizzy Gillespie and Louis Armstrong could not have been more cordial.] —JB

GEORGE T. SIMON

BEBOP'S THE EASY WAY OUT, CLAIMS LOUIS (1948)

Metronome, *March 1948*

"Bebop's the easy out" claims Louis.
"They can give it, but they can't take it,"
insists Armstrong, who threatens to hitch up his mule
if things don't get better soon.

Satchmo sat himself down before his dressing room mirror and tied the handkerchief around his forehead in such a way that the cloth covered the top of his head completely. Immediately sweat began to seep through, soaking the kerchief just the way it had soaked the shirt on his back. Funny, but it didn't seem that he had worked that hard down there on the stage. No, it didn't seem that he had, that is until you stopped to think of what had gone on, the way he not only blew his trumpet, but the way he sang and mugged and hopped up and down and encouraged every guy in his little band as he took his solos. And you began to realize something you had almost forgotten, that Louis Armstrong is not only a great artist, but also a wonderful, hard-working performer, always giving his all.

Now here he was in his dressing room, tired and bothered about something, his trumpet lying on the floor in its case next to the dressing table, his most potent means of expression silent for the moment. Managers and flunkies milled around the little room. There was confusion and yelling, do this and do that, where is he and where is she, and suddenly Louis had disappeared. By the time he returned from the bathroom most of the noise had gone down the hall, into other dressing rooms and out into the street.

Satchmo seemed a bit more relaxed in his clean underwear and his dark blue corduroy dressing gown. Then came the word "bebop" and once again the troubled look returned. "They're always misquotin' me so I don't like to discuss it no more." He walked over to a stack of letters and pulled forth one of those four-page hot club bulletins. "Read this. I never said that. They're always addin' words. What do they want to do that for, anyway? You know, one trouble with the beboppers is that they can give it, but they can't take it! They tear you down, but if you say somethin' against them, they yell you're old fashioned and you don't know nothin' about jazz any more."

Pops didn't want to talk any more about bebop, not yet anyway. Well, then, how about the trumpeters who play the way Louis likes to play? "The best of them? That's easy. It was Bunny [Berigan]. But you know, you can't talk too much about ONE style. Note for note, you'll never find no two trumpeters who play the same. It's impossible. When a guy copies somebody, he only copies what he heard on that one performance. Maybe the first guy'll never play the thing the same way again, so you can't really say the second guy is copying his style, can you? Anyway, what difference does it make who you blow like, just so long as you blow good!"

Other trumpeters who blow the way Louis likes to? "You know who's real good? That's Billy Butterfield. Ever hear what he played on that record Ella and I made together, that 'I Won't Be Satisfied'? Listen to it, man; that's what I think is real good. He don't fake a lot of little notes just because he can't hold a long one. He knows how to blow his horn right.

"This blowin' a trumpet's not easy. Some folks think all you gotta do is hold it to your lips and blow. I'm tellin' you, them babies get so sore sometimes, you can't even touch a powder puff to 'em. And I learned how to play a trumpet right, just the way Bunk and the others did. Trouble today is most of the kids start right off blowin' them real high ones. In a couple of years they won't have no chops left at all, blowin' the way they do. They'll be all wore out. I started blowin' all them high notes to impress folks but I never intended to keep it up."

Louis looked into the mirror and patted his lips lightly, affectionately. They were his way of expressing himself, much more so than just mere words. "I play what I feel, what's inside of me. I don't expect to please everybody. You know a lot of the new cats say 'Armstrong, he plays too many long notes.' They want me to change, but why should I go ahead and change just to please a lot o' cats who are way ahead of themselves, anyway. I listen to what I play, and if it pleases me it's good. That's the only way to judge what you're doin'. I'm my own best audience.

"I'd never play this bebop because I don't like it. Don't get me wrong; I think some of them cats who play it play real good, like Dizzy, especially. But bebop is the easy way out. Instead of holding notes the way they should be held, they just play a lot of little notes. They sorta fake out of it. You won't find many of them cats who can blow a straight lead. They never learned right. It's all just flash. It doesn't come from the heart the way real music should."

The music business has really changed, so far as Satchmo is concerned. "They do such silly things nowadays. Like the time the man from some newspaper calls me up at home, wakes me up out of a sleep, to tell me that Erskine Hawkins challenges me to see which one of us can hold a note longer. How silly can you get? That's not music and I told the man I didn't want to have nothin' to do with anything like that. 'I'm a musician,' I told him, 'and not an acrobat.' He said he guessed I was right at that and the whole thing was called off.

"I've been blowin' this horn a long time and you'd think by now I'd know what it was all about. But the people in the business like to treat me like a child. There's hardly a one among the bookers and managers who knows anything at all about music, and it shows in the things they do, too. They get guys to blow tricks on the trumpet and they push those trick records and all the freaks go ahead and make a lot of money. I play the kind of music I feel is right and do what I gotta do, but sometimes even scuffle to get a week's work when all those other guys are makin' thousands and thousands of bucks. It's getting so that I'm gettin' ready to pack this horn away and go back to hitchin' up my mule. . . . What'cha laughin' at? I'm serious, and you can put that in your paper, too!"

Those were real tears in the big, round Armstrong eyes, tears of despair, of frustration, tears from a man who had always tried to do what he felt was right, in his relations with people and in relation to his music; tears from a man whom everybody loved, who wanted to harm no one, but who wanted to be free to blow his horn the way he wanted to blow it, without interference from bookers, from managers, from people so warped that they could look up at a blue note but down at a brown skin, even from people in his own profession who closed their ears to much of the musical beauty behind them so that they could concentrate better on the involved manipulations that they were trying to create—a new sound which they wanted to supplant the kind of music which Louis and Joe Oliver and others had created and lived.

"I've been blowin' a long time now. My chops get mighty tired sometimes. But I wish they'd let me blow the way I want to. No, I didn't make records when that big rush was on at the end of the year. They didn't give me anything to play that I felt was right, and I'm not goin' ahead and makin' records just for the sake of makin' records. Not me. Not ol' Satchmo. If I can't blow right, I don't want to blow at all, and that's final!"

Louis bent over and picked up his horn, patted it gently, then held it to his lips, very lightly. The next show was coming up. He blew a few warm-up notes. The spit seeped out of the side of his mouth. He reached over for the top handkerchief on a big pile and wiped the spit away. He blew some more, and more saliva started dripping down his chin. The handkerchief again. And a curious thought hit you: how much liquid can the man hold? It comes out of all his pores when he comes on the stage; it comes out of his eyes when he talks about things that mean so much to him, and now, even before he even starts to work, it pours forth from his lips!

What was that he said about the boppers? "They can give it, but they can't take it." They can give it, sure they can, with words. But when it comes to giving of himself, giving what he feels inside, giving warmth and feeling to music and to the world with his body, his spirit, and with his horn, even when "them babies get so sore you can't even touch a powder puff to 'em!"—I'll take Louis Armstrong and give you the rest!

LOUIS ARMSTRONG, BARNEY BIGARD, ERNEST BORNEMAN, AND MEZZ MEZZROW

BOP WILL KILL BUSINESS UNLESS IT KILLS ITSELF FIRST: LOUIS ARMSTRONG (1948)

Down Beat, *April 7, 1948*

(Editor's Note: At the end of the international jazz festival, correspondent Ernest Borneman spent the night in Louis Armstrong's room at the Negresco hotel in Nice, talking to Louis, Mezz [Mezzrow], [Barney] Bigard, Sid Catlett and others about progress and tradition in jazz until the sun came up and it was time to catch the early morning plane for Paris. Others present were Velma Middleton, Louis's featured singer, and Honey Johnson, Rex Stewart's vocalist. Louis asked that some of the things said be considered "among friends." These parts of the conversation have therefore been kept off the record. A transcript of the remaining passages, mainly those of argument between Louis, Bigard, and Mezz, is given below because it seems to cover nearly all the points of opinion that have recently divided the old school of jazz from the novelty school. The interview might also be considered as a fitting reply to Stan Kenton's statement that "Louis . . . plays without any scientific element" and that "all natural forms of inspiration in music have been exhausted." The actual text of

Mike Levin's interview with Stan had, of course, not reached Louis yet at the time of the Nice festival, but some of Louis's statements sound almost telepathic in view of their direct relationship to the questions which Stan raised simultaneously in New York.)

Borneman: Well, now that it's all over, what do you think the verdict is going to be in the cold light of the morning after?

Mezzrow: If it proves anything, it shows that jazz is the greatest diplomat of them all. Did you dig those young French cats playing like Joe Oliver? Man, that's old Johnny Dodds on clarinet and Baby on woodblocks. And that's thirty years later and in another country. If that's not the great leveler, I don't know what is.

Bigard: You mean Claude Luter? You must be kidding.

Mezz: What do you mean kidding? Those cats sound real good to me.

Bigard: They're out of tune so bad it hurts your ears.

Louis: What's that you're saying, man? Ain't you never played out of tune?

Bigard: Sure, man, but I try to do better. I learned a few things all those years since I was a kid in New Orleans. And if you blow wrong you try to keep it to yourself.

Barney Denies Clam

Louis: How about records? How about that thing you made with Duke, the one about the train?

Bigard: "Happy Go Luck Local"? I didn't make that.

Louis: No, the other one. "Daybreak Express."

Bigard: That was the trumpet, and maybe they just cut him off in the end.

Louis: Yeah, maybe.

Louis Admits Clam

Bigard: And how about the one you made with the big band on "Struttin' with Some Barbecue"? How about that clarinet?

Louis: That was half a tone off, but it sold all right.

Bigard: Yeah, but were you satisfied with it?

Louis: It sold all right. Them cats know that a guy got to blow the way he feels and sometimes he hits them wrong. That's better than them young guys who won't blow for fear they'll be off.

Mezz: I'll tell you why he hit wrong that time, Barney. The guy was playing tenor at the time and then switched to clarinet and his embouchure knocked him out.

Bigard: Embouchure, huh! I was playing tenor too. I had two embouchures. For tenor on this side and for clarinet on that one. So what about that?

Louis: That's not what we're talking about. You're always knocking somebody, pops. I say that little French band plays fine. I could take them youngsters up to the Savoy and bring the walls down with them any day.

Bigard: That's because you can take any kind of outfit and blow everyone else out of the room.

Louis: That's a fine band, pops. That little cornet player sounds just like Mutt Carey to me. I can hear all them pretty little things Mutt used to do when that boy gets up and plays. That's the real music, man.

Bigard No Victorian

Bigard: Real music! Who wants to play like those folks thirty years ago?

Louis: You see, pops, that's the kind of talk that's ruining the music. Everybody trying to do something new, no one trying to learn the fundaments first. All them young cats playing them weird chords. And what happens? No one's working.

Bigard: But Louis, you got to do something different, you got to move along with the times.

Louis: I'm doing something different all the time, but I always think of them fine old cats way down in New Orleans—Joe and Bunk and Tio and Buddy Bolden—and when I play my music, that's what I'm listening to. The way they phrased so pretty and always on the melody, and none of that out-of-the-world music, that pipe-dream music, that whole modern malice.

Borneman: What do you mean by that, Louis?

Boppers Money-Mad

Louis: I mean all them young cats along the Street with their horns wrapped in a stocking and they say "'Pay me first, pops, then I'll play a note for you," and you know that's not the way any good music ever got made. You got to like playing pretty things if you're ever going to be any good blowing your horn. These young cats now they want to make money first and the hell with the music. And then they want to carve everyone else because they're full of malice, and all they want to do is show you up, and any old way will do as long as it's different from the way you played it before. So you get all them weird chords which don't mean nothing, and first people get curious about it just because it's new, but soon they get tired of it because it's really no good and you got no melody to remember and no beat to dance to. So they're all poor again and nobody is working, and that's what that modern malice done for you.

Mezz: Because they're full of frustration, full of neuroses, and then they blow their top 'cause they don't know where to go from here. All they know is they want to be different, but that's not enough, you can't be negative all the time, you got to be positive about it. You can't just say all the time "That's old, that stinks, let's do something new, let's be different." Different what way? Go where? You can't take no for an answer all the time. You got to have a tradition. They lost it. Now they're like babes in the wood, crying for mammy. Poor little guys, and one after the other blows his top. They ought to see a psychoanalyst before they start playing music. We made a blues about it for King Jazz, and we called it "The Blues and Freud."

Bigard: But we're in a new age now, man. It's a nervous age, you got to bring it out in your music.

Louis: When they're down, you gotta help them up, not push them in still deeper.

Bigard: You can say that because you're a genius. I'm just an average clarinet player.

Louis: Now none of that, pops. You're all right. You just got off the right track when you were playing with ———— [presumably Duke Ellington]. All that soft mike stuff that can't cut naturally through the brass. You just remember the way the boys used to play way down on Rampart Street and you'll kill the cats.

Vote for Ory

Bigard: You know who has the best band in America now? Kid Ory.

Mezz: Treason!

Bigard: And I'll tell you why. Because they got a full tone and they play in tune.

Mezz: And no mop-mops and be-bops.

Louis: Because they play together, not every prima donna for herself. And not like them cats who got too big for their boots when somebody gave them a chance to lead a band and now they can't play their instruments no longer. Look at ———— starting off "West End Blues" in the wrong key. He don't remember his own solo no more. I remember every note I ever played in my life.

Louis, the Exception

Bigard: But that's what I was saying. It's all so easy for you to talk because you're an exception in everything. We others just got to keep scuffling, and if they want us to play bop, we gotta play bop. It don't matter if we like it or not.

Louis: No, that's because I got some respect for the old folks who played trumpet before me. I'm not trying to carve them and do something different. That's the sure way to lose your style. They say to you "I got to be different. I got to develop a style of my own." And then all they do is try and not play like you do. That's not the way to do anything right. That's the sure way you'll never get any style of your own. Like I was telling you about ————. He had a style once because he played like the old-timers did on their horns, and all he tries now is to play solos and not back up a band or a singer.

Bigard: That's because he was a leader, man, and he just got used to waving a stick.

Louis: Jack was a leader too. You were a leader. I've been a leader for some time now, but don't try and carve you when we play a passage together.

Mezz: That modern malice.

Trumpeters Strain

Louis: You see, pops, it's worst with the trumpet players because the trumpet is an instrument full of temptation. All the young cats want to kill papa, so they start forcing their tone. Did you listen to ———— last night? He was trying to do my piece, make fun of me. But did you hear his tone? 'Nuff said.

Bigard: I won't argue that.

Louis: I'll tell you another. Remember Lunceford? Those first things he did, "White Heat," "Jazznocracy," why, that was wonderful work on reeds. And then the trumpets came in and that was the end. They killed it stone dead every time.

Bigard: That was Steve.

Louis: No, that wasn't Steve. Steve was all right. It was ————. And I'll tell you another one. You know ————? One day he said to Braud I was playing 1918 trumpet and the hell with me. You know that was the wrong man to talk to. Braud nearly killed him for it. Now they tell me he never said it, he loves me too much, but I know those cats. They want to play good trumpet, and they want to show off at the same time. But you can't have it both ways. You can play good trumpet with a pretty tone and a fine melody or you can lay them weird chords. You can't do both at the same time, and if you try, that's when you get unhappy and hate everybody and then you blow your top.

Nuts to Sobsters

Bigard: That's right. I don't go for those guys who get so high they can't work, and then come sucking around you looking for sympathy. Last night ——— comes up to me and says he can't send money home to his wife because the French won't let him. So I say to him, "What were you doing when you were touring—where they let you send money home? Who was buying all your drinks then?" That's the way they talk, and all the time you know they get high just because they're fighting their horns.

Louis: This cat comes up to me last night and says: "Louis, don't you like me no more? You don't ever talk to me." I say: "Pops, don't give me none of that Harlem jive," and I leave him standing there. I don't dig those cats.

Mezz: And ———, how about ———?

Louis: Best white drummer I ever heard and can't hold a job, and that's why he keeps knocking everybody in the business.

Mezz: That modern malice (laughs).

Street Personifies Problem

Louis: Pops, I'll tell you what it's all about. Just look at the Street today. Don't let me tell you nothing. Just look at the Street today. They've thrown out the bands and put in a lot of chicks taking their clothes off. That's what that bop music has done for the business. And look at them young cats too proud to play their horns if you don't pay them more than the old-timers. 'Cause if they play for fun they aren't king no more. So they're not working but once in a while and then they play one note and nobody knows if it's the right note or just one of them weird things where you can always make like that was just the note you were trying to hit. And that's what they call science. Not play their horns the natural way.

Not play the melody. And then they're surprised they get thrown out and have strippers in their place.

Bigard: *Well, I don't know.*

Louis: Well, you oughta know, pops. You've been around long enough. Look at the legit composers always going back to folk tunes, the simple things, where it all comes from. So they'll come back to us when all the shouting about bop and science is over, because they can't make up their own tunes, and all they can do is embroider it so much you can't see the design no more.

Optimists All

Mezz: But it won't last.

Louis: It can't last. They always say "Jazz is dead," and then they always come back to jazz.
[Enter Louis's valet dragging a trunk: "We gotta pack, pops." (Draws the curtain.) "It's daylight, boys. We gotta be at the airport in an hour."]

Mezz: Well, let's scuffle.

Louis: It's always the same thing in all languages. You make a pretty tune and you play it well and you don't have to worry about nothing. If you swing it, that's fine, and if you don't, well look at Lombardo and Sinatra and they're still not going hungry. We'll be around when the others will be forgotten.

Mezz: They'll be cleaning the streets of the city when we eat lobster at the Negresco.

ORRIN KEEPNEWS

CHANGER EDITOR ALSO BLASTS WOLFF (1949)

Down Beat, *July 15, 1949*

In this article, Orrin Keepnews launches a frontal attack on the "nastiness school of criticism" and dismisses the treatment of Armstrong, making an impassioned plea for mutual respect and tolerance. —JB

New York—The moth-eaten old doctrine of dog-eat-dog in jazz criticism, the shrill and often meaningless cries that the other fellow's kind of jazz is a dirty fraud, is back to haunt us again. At any rate, *Down Beat*'s frontpaging of D. Leon Wolff's blast (June 17) definitively headlined "Bop, Louis Nowhere!," makes it look very much that way.

This writer is not overly concerned either with Wolff's demolishing of bop or with his neat trick of knocking off Armstrong in two paragraphs. Others certainly will provide enough angry answers to those attacks.

What Rankles

What does rankle very deeply is the revival of the nastiness school of criticism, which many people had reason to hope had gone out of favor for all time; and what is particularly annoying is that glib, at-first-glance impeccable sentence, punched home in italics, which proclaimed: "No controversy means no standards."

Specifically, Wolff was socking into the *Record Changer* for giving "equal attention" to bop, and for allowing bop, moldy figs, "excruciating" big bands all to "pass for jazz" together. It was nice to be called a gentleman, and on the first page of the *Beat* at that, and thank you, even if no compliment was intended. But it was a bit of a shock to find that what we at *Record Changer* had been thinking of as a minor experiment in furthering jazz by giving all sides a crack at our readers' minds, was in some quarters considered an example of "jazz, criticism (at) its lowest ebb."

We had always thought the lowest ebb came on the night a musician and a jazz critic got into a public brawl at Nick's. We figured that acting like nice people—although on different decks of the same boat—wasn't as sensational as real or fancied muckraking, it was a great deal more helpful to all concerned.

Armstrong warming up backstage, September 1956. Photo: Ted Streshinsky/Corbis.

Some Respect

The suspicion in this corner has always been that most of the good old fights were merely space-filling, circulation-grabbing devices whipped up on and for rainy days. Sure, lots of boppers literally hate two-beat; and they tell me Muggsy Spanier says bop sounds like "Four Chinamen." But most musicians and fans have some respect for the other guy's opinion, and some would like to know why he thinks that way.

This doesn't mean they don't love their own school. What it means is that jazz is not pure emotion, not pure love-and-hate. It also involves the intellect. At the risk of sounding real corny, I'd like to point out that education is a fine old democratic standby.

No controversy means no standards, huh? First of all, the aim is not no controversy. The aim is no ignorant sounding off. No one is enough of a gentleman to like everything or to claim that no one is crazy. Very personally, I don't care for most bop, except maybe for Parker, some Miles Davis, some Thelonious Monk. But some people who I'd swear to be of sound mind are very high on it, and I suspect that if I understand it, which I largely don't, I'd be in a better position to make up my mind about bop.

Information Necessary

If I ever get to be sure I know what the boppers are trying to do, and how, and find I despise it, I intend to fill the air with shrill cries. But information is a most necessary preliminary; it takes knowledge to determine whether the other fellow is right or wrong—if he's operating for respectable reasons or is a dollar-seeking-exhibitionist phony.

Information is what any responsible jazz writer should be seeking to give; his aim should never be to make his readers gasp with his rhetoric, tell them his side of the story, elbow them down with his obviously superior knowledge of the subject, and finish up as the winner of a mammoth shadow-boxing exhibition. If that's controversy, I'll be a gentleman.

This is not intended as a pitch for the *Record Changer;* it is rather a pitch for "gentlemanliness," but possibly the best way to handle the general point by being specific. In the past year and a half, the *Changer* under Editor Bill Grauer and this writer, has stopped being what Wolff praised as a "haven for reactionaries." We figured that jazz didn't really stop dead the night they closed Storyville, so why try to kid people?

Armistice

So what did we do, what awful "armistice" was reached with bop? For one thing, we bypassed the "Man, it's real gone" school of thought. We review new be-bop records, ran an article by Tadd Dameron, are publishing a Gillespie discography. Principally we've run several fairly technical explanatory articles on bop instrumention and the ideas behind bop, by Ross Russell, one of which Wolff quotes and is nonplused enough to call "interesting and constructive." (Come now, Leon, no armistice!)

The whole idea, as this should indicate, is to try giving the moldy figs, and others, some idea of what the supporters of bop—and also of Dixieland and of nice, loud big bands—say lies behind their music, and why they want to defend it to the death.

Likes Fights, Too

Actually, we like a good, shrill fight as well as the next man, which is why I sought this opportunity to jump Wolff. To prove the point, we've just come from under a hot battle in which an eclectic French critic and a leading local moldy traded insults. Reports from the readers were that whole thing was tasteless and quite avoidable, even though both had clawed [the] other's "sham."

There's a lot to be said against any excess of controversy. The late war and the potential next one, fit that description. Controversy without knowledge leads to Southerners who just plain hate Negroes, to people who can't stand Jews or unions. Or to people who object to magazines that try to tell you something about a form of music you don't dig. It's tough to make headlines out of tolerance, but that's not necessarily fatal. What can be fatal—fatal to jazz—is for everyone to run into his own corner, close his ears, and stick out his tongue.

LOUIS ARMSTRONG

TO DIZZY AND LORRAINE GILLESPIE (1959)

Louis Armstrong Archive Series, Letters 3, No. 1/10

By 1959 the musicians were ignoring the media hype and coming to their own terms with regard to bebop's innovations. On January 7, 1959, Louis Armstrong joined Dizzy Gillespie on the CBS-TV Timex All Star Show for a joyous performance of "Umbrella Man." And later that year, when Armstrong wrote to Gillespie from Spoleto, Italy, where he was recovering from a coronary thrombosis, it is clear that the two jazz greats were on affectionate terms.—JB

Grand Hotel
Roma July 1st, 1959.

Dear Dizzy and Lorraine:

Thanks for the lovely wine. But there's one thing that you should always remember—you can't kill a nigger. Ha Ha Ha. Ole Sidney Bechet and Big Sid Catlett were trying to get me to come up there with them and hold that 1st chair down on the trumpet. Probably they would have had a little luck if they weren't so damn cheap. Huh—they only wanted to pay me union scale—shit. I got more than that when I first came up North from down in Galilee. Tee Hee—So I blinded them with (A)——.

We will probably beat this letter home. We are leaving today from Rome—Lucille, Dr. Schiff, my nurse—Doctuh Pugh, a Countess (filthy rich), and the Nurse husband. We all spent our last night with Brick Top—Good Ole Brick. We all took turns (Hmm turns) in doin' a number. I'm back at my old self. Ole Doc Schiff put some kind of jive into me, that's making everything stand up better than before—Wow.

So long for now.

Your Boy, Ol' Lush—
Louis Armstrong.

DIZZY ON LOUIS (1979)

Excerpted from To Be or Not to Bop

By the time Dizzy Gillespie's autobiography To Be or Not to Bop *was published in 1979, Dizzy was prepared to allude frankly to the aspects of Armstrong that had once disturbed him. —JB*

If anybody asked me about a certain public image of him, handkerchief over his head, grinning in the face of white racism, I never hesitated to say I didn't like it. I didn't want the white man to expect me to allow the same things Louis did. Hell, I had my own way of "Tomming" . . . Later on, I began to recognize what I had considered Pop's grinning in the face of racism as his absolute refusal to let anything, even anger about racism, steal the joy from his life and erase his fantastic smile. Coming from a younger generation, I misjudged him.

Part Seven

BOURBON STREET PARADE

IN THE ORBIT OF THE ALL STARS

To say that the year 1947 marked a critical transition in Armstrong's career would be a gross understatement. A number of forces were at work. Much of the change had to do with the collapse of the big bands around 1945, a growing attention given to bebop, a fascination with singers on the order of Billie Holiday and Ella Fitzgerald, and most decisive for Armstrong, the New Orleans Dixieland revival.

Most revealing is what happened within the roughly five-month stretch, from February to August 1947. A February 8 date organized by Leonard Feather saw Armstrong onstage at Carnegie Hall, performing before a packed house in a dual capacity: in the first half of the concert he was accompanied by the sextet of clarinetist Edmond Hall—an aggregation anticipating Armstrong's All Stars in most essential details; Armstrong then closed the evening by fronting his own big band. Reviews were generally favorable and prompted other promoters, such as Ernie Anderson, to make arrangements for another concert, this one in New York's Town Hall on May 17, 1947. On this second occasion, however, only seven musicians, including Armstrong, participated, most prominently the cornetist Bobby Hackett, with whom Armstrong, who was recovering from an ulcer attack, shared top billing. What dramatized more than anything else the nostalgic surge for early Dixieland jazz was the highly publicized premiere on June 9 of the movie *New Orleans,* featuring Bing Crosby, Billie Holiday, and Louis Armstrong, among others. In fact, considerable media attention had been concentrated on Armstrong for close to a year, ever since filming began at the Hal Roach Studios in Culver City, California. Finally, on August 13, 1947, Louis Armstrong and the All Stars premiered at Billy Berg's club in Los Angeles—the ensemble consisting of a front line of trumpet, clarinet, and trombone, backed by a rhythm section of piano, bass, and drums. On hand that night were such celebrities as Hoagy Carmichael, Woody Herman, Benny Goodman, and Johnny Mercer. There was also major press coverage. In its September 1 issue *Time* put it succinctly: "Louis Armstrong has forsaken the ways of Mammon and come back to jazz." Writing in *Down Beat,* George Hoefer was somewhat more equivocal: "The group as a unit does not pretend to be a Dixieland band, nor does it offer anything new or sensational in music. Satchmo's superb stage presence binds together a showcase of jazz stars into a jazz production that warmed the hearts of nostalgic music lovers (Louis is playing and singing with more heart and inspiration than he has for years)."

These qualities of "more heart and inspiration" were to carry Armstrong and the All Stars to the zenith of international fame during the years of the Cold War. Certainly, by the mid-1950s "Ambassador Satch" was a force to be reckoned with, even by the U.S. State Department. What helps make his vital role more comprehensible is the profound influence at the time of the Marshall Plan in shaping both American foreign policy and the general perceptions of the United States abroad. It is indeed of some interest that the basic concept of the Marshall Plan was initially proposed on June 5, 1947, some two months before the All Stars first opened at Billy Berg's. In any event, it helps put in proper perspective the high visibility of Armstrong at this time, his highly publicized tirade at the Newport Jazz Festival in July 1957, and his cancellation that September of his State Department tour of the Soviet Union over the issue of public school integration in Little Rock, Arkansas. The pieces by Dan Morgenstern and David Ostwald included here are especially compelling on these points.

Preceding them are excerpts from four separate interviews with various All Stars sidemen. Three of them—trombonist Russell "Big Chief" Moore, bassist Arvell Shaw, and clarinetist-tenor saxophonist Barney Bigard—had the distinction of working with Louis in his big bands and other settings prior to the creation of the All Stars. Trombonist Trummy Young, who replaced Moore, was associated with the All Stars for some twelve years, from 1952 to 1964. —JB

RON WELBURN

INTERVIEW: RUSSELL "BIG CHIEF" MOORE (EXCERPTS) (1980)

Nyack, New York, March 13 and 14, 1980

Russell "Big Chief" Moore, born on the Pima reservation near Sacaton, Arizona, recalls in his interview with Ron Welburn how as a seventeen-year-old he first came to hear Armstrong in the Chicago of 1929; this was long before he began playing with Armstrong in December 1944. The excerpts have been transcribed from the Jazz Oral History Interviews on file at the Institute of Jazz Studies at Rutgers-Newark. —JB

Russell: . . . at that time I was in the 124th Field Artillery Band, the National Guard across from White Sox Park on Wentworth Avenue. I roamed the streets of Chicago, I didn't have any job or any money, and I was begging [for] food and trying to survive, and I was sleeping in a burned-out coffin factory. And I would go to sleep in a coffin with excelsior [thin wood shavings used in packing] that was in there and cover myself for warmth. (I'm telling you it was rough.) I always figure that someday my ship will come in. And I'm beginning to, at that time, beginning to see the dawn comin' up by listening in front of the Sunset Cafe and hearing this trumpet blowing through the walls. It looks like the wall's gonna crumble. And I wasn't the only one in front of the Sunset. There was other people that came back—they didn't have the money to go in. Just listening, just, just listen and see who was blowin'. About the second or third night I was there I finally got nerve enough to ask one of the listeners outside on the sidewalk. I said, "Who was that blowing?" "Oh, you don't know? There, I'll show you." He took me over in front of the place, and I saw the picture, and under the picture with horn, the trumpet, under there was the name "Louis Armstrong". . . . when I heard Louis, that was the most beautiful. I was more determined to be a jazz musician. (He's the prince. He's one of the greatest.)

—

Russell: At this point, when they asked me to come join Louis, (I've thought about the times in front of the Sunset when I was seventeen years old) I never dreamed I would be with Louis Armstrong. It was a privileged opportunity. It was great to be asked to join the band. When they left St. Louis, I was in St. Louis for a week, and Joe Glaser called me to come in. So I came to New York and I talked to Joe; Joe said to go to Karnak Tailor Shop at 48th and Seventh Avenue. So I was fitted with three uniforms, one was dark blue with white buttons, and another was light blue, sky-blue, and the third one was gray, gray pants and gray sport coat. That night I opened with Louie at the Zanzibar on 49th and Broadway. And on the same bill at the Zanzibar was Bill Robinson, the Delta Rhythm Boys, the Peters Sisters, Maurice Rocco . . . Pee Wee Marquette. The intermission band was Claude Hopkins, and our band played the show, some dancing, and then we'd get off, and then we'd get Claude Hopkins to take over. . . . He [Claude Hopkins] had about seven men. We had the big band. It was beautiful to hear Louie play. I'd be listening while reading my music and we had a head arrangement. . . .

. . . There was no rehearsal . . . all the stuff was written . . . some head arrangements . . . and in charge of the band was Ted McRae, and it was beautiful being in the band . . . every time that Louie would be in front of the band . . . he would be singing and I'd be with the section . . . did some hard work with Louie . . . we would open up in the afternoon, we'd play the first show at the Roxy and then . . . the second show. Then after the second show we'd have to report back to the Zanzibar to play the Zanzibar. So . . . the rest of the night we alternated between the two shows; and it was quite hard to go back and forth. Each performance we had to change clothes and come back.

⌐

Ron: With that . . . big band . . . he recorded in 1946 for RCA.

Russell: Those records were the tunes out of the picture *New Orleans*. We were in Hollywood . . . and one of the trumpet players who always loved brown shoes . . . instead of wearing black shoes. We were having dark suits with tails; and I remember every one of us went over to a costume building where all the clothes for the movie stars were stored away . . . So they fitted me with tuxedo and tails, and right on the inside of the lapels it said "Sidney Greenstreet." I'll never forget that . . . anyway . . . I remember one time we were on a huge stage and the whole setup . . . the director was right in front looking over the scenes . . . how it was going to look and all he did was come to this guy who liked these brown shoes.

Russell: When I first joined the band [we were using arrangements by] Teddy McRae and then . . . Joe Garland took over. It was Joe Garland who was on those records. Joe Garland supervised that recording session. Louis was just there to play his parts . . . we were in St. Louis because the Armstrong band was going to play The Plantation . . . and then that same night the bass player had to leave . . . to go back to Philadelphia. I think it was Al Moore. So Joe Garland asked me: "You've been here before with Jeter-Pillars. Do you know a good bass player in town? We need a bass player right away." So I said, "I know Arvell Shaw; he lives in St. Louis." . . . I put Arvell Shaw in with Louis.

Russell: . . . later [around 1963] I get a call from Arvell Shaw who was with Louie. "Chief, Chief. Go to Glaser. They want you in the band." I said: "What about Trummy. Isn't he with you any more?" He said: "Trummy is in Hawaii, he left for Hawaii . . . he didn't give us notice. . . ." So I was thinking about the time that I put [him] in the band during the early years . . . he kind of spoke up for me . . . "Let's get Chief!"

JOSHUA BERRETT

INTERVIEW: ARVELL SHAW (EXCERPTS) (1997)

Roosevelt, New York, March 21, 1997

Arvell Shaw first began playing with Armstrong around 1946 and was to remain his loyal friend and regular bassist—allowing for some minor interruptions—to the very end. Shaw married Swiss journalist and photographer Madeleine Berard—Armstrong's letter to her appears earlier in this book. What follow are excerpts from an interview with Shaw that I conducted in his home in Roosevelt, Long Island, New York, on March 21, 1997. Included are not only Shaw's reminiscences about how he first began working with Louis, but also vivid memories of the excitement that greeted the All Stars on their international tours. —JB

In my very early career—I was still in high school—I wasn't playing bass yet; what I played was cymbals. You used to play that cymbal like a hand-held sock cymbal . . . I was like thirteen or fourteen. Fate Marable, he was a very old man. He would maybe come in once or twice a week, like on a Saturday night, and play like one set and then go. But the band was cooking. . . .

The riverboats would go up and down the Mississippi . . . they would go up to Alton, Illinois . . . they were excursion boats, the SS *Admiral,* "part of" the Streckfus line . . . the family still ran it.

The first time that I remember seeing Louis . . . there was a theater in St. Louis—St. Louis in those times was a completely segregated town— there was a black theater that had all the big bands; it was called the Comet Theater. And the first time I saw Louis he played there for a week . . . I remember Louis then had Big Sid Catlett with him, and J. C. Higginbotham . . . and George Washington. I was so impressed. My father took me to see him; I told my father: "One day I'm going to play with him." All bands played there at least one week out of a year.

———

The first time I joined Louis I had just been discharged from the Navy after the Second World War. I went back to St. Louis to see what I was going to do with my life. Just by chance Louis and the big band were playing at a club in St. Louis called Club Plantation. The bass player that was with Louis, Al Moore, his wife was pregnant, and he was from Philadelphia. He had to go to Philadelphia for the birth of his child. So they called the union and asked them: "Who is the best bass player in town?" Not only was I the "best one," but I was about one of the only ones there. . . .

The union sent me to the Plantation. So the manager said to me: "So, you're the bass player! You know, it's only for two weeks . . . we have another ten days here and then we're going on one-nighters, and the first one's in Kansas City." . . . I was happy. We got to Kansas City and the bass player—he had been there so long—he never looked at the arrangements. He made up his own parts; he didn't think about what the rest of an eighteen-piece band was playing.

First thing, I was scared to death, I was so nervous. Joe Garland was the straw boss—he's the guy who wrote "In the Mood," "Leap Frog," and those tunes—he was the straw boss conductor. He called out the first set, about four or five numbers for each set. The "book" was all screwed up. I couldn't find not one tune . . . the beginning of the "book" was in the back and the middle. So finally, he came and helped me find the set . . . In this first set we started playing . . . I was reading the parts and noticed everybody looking. Before that, Louis, he just came on stage and he didn't look at me. And [now] everybody started looking at me; Louis looked back at me.

At the end of that set Joe Garland came and said: "What the hell, what are you playing?" I said: "I'm just playing the notes as written." They had never heard the notes from that arrangement. And the arrangements were written by Don Redman; some of them were written by Benny Carter.

So, to make a long story short, at the end of the two weeks something happened. He (Al Moore) couldn't get back. So that's when he (the manager) said: "Look, can you stay for another two weeks?"

I said: "Of course. I can stay for ten times that!" So pretty soon they said: "We'd like to have you stay with the band; would you be interested?" That's how I started with the big band.

Of course, that was the end of the era of the big band. The big bands were disbanding because it was too expensive and bebop came in; the small bands came in. So the big band lasted for a year. We got to New York and the band disbanded. I just stayed in New York. I wouldn't think about going back to St. Louis. I was gigging around, around Harlem with Art Blakey and different [guys].

Louis went out to Hollywood to make a movie, *A Song Is Born*. Anyway, we did a concert at Carnegie Hall . . . and the first part they got Edmond Hall's band and Louis was playing Dixieland. That's what the people had been waiting for; they wanted to hear Louis. It was such a sensation. Leonard Feather told Louis: "This is what you should be doing now. The big band is over. . . ."

So he got together with Joe Glaser during the time they were filming *A Song Is Born*. They said: "While you're out here why don't we try and see what happens. There's a jazz club in Hollywood called Billy Berg's. We'll book in that for three or four weeks. . . ." By that time Jack Teagarden, he was in trouble with his band; he was bankrupt. Earl Hines was bankrupt with his big band. Barney Bigard, I don't think he was doing too much. . . .

So they tried Louis playing New Orleans–type music. So they said: "Who you gonna get on bass?" So Louis said: "Well, I have a young kid who can really play. Why not get him?" They said: "We've never heard of him." He said: "So what! At one time nobody never heard of me." So I got a call from Joe Glaser. "Would you like to join Louis out in L.A.?" I said: "Is the Pope Catholic?" I had no idea what I was getting into. . . .

We flew out (with vocalist Velma Middleton), went down to Billy Berg's, looked up on the marquee and I saw "Louis Armstrong and the Esquire All Stars" with Jack Teagarden, Dick Cary—Earl Hines had some commitments to fulfill before he could join the band—Barney Bigard . . . and then I saw my name down there, "Arvell Shaw." Man, I almost fainted.

I'll never forget the first job. I didn't know anything about New Orleans jazz. I had heard about it because Fate Marable played some of that jazz. And then there was another street parade band in St. Louis called Simms Band . . . they were a New Orleans–type funeral band—the "cookingest" [sic] band I ever heard in my life.

~

The first Europe-wide tour [in 1949], we played from Helsinki all the way down to Palermo; 'cause the first time we went to Europe we went to the first Nice Festival in 1948. We were, on the '49 tour . . . the first concert was in Stockholm. When we went over we broadcast from the plane and everything. The last stop [in North America] was in Gander, Newfoundland. Then in Ireland. Then, going to Sweden, we stopped in Copenhagen. We were supposed to leave in forty minutes, just refuel or something. So two hours later we were still sitting there. So everybody started getting [restless]; then three hours. Everybody said: "What's goin' on?" Then they announced: "Ladies and gentlemen, we cannot go to Stockholm; there are something like 100,000 people at the airport to greet Mr. Armstrong and his band, and there is only one runway; we cannot get them off so we can land there."

So they finally got them off so we could land. I'll never forget coming in and looking down. They had all the lights going, the press was there, and it looked like ants, thousands of ants. We finally landed and they had a parade. . . . Anyway the whole tour was like that and we were broadcasting every night.

I guess the people and the Pope had been listening to the broadcasts. He found out we were going to play Rome so he asked to meet Louis and Lucille Armstrong 'cause he said that when he was a young priest he was a fan, he had Louis Armstrong records. He liked jazz—this was Pope Pius XII. So he would like to talk with Louis. So it was arranged through the

American Embassy in the Sistine Chapel. And all the diplomats and all the press was there. The Pope was telling Louis how he loved his records and how he had his records from when he was a young priest and everything. And he was asking Louis and Lucille about their life in the U.S. And he said, "Mr. Armstrong, you and Mrs. Armstrong, do you have any children?" And Louis said, "No, but we're having a hell of a lot of fun trying." There was complete, shocked silence for a minute. It could have been a disaster. Then everybody looked at Pope Pius; he burst out in a guffaw, then everybody . . . I bet the American ambassador must have lost three years of his life.

Playing with Louis there's no way you can improve on anything. But, what it did (studying in Geneva, Switzerland) . . . my appreciation of him and the music we played was enhanced. I learned to appreciate it more than before I went. When I studied European music I realized just what a great art form jazz is—America's gift to the arts of the world.

Louis's first thought was to entertain the public. That's why he was so great; he was more than just an innovative jazz musician. What Louis's contribution was, I think what Louis did by himself, was to make jazz into a soloist's art form. Before Louis, when they improvised they would just state the melody and then what they would do, they would get "hot"; they would heavily syncopate the melody. Louis started improvising on the chord structure of a tune. The old guys used to think he was crazy.

That's why he understood Charlie Parker so well. Because when they used to put down Charlie Parker, Louis understood, because they used to put Louis down just like they did Charlie Parker. Louis was so far ahead of his time, [but] didn't frighten so many people.

Dizzy and Louis lived maybe two blocks from each other in Corona. They were very dear friends. Louis, Dizzy, and Bobby Hackett, they all lived around there. That competition, that thing that Louis was against bebop, that was something created by the jazz writers to have something to write about—"the moldy fig" thing. They were not capable of criticizing jazz because jazz was from another people and another culture in those days. They didn't understand it themselves, the jazz, the writers like Leonard Feather or Nat Hentoff. The only thing they knew about jazz is what the musicians told them and that's what they wrote. They created that thing for publicity just to have something to write about—that Louis and Dizzy were feuding.

—

We worked continuously [the All Stars]. We'd play a tune a couple of times then everybody would figure out their own part. And Louis was the fountainhead. He was the star and he was the leader. Whichever way he went, we went. He always went the right way; and everybody knew what he wanted. . . . Anything that happened in my life after that is anti-climactic. . . .

Traveling with Louis was like traveling with the President of the United States. That's how he was looked on, especially all through Africa, and all through the Orient . . . It's a funny thing. We played the most technically advanced countries, like Europe . . . we'd go into some small villages. In Africa we'd go out into the bush . . . we'd go play concerts. And no matter what language or culture we played, the people reacted the same way to the same things that Louis did. No matter whether they understood what he did. For instance, all he had to do was walk on stage and flip that handkerchief and smile; and the audience was his.

That's why a lot of band leaders, if you went out and played a solo, and you got too big a hand, you didn't play no more. But with Louis, everybody had a featured spot, and he'd tell you: "Go out there and tear up the house if you can"; 'cause he knew that you can stand on your left eyelash and get the biggest applause in the world. All he had to do was walk out there with that handkerchief and smile; and he'd wash you away. That's one of the things I admired about him. He gave everybody an equal chance, and he was different. He wasn't all the time with the smile. Before he went on stage he was strictly business. He never asked you to do anything he wouldn't. . . . He was always the first one on stage and he worked hard, harder than anybody else. Nothing can top that.

One concert we played on the Gold Coast . . . I think we had one of the largest crowds; we played to almost 200,000 people in a soccer stadium. In the Congo [Republic of Zaire], we got there three days after they had assassinated Patrice Lumumba and they were at each other's throats. You know what happened? When Louis came we played three concerts. They called a truce; both armies came to the concert and sat side by side, and had a ball. As soon as we left they were fighting again. That's why Louis was so invaluable to the State Department. That's why when he had this flap with President Eisenhower they forgave him because they needed him. He didn't need them. Most people when they have a flap with the president, man, you're finished, especially a president that was as popular as Dwight Eisenhower. But Mr. Eisenhower and the State Department realized this man . . . made more friends for this country than all of us put together.

PATRICIA WILLARD

INTERVIEW: BARNEY BIGARD (1976)

Los Angeles, California, July 1976

New Orleans reedman Barney Bigard is perhaps best known for his fourteen-year tenure with Duke Ellington (from around 1928 to 1942), during which time he helped create such pieces as "Mood Indigo" and "Saturday Night Function." But in 1946, following the filming of New Orleans, *he began an important association as clarinetist with the All Stars that was to last on and off for some fifteen years. Excerpts from this interview, conducted by Patricia Willard in Los Angeles, have been drawn from the Jazz Oral History Interviews on file at the Institute of Jazz Studies at Rutgers-Newark. Bigard not only talks about what it was like playing with Louis onstage as compared with Duke; he also reveals something of what went on behind the scenes, and how Armstrong's generous, but gullible nature could lead to abuse as well as self-delusion. As an example, Bigard touches on Armstrong's affair with "Sweets"—the major topic of the letter Armstrong wrote to Joe Glaser that appeared earlier in this book. —JB*

Willard: *What about the difference in the music of Armstrong and Ellington?*

Bigard: I used to enjoy Louis a lot, if you wanted to play longer, you [could] play longer; if you didn't want to play at all, you didn't have to play at all. It was just beautiful. Duke, on the other hand, would write arrangements . . . and it'll have an open space and just say "Solo." Now, that's an original tune. What are you going to solo if you don't hear it? What's going on, you know? Then there will be about eight bars or sixteen bars, and that's it. Then probably, just about the time you're getting used to what you're hearing, you're off, your solo's gone. See, that's the difference.

—

Willard: How was the spirit of the members of the band in Ellington compared with Armstrong's? The feelings of the men for the music and each other?

Bigard: Oh, I guess the feeling was all right. But I think that they were more close in Louis's aggregation because it's smaller, where Duke's is larger and they go like—I hate to say that—I mean, like cliques. . . . But Armstrong's band's too small for that kind of business. You know what I mean.

Willard: Was there a competitive feeling in Duke's band among the men?

Bigard: Oh, I don't think so. I mean, I think it could be a little jealousy feeling.

Willard: How about with Louis Armstrong?

Bigard: No, you don't have time to think about anything like that with Louis. I mean, he was wonderful.

—

Willard: What kind of a person was Louis?

Bigard: Louis was a wonderful man to work with. I mean, he'd say a lot of things. He can raise hell with you. Now in two seconds he's forgotten all about it and even what it was all about. I kidded him. One time, for no reason whatsoever, we were at the Blue Note in Chicago—and he came off the stand. He said, "Cats think because they played in a big band that they are the best musicians in town. . . . They think they're hell and every-one thinks he was with Paul Whiteman, he thinks he's hell too." So I'm listening. I said, "What's all this about?" And I hadn't even said one word to him. Neither has Jack [Teagarden]. Nobody. And he's mumbling all this in his dressing room. So I said, "Well, I know you must be hinting at me . . . I'm sure glad I was with the greatest band in the world, because your band wasn't nothing." I said, "You had the world's worst band." And he kept quiet . . . Oh, boy. That's the truth. He had good men in his band, but they didn't have no good arrangements, nothing. I was surprised. If it wasn't for him, there wouldn't be any band. And you're talking about a man that can remember tunes of the past years and people of the past years. He had that memory. He was phenomenal. I've never seen anybody like that.

Bigard: Money didn't bother him. That's funny. And he had women strung all over the world, put them in business, even. He had one guy that used to live here [Los Angeles] called Stuff Crouch . . .

Willard: Stuff Crouch, Julius Crouch . . .

Bigard: He put him in business; gave him an after-hour place.

Willard: The Backstage, Vernon and Central.

Bigard: So he came over there at Billy Berg's after the place opened up. He invited the group over to the place for some drinks and a little snack if they wanted. Now, Louis put him in that business . . . And by a quirk, I didn't feel like going. (And the guys that went—Earl Hines, Jack Teagarden, and all the rest of them—went over there.) And when they were getting ready to leave, Crouch gave them a check. And that burned Louis up. And he used to send his kid, like, go to Billy Berg's—he'd send his [own] kid to talk to Louis . . . telling Louis he's her uncle and all that business.

Willard: Yeah, well, he was the godfather to one of his daughters . . . and his daughters—Julie and Cheryl. And then he had a son, Howard, who sang under the name of Dave Howard, and Louis helped him too.

Bigard: He helps everybody—money doesn't mean nothing to him. He wanted a kid so bad, and this is real funny. He had a little girl called Sweet, Sweetie, something, and she got pregnant, but not by Louis. But Louis thought it was by him, because she was telling him that, you know? And, oh, he was proud. He's going to be the daddy.

So he had a bag. We were traveling by bus now, and he had a

bag . . . when he was getting ready to go to sleep, all the change he had in his pocket plus dollars, he'd take it, put it in his bag. I asked him what he was doing that for. He said, "That's for my kid when it's born." Okay, so by the time this kid was born that bag was stuffed with coins and dollars and fives and tens, just stuffed.

So he gave it to this little gal. Now the baby was born. Oh, he was walking around like a peacock. So he started talking to Lucille again. He said, "Lucille, how'd you feel if you adopt my kid?" She said, "What kid?" He said, "My kid. I got a baby by Sweetie." She said, "Who told you you got a baby by Sweetie? You better not bring no baby around here." She says, "You couldn't make a baby with a pencil. Now you're talking about your kid. She done fool you and she's got a boyfriend. He must have did it and he's telling her to tell you that you're the father." She said, "You sure are stupid."

Well, that's how he was. He'd go for anything.

PATRICIA WILLARD

INTERVIEW: TRUMMY YOUNG (EXCERPTS) (1976)

Washington, D.C., September 18 and 20, 1976

Trombonist Trummy Young played with the All Stars for some twelve years, from 1952 to 1964, and he has valuable remarks to share about Armstrong's prior history with big bands and his ongoing dependence on arrangers. Most compelling is what he has to say about the All Star years, the making of various movies, Jack Teagarden and "Rockin' Chair," a confrontation with Benny Goodman's band during a six-week tour in 1953 that had been ill-conceived by Joe Glaser, how much Louis taught him about timing and relaxation, Louis's views on modern painting, his antics on tour, and more. These excerpts have been taken from an interview conducted by Patricia Willard as part of the Jazz Oral History Interviews on file at the Institute of Jazz Studies at Rutgers-Newark. —JB

Willard: *I was going to ask you, in 1930, when you saw Louis in Washington, whom was he working with? Did he have a group, or would he appear in front of a local group?*

The Louis Armstrong Companion
172

Young: I think Louis was playing in front of Luis Russell's group at that time. Of course, Louis had a lot of bands of his own back at that time, but I'm . . . pretty sure . . . I think he was fronting Luis Russell's band at that time. You see, Louis never did rehearse bands much himself. He always had a musical director, somebody in the band who was an arranger to do this for him.

I know once with his big band he had Joe Garland, the saxophone player, the guy who wrote "In the Mood." He had Joe Garland to conduct his band, and Luis Russell used to be his musical director. Even with the little band . . . when I was with him, he had Billy Kyle as musical director. For instance, if we went in a town and Louis had to rehearse for a TV show or something, well . . . Louis didn't have to go out, but Louis could go home and relax. Billy would go and tell them what songs Louis was doing, and most of the stars do it that way, you know, and they don't fool around there all day doing that. But we would go, and Billy Kyle would instruct them on just what key Louis did this or that in, and how many choruses, this and that, how he went out, and Billy Kyle would probably write out a little sketch for him and give it to him—just what we were doing, you know. And we would rehearse. Sometimes Louis would rehearse with us if it was something very important; but usually he went to the hotel, and he relaxed, you know. And most of them do; that's the way they do it today. (With Louis it was just one big thing after another, because you never knew when he had all these big things coming up. If we weren't doing a movie, we were doing a big TV show or something of this sort, and, of course, he never was on real long, but he always had an important spot in these things. . . .)

Willard: How many movies did you make with Louis?

Young: Well, the first movie I did with Louis was *The Glenn Miller Story.* I think I did three or four movies with Louis. I did several in Europe . . .

———

Young: I ever tell you about some of interviews Louis had over there [Middle East]?
. . . [W]e went to Beirut with Louis . . . Well man, these guys were high all the time. They'd be smoking that hashish; so he's smoking it along with them. So they [asked] us one day, "How come you guys going to Israel?" So you know, they cornered Louis, got some newspaper guys down in the basement dressing room. "How come you going to play for

them Jews down in Israel?" So Louis sort of looked at them, and he said, "Let me tell you something. When I go down there, the first thing they're going to [ask] me is, 'How come you played for them Arabs over there?'" He says, "Let me tell you something, man. That horn. You see that horn? That horn ain't prejudiced. A note's a note in any language."

Willard: . . . [Y]ou mentioned . . . one of the times Louis came to Honolulu he had Tyree Glenn with him on trombone [replaced Trummy Young upon his departure in 1964], and asked you to show Tyree a good time.

Armstrong and Lucille serenading the Sphinx in Giza, Egypt, January 28, 1961. Photo: UPI/Corbis-Bettmann.

Young: He kept me up all night. Louis didn't like to sleep, for one thing. I tell you something about Louis. Louis and Duke had similar qualities. They always want people around them. And Louis—he didn't like to sleep. So he called me up, and he had me with him all night to show Tyree Glenn how he should be singing some of those things. "Old Rockin' Chair" and some of the things that I used to do with him. I didn't do this originally with him. Jack Teagarden did . . . Louis always wanted somebody to sing, you know, sing things with him, because he had Velma over there as a foil . . . ; they were a fantastic team together. Velma [Middleton] wasn't a great singer or nothing like that, but she certainly was the right foil for Louis. I would have hated to follow them two on stage, man.

But Louis kept me up all night, up until nine o'clock in the morning, showing Tyree how to do these spots with him . . . He'd say, "Now when I get . . . when I mug like this, you do that or you do this . . ." And over the long period of time I worked with him, I picked up a lot of those little mannerisms to do with him . . . And so he wanted me to show Tyree, and I showed Tyree. I was helping Tyree on a lot of things. See . . . anybody could have learned from Louis. I had a long discussion with Jon Hendricks one time . . . we had a long discussion after rehearsal. He said, "You know, I kind of envy you. Man, you're sitting there working under the greatest teacher you can find." I said, "I know it." He's speaking about Louis, because you could learn an awful lot from Louis if you were observing . . . if you were aware. Anybody could, not just me, but anybody else. The guy knew, he knew phrasing, he knew timing. He was a master of timing and phrasing and little innuendoes that he would put into things—I thought I knew something about the stage and all. I knew nothing . . . He was a master of that stage. You had a hard time following Louis on that stage. I don't care who you were.

I tell you something that happened when I was with Louis. We had a tour with Benny Goodman's big band, and so Benny had some money put up in the tour. Joe Glaser's office was booking it. And so they decided to put, Benny decided to put, Louis on first. You know, that old show business thing. I'll get that last shot at you. So he did. And when he put Louis on first he could hardly get on afterwards. . . . So after about a week of that going on he said, "Let's put Louis on last." So they did. And I don't know why he ever did that. So . . . when Benny went on, people would be out in the lobby smoking. And Benny got so mad one night; he took his glass— he had some scotch and soda—[and] he threw it against the wall. So he told them: "Hey, that guy ain't doing nothing but clowning out there." He was talking about him and Velma. "That's not music, you know!"

Well, you see, what he forgets is Louis wasn't only a great musician, Louis was a great showman on top of it. So there isn't nothing wrong with using showmanship out there along with your music—a combination, and this is what Louis had. This is one of the things that made him so great. He could play one of the greatest choruses you ever heard in your life, and after he got through, he could give some little mannerisms that was greater than the chorus, you know. So he'd shoot you down one way or the other. And these are things that he naturally had. Nobody taught him that.

—

Young: . . . [I]t was in Paris, and some people had just took us down to the Louvre. So he told me when we came out. He said, "Trummy, you see all them pictures with the eyes and all coming out?" He was talking about modern paintings. He said, "Did you see all those things?" I said, "Yeah." He said, "What did you notice about them?" I said, "Well, it's real modern, Louis, you know." He said, "Let me tell you something. You know who put those things up? The Russians put them things out to confuse the Americans."

—

Young: And I used to look at him. We went to Japan, and you know, we played a little thing at an American club over there. And this night the Prince and his wife were there, and he wound up out there dancing with them, and you just don't do that with the Prince's wife—and this is against all protocol. But everybody was just laughing and dying laughing. The next day he had got with some newspaper reporters. He was drinking, so they had had him pull off his shirt. You know, and he had a little round belly. So they took his picture; he's sitting on the floor. They had a thing in the newspaper: "Black Buddha."

—

Young: I would say I learned a lot about timing from Louis. I learned a lot about building, like not starting out too strong, just building things and you know, starting easy and building things up. And these things are important. But timing I think the greatest thing I accomplished from Louis was not trying to put everything . . . right away into something, not trying to do all the things I knew right away into a chorus, but taking it easy and building the thing up to a climax. And he was a master at that . . . he was relaxed.

He had the whole thing going there.

COMMENTARY

Liner notes, Louis Armstrong: Chicago Concert, *Columbia CS 36426*

The following piece by Dan Morgenstern, esteemed critic and director of the Institute of Jazz Studies at Rutgers University, was originally written to accompany the release on Columbia Records of a two-record set featuring the All Stars performing a benefit for the Multiple Sclerosis Society in Chicago's Medinah Temple on June 1, 1956. Morgenstern covers in loving and perceptive detail the trajectory of Armstrong's career, the origins of the All Stars, the qualities of its various sidemen, the reception of the group in the United States and abroad, not to mention some of the telling moments at the Newport Jazz Festival in 1957 and 1958. Here stands a conquering hero and "one of nature's true noblemen." —JB

Step right in . . . the show is on! And what a show it is: Louis Armstrong is performing with his All Stars—ready to entertain you royally. To be entertained by a King is not an everyday event. Show Entertainment. Those are the terms which, when Louis was making the music heard herein, jazz critics were wont to hurl at him, as if they were invective. And to the hurlers, they were. By 1956, jazz had become an art form, serious business. (The more serious, the less business, but the gentlemen of the pen couldn't care less.) After all, hadn't they decreed that jazz was "A Serious Art Form"? Louis Armstrong, of course, had been "A Serious Artist" in the 1920s, when he recorded with his Hot Five, playing The Real Jazz. But then Louis became a star. He fronted big bands (bands of which the critics disapproved even when other big bands were in). He sang and played pop tunes. He appeared in films. He had fallen from grace.

Never mind that musicians admired him more than ever, that he continued to refine the astonishing creative and instrumental powers that had stunned all within hearing of his horn from the time he'd come to Chicago to join King Oliver. Never mind that his magic ways with an ordinary song had enraptured a generation of singers, starting with Bing Crosby, and changed the way everybody in America sang, whether they knew where the new way came from or not.

Never mind all that: Louis Armstrong had become an entertainer.

It could not be denied that he still played the trumpet well—but all that other stuff. Good heavens!

Today almost everyone with access to print fawns over Louis Armstrong's memory, including those who jabbed and jived him when he was around. Not that it bothered him much. He had the love of his audiences, and those audiences outnumbered and outloved those of any other living artist. Only Charlie Chaplin could rival his worldwide fame, and Chaplin did not perform in person. Yet it did get under his skin, and sometimes he fought back—Louis was a counterpuncher from the start; had to be in order to survive.

It didn't rub him that he was criticized. "As long as they spell my name right and keep it before the public," he used to say to friends. And though he was held responsible for such presumed flaws in his "act" as the unchanging repertoire (a canard: what working jazz group doesn't have a set repertoire?); the "tasteless" jokes (Louis had the capacity to genuinely enjoy his ability to make people laugh, and besides, his timing was superb); the flashing teeth and rolling eyes (judged suspect, though they came naturally to Louis: could or should he have hidden those magnificent teeth that supported his horn for all those blowing years, or those battle-scarred lips he cared for so tenderly with the special salve made for him by a German master craftsman, an instrument-maker who understood what went into playing the most demanding horn yet devised by man), so clearly reflected in the expressions and mannerisms of the people of West Africa (the former Gold Coast) whence he proudly traced his ancestry, long before *Roots*, always ahead of his time, and in every way— he didn't let all that get him down. Not even when some whites (who had no right to) and some blacks (who had no right to) called him Uncle Tom, aggressively or apologetically, maliciously or misguidedly, did he let it frustrate him, though it hurt him deeply. (He spoke of "the modern malice" and was misunderstood.)

No, it was when the musicians in his band were disparaged, that was when he became furious. Not only because it was unfair: his people did their job, or they left the band. But because it destroyed morale, and in a band that traveled and worked like Louis's did—more than any other organization, perhaps with the exception of Duke Ellington's orchestra— morale was a crucial factor. Steady work and good pay made up for a lot of barbs, as did the sheer fact of working with Louis and basking in his glory, but musicians are not the world's most thick-skinned people.

Newport, July 4, 1957: Louis Armstrong's and the nation's birthday.

Louis Armstrong Night. Louis and his group arrive at Freebody Park in mid-afternoon, straight from a one-nighter somewhere in New England. That they're used to; routine. Sometimes they go on within hours after a flight of thousands of miles, in places they've never been to before. All in a year's work: get on, do the show (always a hell of a show; nothing less than all you've got with Louis, who never gives less than his all). But this time, in the tent behind the stage that is the Newport Festival's star's "dressing room" at this stage of the game, Louis hears from the producer, and the producer's advisory board, and his own manager, that he is to appear with almost every act on the bill except his own group, with people he hasn't played with in years, a parade of figures from the past: Henry "Red" Allen, once or twice in his band; Buster Bailey, a 1924–25 colleague from Fletcher Henderson's band; J. C. Higginbotham, who was with Louis's big band in the '30s; and Jack Teagarden and Cozy Cole, alumni of his All Stars. Plus special guest Kid Ory: the septuagenarian trombonist who gave Louis his first important gigs and was in his Hot Five recording group. And with Sidney Bechet, a boyhood acquaintance and 1924 and 1940 recording partner. Then with Ella Fitzgerald, friend and recording partner. Then with everybody for a Happy Birthday jam.

Louis, who never in his career has favored unrehearsed public performances, especially on stage before thousands, is stunned. While press and musicians and backstage hangers-on mill about, he considers a compromise. "Maybe a number [or] two, but I go on with my band to close the show—no other way." Meanwhile a telegram from Bechet (the one he might have secretly wanted to play with; they are old rivals, and Louis has not had many such): "Sorry, but unable to come to America. Happy birthday to Louis." Now there is room for Louis's band—even a need. OK, the band will close the show ("We don't do less than an hour," says Louis), but—without Velma Middleton, the All Star's singer. Louis can't believe what he hears. Velma has been with him almost uninterruptedly since 1942. He knows the critics find her distasteful. (Many men have problems with fat women, especially if they are attractive. Velma has a pretty good face atop her robust 250-pound body, and she's light on her feet. Before she joined Louis, she was a solo turn—singing and dancing. She does a mean split. She also sings nicely, with feeling, and is a perfect foil for Louis's comedy—perfect because she is funny but not ridiculous.) The rationale, of course, is that Ella is on the bill and one female singer should be enough.

Louis has had it by then; and he withdraws behind the tent flap that contains his "private" area. Soon Velma hears the news, and bursts into tears. Louis, who has fantastic ears, hears her crying. Suddenly he appears from behind the flap, wearing nothing but a handkerchief tied around his scalp. Shouts and alarums. Women shriek, grown men flinch, and everyone scatters to the winds, Louis's curses in their ears. Like an ancient African king, he smites them with his righteous wrath.

A special Newport society dinner party has been arranged, with Louis as guest of honor. (That it would take the place of his only chance to rest before the performance did not occur to the well-bred planners.) Louis does not appear, nor does he play with any act but his own. Velma performs. The show goes down in style; no one not in the know senses anything wrong. At the end of Louis's set, a giant birthday cake is wheeled on stage, and Ella and Johnny Mercer sing "Happy Birthday." Louis has fine manners; he joins in, backing them up on his horn. As Ella cuts the cake, someone (perhaps the producer himself) whispers to Louis that Ory and the other musicians are waiting to come on stage with him for a jam session finale. "No one hangs on my coattails," says Louis, and intones the National Anthem, his band falling in behind him. He doesn't taste his cake. That night, Louis Armstrong didn't eat anything they were dishing out.

The next day, Murray Kempton, then an influential newspaper columnist, who—like so many members of the press—had discovered jazz when Newport became a fashionable media event, wrote a piece attacking Louis for his boorish behavior. His sentiments were echoed by other writers. The musicians knew better. "Some of these people seem to be trying to crucify Pops," said Jack Teagarden.

Louis never bore a grudge. . . . At next year's Newport, he played with the Youth Band (they had rehearsed that afternoon) and Teagarden and Bobby Hackett guested with the All Stars—as those two good friends were always welcome to do. The press was cautiously laudatory.

All this to say that Louis Armstrong was a complex and proud man, who gave his life's work (I should say his calling) everything he had—a reasonable man, but not one to be pushed around, and a tiger when his special people were pushed. And also to say that Louis Armstrong was the greatest musician of his day (which means our time) and, one of the greatest entertainers of his day, both things (not contradictory, fashionable esthetics to the contrary notwithstanding) rolled into one. To know Louis was to understand that, and these who knew could find untold joy in hearing, yes, again and again, how he had perfected those same pieces—the way you could tell, from the way he kicked off the opening "Indiana," or even the way he intoned his theme song (written especially for him by a team of black songwriters including the famous actor Clarence Muse, and a thorn in the side of confused liberals), "Sleepy Time Down South," if this was going to be an extraordinary night or just (just!) an ordinary very special one. Every encounter with Louis Armstrong, every note from his horn or vocal cords, was special—from first to last.

So come on in—the show is on!

Louis Armstrong's official, certified jazz-historical fame rests chiefly in his seminal recordings of the 1920s with his small studio groups, variously called Hot Five or Hot Seven or Savoy Ballroom Five. These are supposed to be representative of his work in the mid-to-late 1920s, but it is seldom considered that the small groups were strictly studio units, and that from the time he left King Oliver's Creole Jazz Band in 1924 to join Fletcher Henderson, his day-to-day work was with big bands, including his own. The small group records represent some twenty-five days in the years between 1925 and 1929, of his musical life. And not complete days at that, just a few hours before starting the night's work.

The more incongruous, then, that because he ceased to make such small-group records in 1929, he should have been judged to have radically changed his approach to music. The fact is that Louis Armstrong did not head up any working small group until the first All Stars were formed in late 1947. By then, big bands had fallen on evil days economically. Even so, it took all of manager Joe Glaser's persuasive powers to convince Louis to lay off his sixteen men and one woman. He knew that he was their meal ticket, and he was a compassionate man.

The All Stars grew our of some New York concerts in 1947 with hand-picked small groups that were ecstatically received by press and public. According to the scribes, Louis was returning to his proper element. In truth, he was going through a major adjustment. Long accustomed to the role of featured soloist and singer backed by scores devised for a big band, he now found himself playing ensemble lead, as with King Oliver. The music he had played for more than twenty years had moved with the times, and by the mid-40s was by no means untouched by "modern" tendencies. Not that Louis played bop. But his 1944–45 band featured a young tenor player named Dexter Gordon. The New Orleans revival that was also an aspect of the jazz world of the day had not reflected itself in Louis's music, except when he was featured in a 1946 Hollywood epic called *New Orleans.*

Yet he had never lost his love for the music of his hometown, and the All Stars, at first more or less a swing group, gradually moved toward incorporating traditional pieces in its repertoire. It never became a "Dixieland" band, however. On records, Louis continued to work with groups of all sizes, sometimes with strings, playing current material. If the results became successful sellers, they were incorporated into the All Stars' book. ("Blueberry Hill," for example; or "La Vie En Rose" and "C'est Ci Bon.")

The core of the first All Stars was the empathy between Louis and Jack Teagarden, and the superb drumming of Big Sid Catlett, who'd been in Louis's big bands. Earl Hines, with whom Louis had collaborated so excitingly in the late '20s, came aboard for a while, another victim of the declining market for big bands, but he'd been a leader too long to play second fiddle, even to Louis. Teagarden had been a leader, too, and he also left, after some four years. Clarinetist Barney Bigard, from New Orleans, and Duke Ellington, stayed longer, though his style was not ideal for the group.

The All Stars visited Europe for the first time in 1948—Louis hadn't been there since the spring of 1935—and made the other long journeys from time to time. But it was not until 1954 that the constant worldwide touring began in earnest. Louis now stood on the threshold of his greatest fame, and 1956 was the year in which he crossed it.

First, there was a tour of Great Britain, where he had not appeared since 1934. The warmth of his reception was overwhelming. The tour climaxed in a typical Armstrong escapade. Performing in London's Empress Hall before an audience including Princess Margaret, he "broke all rules of theatrical protocol," according to the Associated Press report, by acknowledging the presence of a member of the royal family. "We've got one of our special fans in the house," he announced, "and we're really going to lay this one on for the Princess." The audience gasped and the object of Louis's affection applauded enthusiastically. It was further reported that she "started to beat her feet up and down in full view of hundreds" as the All Stars swung into "Clarinet Marmalade"—another breach of protocol. Such things made worldwide news.

It also made news when Louis played in West Berlin and a sizable contingent of fans crossed over from the Eastern sector, including a number of Russians. And it made more news still when, in May, Louis made his first visit to Africa, to what was then still called the Gold Coast, soon to become Ghana, and already was run by Nkruma. Tens of thousands received the All Stars at Accra airport, and at an outdoor concert, a crowd estimated by *Life* at half a million, turned out to hear and see them. Louis was more than pleased to find traces of his ancestry here, and was particularly moved by a dancer who strongly resembled his mother, in features and movement. Black had not yet been officially declared beautiful, but Louis knew.

The All Stars, accompanied by Edward R. Murrow and his CBS-TV crew (shooting the documentary later theatrically released as *Satchmo the Great*) left Accra on May 28. On June 1, they were in Chicago for the concert captured on this album. Billed as "50 Years of Jazz," it was a benefit for The Multiple Sclerosis Society, narrated by Helen Hayes, and "illustrating the development of American jazz from New Orleans to Chicago, New York, Europe and back to America again," according to a contemporary newspaper account.

Louis had little patience with such gimmicks. Basically, he and his band just did their show—a long and full one—with a few token gestures toward the format. Apparently, the concert opened with the band marching through the hall (Medinah Temple) to the strains of "Free as a Bird" and "Didn't He Ramble" (part of the group's standard repertoire). We pick them up as they reach the stage, playing a single chorus of "The Memphis Blues," pianist Billy Kyle reaching the keyboard *in medias res*. In medley style, "Frankie and Johnny" and "Tiger Rag" follow. Miss Hayes's stilted narration has mercifully been omitted, so what we hear is an unadulterated Armstrong show by what was arguably the best edition of the All Stars.

On board were trombonist Trummy Young, the erstwhile star of the Jimmie Lunceford band, who had joined in 1952. Favored by the critics during his Lunceford days and when he later worked and recorded with Dizzy Gillespie on 52nd Street, his playing with Louis often came in for critical knocks as overly emphatic and crude. But Trummy had always been an extroverted blustery player, and he did what Louis wanted and needed. He soon became Louis's mainstay in the group, musically and personally, and it was a sad day for both men when he left in early 1964 to return to Hawaii, his wife's native state, at her request.

Trummy loved Louis, and understood his role in the band even better than Teagarden had. Like Jack, he also sang and entertained.

Clarinetist Edmond Hall had joined in the summer of 1955. From Louisiana, and just a year younger than Louis, he was a man with his own style and his own mind. He never called Louis by anything but his first name, with a sibilant "s," and referred to him as "Armstrong." That was very much old New Orleans, and so was the Albert system clarinet he favored. He fitted into the band and was an inspired and inventive soloist. But he was restless and quit in 1958, using the band's fixed repertoire as a convenient excuse.

Pianist Billy Kyle had been aboard since 1953. A brilliant stylist (and a favorite of Bud Powell), he also knew a thing or two about arranging, and was a flawless accompanist. He stayed with Louis until, in his fifty-second year, he died on the road in early 1966. During his thirteen years with Louis, no record company offered him a date outside the All Stars—a great pity and a symptom of the benign neglect in which the jazz establishment held Louis's sidemen (Trummy had no offers, either).

Bassist Dale Jones, the least known of these All Stars, was also an old-timer, born in Nebraska in 1902. An early associate of Jack Teagarden, he came to the All Stars in 1951, when Arvell Shaw took a sabbatical, and rejoined from time to time in ensuing years, not willing to stay on the road. A sturdy player, he led his own groups in California and Las Vegas.

Barrett Deems had been billed as "the world's fastest drummer" when he broke into the big time with Joe Venuti's band in 1938, at the age of twenty-four. With Louis from 1954 to 1958, he was a special target of the critics. Being white, he was fair game for white critics, with their prejudices bred of guilt and insecurity. Still active in Chicago, Deems is a brilliant technician with a firm beat who counts Tony Williams among his fans. Barrett played loud and strong when Louis wanted it that way, but was a good man with brushes, too—as on "Perdido," Billy Kyle's feature, and, more unexpectedly, on Hall's fiery "Clarinet Marmalade."

As for Louis, he had long since taken to heart King Oliver's advice to play the lead and let a good melody speak for itself. Gone were the striking flights of fancy from the days when, by his own account, he was more interested in impressing "the musicians in the house" than in playing for the public's benefit. With Louis, there was never any doubt about what tune was being played. His majestic phrasing and matchless gift for melodic construction enhanced the most banal material, and when he sang a lyric, the words attained poetic loftiness and weight.

No wonder Billie Holiday loved him—and not just as a girl. As he became more stylized, more deliberate, so did she. Fittingly, her very last album contains a beautiful version of "Sleepy Time Down South." (For one example, hear what Louis does with the word *else* in "The Gypsy," a song which he and Charlie Parker were the only jazzmen to favor.)

A Louis Armstrong show was a masterpiece of pacing. As he says somewhere along the way, "We've got to keep it rolling." Which he did. Changes and contrasts in mood and tempo abound, and the variety of material is astonishing: from "Bucket's Got a Hole In It" to "Tenderly," from "Black and Blue" to "Ko Ko Mo," from "West End Blues" to "You'll Never Walk Alone." About that last tune: played as a medley with "Tenderly," with a strictly New Orleans beat, slow and stately, yet great for dancing (this medley was always a highlight of Louis's dance sets), it is transformed by Louis's respect and artistry from Broadway bathos to true pathos.

As he told a young journalist named David Halberstam, who spent a few days on the road with the All Stars in 1957: "When we hit Savannah we played 'I'll Never Walk Alone' and the whole house—all Negroes started singing with us on their own. We ran through two choruses and they kept with us and later they asked for it again. Most touching damn thing I ever saw. I almost started crying right there on stage. We really hit something inside each person there."

(Louis had a way of "hitting something" inside people. At Newport in 1958 I was listening to Louis's set with James Baldwin. As always, Louis concluded the set with the National Anthem. It was early in the morning— the show had run very late—and the music carried beautifully in the damp air. The crowd had roared for more, but now they were still. After Louis's final golden note had faded, Baldwin turned and said: "You know, that's the first time I've liked that song.")

Forget all the nonsense about this or that stage of Louis, about commercialism and redundancy, and hear Louis Armstrong imbue each note he plays with the essence of music and life. Hear his ensemble variations in the several da capo sections of "Bucket's Got a Hole In It" (in perhaps its best versions ever here) and hear a master of the blues, and of spontaneous, amazing invention. Never mind that his "West End Blues" doesn't (couldn't, and shouldn't be expected to) measure up to the 1928 version. Never mind the brief confusion on "Manhattan," put in strictly for this concert. But do hear Louis's lead and solo on "Struttin' with Some Barbecue," hear the background riffs and obbligati (how about "That's My Desire"?) he fashions throughout, and hear how he knows to build to a climax.

And since it comes last, hear him take "Ko Ko Mo" from Harlem through the Caribbean to Africa, quoting "The Peanut Vendor" and singing the blues, free as a soaring bird. Then you'll hear the father of all that is good and great in this music called jazz, one of nature's true noble-men, and one reason why this sad, monstrous century will he remembered well.

And then, listen to some more Louis Armstrong music. I've been doing that for more than thirty-five years, and still discover new and magic things about the mystery of Louis Daniel Armstrong.

DAVID H. OSTWALD

LOUIS ARMSTRONG, CIVIL RIGHTS PIONEER (1991)

New York Times, *August 3, 1991*

While on the road in Fargo, North Dakota in September 1957 Armstrong caught some late-breaking TV stories about events in Little Rock, Arkansas. He then summarily canceled a State Department–sponsored tour of the Soviet Union, telling reporters, "The people over there ask me what's wrong with my country. What am I supposed to say? The way they are treating my people in the South, the government can go to hell." He refused to take back a word, despite less than unanimous support from fellow blacks, among them entertainers like Sammy Davis, Jr. The impact of Armstrong's strong stand against racial discrimination and his putting President Eisenhower on notice is seen in what David H. Ostwald has to say about Armstrong's role as civil rights pioneer. A lawyer and leader of the Gully Low Jazz Band, Ostwald wrote the following Op-Ed piece to mark the occasion of Armstrong's 90th birthday the following day. Ostwald's article also helps one understand why it was only in 1995, fourteen years after Armstrong first became eligible in 1981 and ten years after his death, that the U.S. Postal Service finally issued a stamp in his honor. What is more, it happened only after a heroic effort initi-ated by Lucille Armstrong, a battle against a bureaucracy that would sooner accord the honor to the likes of Elvis Presley, Hank Williams, and Howlin' Wolf. —JB

In the clamor over the Supreme Court nomination of Clarence Thomas, the civil rights struggle is again at the forefront of the national conscious-ness. The names of black heroes—Thurgood Marshall, Martin Luther

King Jr., Rosa Parks, Jackie Robinson—are seen and heard everywhere. One person has unfortunately been omitted from this pantheon—Louis Armstrong, whose 90th birthday would have been tomorrow.

Before black ballplayers and political activists became household names, musicians were the only blacks able to attract white America's attention, and Satchmo was the first to make it big. He was the first black man to be featured in Hollywood movies made for white audiences, as well as the first to serve as host on a sponsored network radio show. The power of his genius, combined with his loving manner, forced whites to rethink their racism, whether they knew it or not.

For five decades, he was a huge public presence. In February 1949, wearing a crown of trumpets, he was on the cover of *Time* magazine. In 1957, Edward R. Murrow's CBS documentary *Satchmo the Great* followed Armstrong from a tour of Europe and Africa to a New York performance with Leonard Bernstein. Armstrong had hits from the 1920s to the 1980s, the longest string in recording history. In May 1964, "Hello Dolly" toppled the Beatles from the No. 1 spot on the *Billboard* chart.

Armstrong was rarely overtly political, but as a black artist of universal popularity he had an inevitable social impact. The trumpeter Lester Bowie recently told Gary Giddins, Armstrong's biographer: "The true revolutionary is one that's not apparent. I mean the revolutionary that's waving a gun out in the streets is never effective; the police just arrest him. But the police don't ever know about the guy that smiles and drops a little poison in their coffee. Well, Louis, in that sense, was that sort of revolutionary, a true revolutionary."

But Armstrong was more than just visible. As early as 1929, his celebrity allowed him to shrewdly inject the issue of race into the mainstream. His recording that year of "Black and Blue"—a song with the lyrics: "I'm white inside, but that don't help my case / 'cause I can't hide what is on my face"—was made and publicized at a time when such sentiments were unheard of in white America.

In his early films, in which he portrayed potentially demeaning black characters, he used his awe-inspiring artistry and gift for satire to overcome stereotype and rise above the material.

In September 1957, Armstrong finally lost his cool. "The way they are treating my people in the South, the Government can go to hell," he announced as he canceled a State Department–sponsored tour of the Soviet Union upon learning that Governor Orval Faubus had called out the Arkansas National Guard to prevent the integration of Little Rock's schools. He charged that President Eisenhower had "no guts" and was "two-faced" for allowing it to happen.

This outburst resulted in some bad press and canceled engagements, but his popularity was too great to allow permanent damage to his career. And when Eisenhower sent Federal troops into Little Rock, Armstrong sent him a telegram saying: "If you decide to walk into the schools with the little colored kids, take me along, Daddy. God bless you."

Charles L. Black Jr., a white Southerner who was a member of Thurgood Marshall's legal team that won Brown v. Board of Education in 1954, attributed his own civil rights involvement to having heard Armstrong live at a 1931 dance. "It is impossible to overstate the significance of a sixteen-year-old Southern boy's seeing genius for the first time in a black. We literally never saw a black then in any but a servant's capacity. It had simply never entered my mind—that I would see this for the first time in a black man. But Louis opened my eyes wide, and put me to a choice. Blacks, the saying went, were 'all right in their place.' What was the 'place' of such a man, and of the people from which he sprung?"

Happy birthday, Pops, you'll not be forgotten.

Part Eight

HIGH SOCIETY

ACTOR AND MUSICIAN

All too often, Armstrong's place in jazz history has been identified pure and simple with what has become something of a fetish—his body of Hot Five and Hot Seven recordings (they were exclusively studio groups) made in Chicago between November 12, 1925, and July 5, 1928. Though these sessions were seminal to the future development of jazz, there are several problems here. Not only do these recordings represent a mere twenty days of recording activity spread out over some thirty months; they took place within the context of a feverishly busy career, whether in the recording studio, nightclubs, movie theaters, and more. In the studio alone during this time, Armstrong recorded with such groups as Erskine Tate's Vendome Orchestra, Jimmy Bertrand's Washboard Wizards, Butterbeans and Susie, and with such vocalists as Hociel Thomas and Sippie Wallace.

Even more important, what is rarely considered is how inclusively Armstrong perceived jazz itself. In an interview with Richard Hadlock Armstrong says, "Anything you can express to the public is jazz." It is a deep-seated conviction stemming from his self-image. We know that when applying for a passport in anticipation of his first European tour in 1932, Armstrong identified himself as "actor and musician." Thus it is that dichotomies superimposed by misguided or ill-informed critics lose any solid basis. It is, in other words, patently absurd to separate "art" from "entertainment," "high" from "low" art, or jazz from popular music, when considering Armstrong's total output and how he perceived his role as a creative performer. Here was an entertainer in the best sense, for whom the widely popular dancer and comedian Bill "Bojangles" Robinson was a major role model.

At best, Armstrong's personality and career remain enigmatic. In a perceptive *Village Voice* article entitled "Laughin' Louis," (August 14, 1978) Stanley Crouch makes the point that Armstrong was no lap dog to Joe Glaser and that there was a lot more to him than was communicated by the public persona of mugging and singing. He refers to an incident when Armstrong was reportedly found in his dressing room holding a knife to Glaser's throat, threatening, "I can't prove it, but if I find out you've stolen one dime from me, I'll cut your goddam throat." This was also a man who could knock trombonist Jack Teagarden out cold backstage for becoming too familiar, and then blithely wear his grin onstage while making the following announcement: "Thank you very much, ladies and gen'mens. Our first number this evening is dedicated to our trombonist brother Jack Teagarden, who won't be playing this show with us, and it's called 'When It's Sleepy Time Down South.'" But what is quintessentially enigmatic Armstrong is his recorded performance of "Laughin' Louie" of April 24, 1933. Opening with a trite theme, it almost immediately falls apart only to lapse into burlesque, buffoonery, and banter with the band. But after a series of false starts Armstrong, seemingly out of nowhere, decides to play a melody from his New Orleans past. After some sputtering and more laughter he quiets the band down to play "the beautiful part" and we find ourselves touched by a haunting unaccompanied melody. In the words of Crouch: "Its rich tone conveys a chilling pathos and achieves a transcendence in the upper register that summons the cleansing agony of the greatest spirituals. The band drops a chord under him and it's over. The feeling one is left with is one of great mystery."

Much of what is said in the two following articles has to be understood against the background of what has just been discussed, not to mention the marketing strategy of strong-willed record producers. In the first, Will Friedwald, one of the most articulate and best informed writers on the subject of jazz and popular singing, examines Armstrong's singing career in the context of his work with Bing Crosby. Friedwald's observations have been excerpted from the chapter "Mr. Satch and Mr. Cros" appearing in his book *Jazz Singing*. He begins here by commenting on Lester Bowie's phrase to the effect that Louis Armstrong created "jazz as we know it." —JB

MR. SATCH AND MR. CROS (1990)

Excerpted from the book Jazz Singing

How to top an act like that? For Armstrong, the logical next step after reinventing jazz was to reinvent popular music in his own image—to apply his discoveries as a jazz musician to mass market pop. To speak diagrammatically, from 1929 onward Armstrong works just as hard at expanding outwardly as a performer as he had at growing upwardly from 1925 to 1928, the years of the Hot Fives. The opinion of some of his critics to the contrary, this expansion did nothing to lessen the internal content of Armstrong's art; it altered his music only in terms of its outward manifestations in three specific areas: on records especially, Armstrong now works almost exclusively with big dance bands as opposed to Hot Fives and Sevens; he concentrates more on popular songs instead of original compositions and material out of the jazz tradition; and he gives equal time to singing.

To be sure, Armstrong had sung quite a bit on his earlier small-band records, his vocals on these coming off more like a direct extension of his horn work than the other way around (as was actually the case). On "Hotter Than That" (1927) and "West End Blues" (1928),[1] for example, Armstrong experiments with transposing the functions of the voice and the trumpet: He trades call-and-response phrases with another musician; but sings back his answers where you expect him to play them. Armstrong also sings a trumpet-style obbligato behind Lillie Delk Christian, the main vocalist on "Too Busy" (1928).[2] Many Hot Five sides also contain stop-time breaks sung instead of played, but the most revealing glimpses into the future occur on Armstrong's longer scat choruses. Cliff Edwards had been the first to apply scat to pop singing,[3] and he had done as much as it was possible to do with the technique in the pre-Armstrong world. Armstrong not only brought scatting into his universe, he devised new contexts for it.

"Heebie Jeebies" (1926), the most celebrated of his vocal improvisations, transliterates patterns Armstrong had conceived for instrumental music very directly into vocal terms, starting with lyrics, then modulating into scat phrases, and returning to the words at the conclusion, which all lends credence to the trumped-up tale of the record's scat sequence not being deliberate. No one could make such a claim with Armstrong's two equally remarkable 1928 scat vocals, "Basin Street Blues" and "Squeeze Me"; so in place of an extra musical explanation, Armstrong "excuses" his scat episodes by having two other members of the band hum in harmony behind him—as if to somehow normalize them. In doing so, Armstrong unearths the folk origins of each tune, investigating what they might have sounded like before W. C. Handy and Clarence Williams codified them into song form.

Other indications of things to come can be found in his more or less conventional vocal refrains. There's the monumental sense of humor that produced the comic duet of Mr. and Mrs. Lil Armstrong (then also his pianist) on "That's When I'll Come Back to You," and the mastery of the blues in spirit and form on "I'm Not Rough" (both 1927), which contains the single most powerful blues ever sung by a man (or anyone besides Bessie Smith) in this period, authenticated by the presence of blues guitarist Lonnie Johnson, here serving as guest accompanist.

By 1929, Armstrong had all the elements necessary to become a great singer. The next move in the evolution of jazz-influenced popular singing would then be a matter of integration.

—

Simultaneously, Armstrong's 1929 recordings, especially "I Ain't Got Nobody" and "I Can't Give You Anything but Love" (Okeh), show that interpreting lyrics is gradually becoming as important to him as scatting, though at this early stage his vocals still serve as mere interludes between more crucial trumpet solos. Armstrong's 1930 "I'm Confessin'" (Okeh), selected by Gary Giddins as the Armstrong record that most strongly reflects Crosby's reciprocated influence,[4] represents a milestone of the latest stages of the new art's development. Armstrong gives out with as many Bing-ish trills and extended line-ending notes as he does his own devices, like roars, repeated phrases, and personal interjections, playing off the guitar accompaniment in the same manner that Crosby had done with his guitarist, Eddie Lang. (Armstrong's November 1931 "Star Dust" includes a line of "boo-boo-boo"-ing inspired by Crosby's May 1931 record of "Just One More Chance.")

The early thirties saw the Crosby and Armstrong styles at their most convergent, although their individual personalities were strong enough to pull them away before too long. Nevertheless, they would retain enough of their mutually developed bag of tricks to make their later performances together high points of both careers. More importantly, now that they had put all the pieces together, no man could tear them asunder, and hundreds and hundreds of singers, arrangers, and songwriters would use the vocabulary developed by Armstrong and Crosby in the late twenties and early thirties. The spread of the new language was hastened by the rising popularity of each man in two of the only cases in Western history where an artist's fame and fortune came to equal his talent. They were so perfectly a part of their time and culture. By the mid-1930s all of the problems had been solved.

Crosby's improvisations on three standard tunes—"Sweet Georgia Brown," "Some of These Days," and "St. Louis Blues" (all Brunswick)—make clear how far his ability to spontaneously create melodies had developed by 1932. The jazz content is extraordinarily high even on the "straight" melody statements (the first choruses), and in time we will value these even more than the scatted portions. He embellishes each melody with the full stock of stop-time breaks and passes, grace notes, passing tones (a device he would be fully comfortable with for a few more years), syncopes, and irregular and middle-of-bar entrances.

But more than melodic and rhythmic ingeniousness, there's a sense of just plain rightness to everything he does, from the way he states the lyric and tune and makes you feel the meaning of each deep inside, without being maudlin or hammy, to the amazing architectural skill he displays—clearly he has learned Armstrong's lessons well—in the way he organizes an improvisation.

Armstrong's "Basin Street Blues" (1933, Victor), one of the most thrilling records of the decade, shows the singer taking the scat technique to its limits. It owes little to the melody Handy wrote (or transcribed) and even less to the limits of the blues. Armstrong had recorded the piece five years earlier in a small-group version that serves as a blueprint for this 1933 big-band masterpiece, passing on to it its relaxed tempo, tinkly celesta introduction, scat vocal with background voices, and overall structure. The arranger (probably Budd Johnson) has divided the piece into five sections with stop-time breaks running throughout. The first of these, which follows the celesta vamp (here played by Teddy Wilson instead of Earl Hines), has trombonist Keg Johnson playing the melody and a clarinet break halfway through. Louis takes most of the remaining four sections for himself, and on these alternates between playing and singing.

The two vocals here bespeak Armstrong's mastery of the human instrument for two separate, though related, reasons. Armstrong sings on top of a choir of sidemen who hum the harmony line, an effect he tried in the 1928 version but couldn't quite pull off with only two hummers. The effect he gets of voice-over-voices has metaphoric counterpoints that stretch across the whole history of jazz, from its church roots to the parallel of big-band swing, where a soloist plays in front of a choirlike ensemble of horns (Herschel Evans's chorus in Count Basie's "Blue and Sentimental" [1938, Decca] being the most vocal I can think of). Equally important, Armstrong scats both vocal refrains. Why is scatting so appropriate here? Because Louis Armstrong has tapped into his own core of emotion, gone back and released feelings so deep, so real, and so full of meaning that they can't be verbalized. To try to connect them with lyrics would only change them. We receive these messages the same way Armstrong transmits them; they bypass our ears and our brains and go directly for our hearts and souls.

At the end of the side, Armstrong voices aloud what surely must be going through the heads of everyone listening: "Yeah, man!"

Crosby and Armstrong would go on perfecting their craft until their deaths, but by 1935 most of the dragons had been slain. And it's from this point on that they do their best and most consistently exciting singing—here the mature period in the lives of each man begins.

The single most important event that marks the mid-thirties as the halfway point in the recording careers of both men is that they now came under the control of Jack Kapp. Joe Glaser, Louis's manager, had also begun encouraging him in Kapp-like directions, and Crosby had worked with Kapp since 1931, but it was not until 1935 that Kapp had both men under contract and complete freedom to carry out all his ideas on his own label.

Jack Kapp is possibly the most controversial figure in all of popular music. He is revered in as many histories of the record business as he is vilified in histories of jazz. At the same time, he is the ultimate philistine, forcing artists to record material that critics charged was trashy and beneath them, and the ultimate highbrow snob, going bananas when anyone tried to jazz up the classical repertoire. Kapp was the crook to end all crooks; he was the man who shamelessly cheated the young Count Basie as he twisted his arm to record inane novelty tunes while simultaneously acting the benevolent patriarch who was the first to give Billie Holiday a royalty check. He was also indirectly responsible for Holiday's "Lover Man" and "Good Morning Heartache." You can credit Kapp with such innovations as the girl band singer (all three of the first great canaries—Mildred Bailey, Connee Boswell, and Lee Wiley—ran up against him at one point or another) and also justifiably accuse him of a shortsighted point of view that was directed, in the main, against jazz. As Lee Wiley said, "At Decca they had a sign above the door that said, 'Sing the melody.'" But whatever you think of him, you have to admit that, as far as Bing Crosby and Louis Armstrong are concerned, his ideas were 100 percent dead on target.

Realizing that in Armstrong and Crosby he had the two founding fathers of modern pop music, Kapp devised a way for them to expand both their musical horizons and their popularity, turning them into all things for all people, covering all musical genres. Under Kapp's aegis, the two men continued to record current mainstream popular songs (and Armstrong continued with jazz instrumentals), but between the two they also took on country and western (then called "hillbilly") music, sacred music, Hawaiian harmonies, rhythm numbers, novelties, French chansons, folk songs, nostalgic "good-old-good-ones," cover versions of other artists' hits (including each other's), light classics, kiddie ditties, comic pieces, and a limitless number of duets with other singers and vocal groups as well as team-ups with popular name bands. In the midst of this ocean of vinyl, which nearly drowns us in sheer variety, Armstrong and Crosby tackled a fair amount of small-group jazz performances of the kind that had initially made both reputations.

The Kapp principle worked for each man for different reasons. It worked for Crosby because, as it turned out, he really was the ultimate musical everyman, and he and Armstrong were able to use this over-whelming plethora of performance modes to convey the full range of human experiences. Slowly, a persona evolved out of the records, and the writers of Crosby's radio shows and movies gradually fashioned an every-man character for him. Whether or not this actually was the case isn't important, for he played it so well for so long that it must have had some ring of truth to it. No one ever found a limit to the kind of songs he could sing. Unlike Frank Sinatra, his only rival to the title of the century's most identifiable voice—though not in intonation—Crosby (or was it Kapp) believed there was no such thing as a bad song, and he could prove it, too. Whether singing "Just a Kid Named Joe," "The Hut Sut Song," or "Aloha Oe," he could leave you touched.

The Kapp principle worked for Armstrong because, as it turned out, he was a genius. The only other improviser in all of music who truly deserves this accolade, Charlie Parker, also proved that geniuses are simply above such "mortal" considerations as repertoire and accompaniment. Armstrong was the only singer who ever lived who didn't care anything about material or backing.

One point mentioned over and over again concerning Armstrong is how he "makes gold out of mere sentimental dross." If Armstrong can make gold out of a second-rate pop tune, then he ought to be able to get something even better from an immortal, beloved standard. But he doesn't. Armstrong makes "Red Cap" sound just as good as "Love Walked In," because the Satchmoification of a piece of music is an equalizing process, and the innate quality of the notes and chords before Armstrong gets to them has absolutely no effect on the quality level of the music he makes.

Some writers attacked Louis for singing songs like "Little Joe" (1931, Okeh), a typical though somewhat extreme mammy song that refers to kinky-headed babies, little pickaninnies, and colored sonny boys, but also contains lines like "Although your color isn't white, you're more than mighty like a rose to me." As Dan Morgenstern says, "If that's not black-is-beautiful, I don't know what is." Whatever the case, Armstrong would leave his sense of humor as a legacy for jazz's other great clowns (to use Morgenstern's term, in the Elizabethan sense) like Fats Waller, Gillespie, and Sun Ra—who said that Armstrong "always had a sense of humor so lacking in many musicians of today. He is part of my destiny."

In the art of Louis Armstrong, humor connects rather directly with religion; the shortcomings of mankind forever underscore the perfection of the divine. He makes the point with both reverence and irreverence: Collection-conscious clerics provide ripe targets for ribbing, but the Almighty Himself is not to be jived with. On the first recording of "The Saints" ("Oh, When the Saints Go Marching In" [1938, Decca]), the spiritual that Satchmo took out of the Sunday services and into the Dixieland canon, and on "Bye and Bye" (1941, Decca), Armstrong introduces trombonist J. C. Higginbotham and other soloists between strains and plays and sings jubilantly with the band, which doubles as choir (according to Rex Stewart, when Armstrong sang this type of number in person his audiences filled this function). A professional chorus backs Louis on his first "legitimate" sacred recordings (four from 1938, Decca), including the sublime "Shout All Over God's Heaven" and "Nobody Knows the

Sarah Vaughan, Louis Armstrong, and Billie Holiday, c. 1950. Photo: Joseph Schwartz, Joseph Schwartz Collection/Corbis.

Trouble I've Seen," and he doesn't even need to take his trumpet out of the case. None of these would have been made without Jack Kapp.

Taken another way, the religious sides illustrate the evolution of Armstrong (like Crosby) from a revolutionary to an establishment figure. On his first church-styled record, "The Lonesome Road" (1931, Okeh), he ruthlessly lampoons down-home deacons with lines like "Thank you for your contributions, Sisters and Brothers. It could've been bigger, two dollars more would have got my shoes out of pawn!" But by 1958, when Armstrong had made his ultimate religious statement in the classic *Louis and the Good Book* (Decca), he no longer satirizes preachers. Instead, he has become one of them: the Reverend Satchel-mouth. He plays both roles, the saint and the sinner, to the hilt.

———

When Armstrong became a hero to blacks across the nation and "There wasn't a jukebox in Harlem that Louis wasn't scatting on," as Mezz Mezzrow reports, the only other artist whose records were permitted on Harlem jukes was Crosby. In 1936, Crosby worked Louis into his movie *Pennies from Heaven,* which launched Armstrong's career as a motion picture performer, and Armstrong probably guested on Crosby's radio shows at this point at well. Paramount Pictures filmed an Armstrong sequence for Crosby's flick *Doctor Rhythm* (1938), but their editing of it from the release print became no real loss as the song they gave Armstrong, "The Trumpet Player's Lament," was no great masterpiece. Armstrong went into the Decca studios in 1939 to cut a special private recording of "Happy Birthday" for Crosby's thirty-fifth, and it shows that even then he called him "Papa Bing."

It is important to note that in none of these early ventures did Mr. C. and Mr. A. sing together—undoubtedly fear of the dread color line kept them apart. But between 1949 and 1951, when Armstrong had broken the line with top-ten hits like "Blueberry Hill," he made no less than eight appearances on Crosby's program, sang with him in Frank Capra's comedy *Here Comes the Groom,* and made one hit record with him, "Gone Fishin'."

A lot of time is wasted on these shows; they were, after all, not made for connoisseurs who remembered "West End Blues," and they constantly remind us of the sacrifices jazz had to make to remain a popular music. But they also feature some of the most heart-warming, crowd-pleasing entertainment either man was ever to produce. Their duets, "Lazy Bones," "Blueberry Hill," "Gone Fishin'," "You're Just in Love," and "Kiss to Build a Dream On" do not fit within the prescribed notions of what "music" and "comedy" ought to be, but are examples of pure, undiluted entertainment that simply and utterly move us.

"Kiss to Build a Dream On" had originally been written for the 1935 Marx Brothers movie *A Night at the Opera,* but lingered unsung until Armstrong introduced it in *The Strip* (1951). The radio version starts out as a solo for Crosby, who unexpectedly entreats Armstrong to join him, and then the two spend the first chorus trying to figure out just who will sing what. On the second round, Papa and Pops pick up on each other's mannerisms with humor and love. When Satch substitutes "chops" for "lips" (he did this regularly on "That's My Desire") in the last eight, the crowd gets ecstatic. When Bing repeats the device in chorus two, they nearly fall out of their seats en masse. How could they not? "If you don't like Louis," said Mahalia Jackson, "you're not human."

Though the 1949–51 period saw the most heavily concentrated amount of tandem activity between the two, they would combine frequently right up to the end. Cole Porter's "modo-hip" tune "Now You Has Jazz," though no one could have predicted Porter would turn out to be such an expert on the subject, gave Armstrong and Crosby an excellent excuse for a duet, which they did in the 1956 picture *High Society* and even better in numerous TV appearances from the same period. But their one full-length album collaboration, the 1960 *Bing and Satchmo* (MGM), has only a few good moments, due to overdubbing and overarranging (why does Billy May have to throw in background voices, even if he did have the panache to transcribe Armstrong's lovely 1931 trumpet solo on "Lazy River" for the choir?).

Their work, together and apart, did not triumph so much because of their similarities as because of their differences. Each took up where the other left off, and this allowed them to create virtually the entire vocabulary of twentieth-century vocal music. Armstrong, who had grown up virtually parentless, had only the family he created for himself out of the millions of people who loved him and his music. Crosby grew up seeking individuality and inner strength in a family where the family was all-important, and eventually became the musical patriarch of the entire world. Armstrong's great strength was his freedom and ability to express emotion, and the key to the success of Crosby's singing is the way in which he controlled emotion. It was said that Crosby never invited Armstrong (and hardly anyone else) to his house, but the same way that Louis sang the glories of God in a way that counted for more than his going to church each week, their relationship and their empathy transcended that consideration. In Crosby's personal life, he lived the words of the poet Percy MacKaye: "Because he never wore his sentient heart / For the crows and jays to pick, oftimes to such / He seemed a silent fellow."

"Like everyone else, Louis loved my father," Gary Crosby told Ross Firestone. "Between shows he'd tell me endless stories about him. 'Your old man is the greatest singer,' he'd say. 'Really, he can wail.' Then he'd go on to reminisce about all the funny things that happened when they crossed paths in the old days, and how much he enjoyed working Dad's radio show and being in his movies. 'Well, Dad loves you, too, Louis.' And that was so, Louis was always one of his favorites."

NOTES

1. All Armstrong records discussed on this and the next few pages, unless otherwise noted, were originally recorded for the Okeh label and were reissued by CBS in America or Europe.

2. Unfortunately, he doesn't sing it loud enough, as Miss Christian is still audible.

3. There are, however, a few isolated examples of the technique being used in a jazz or pop context that undoubtedly precede any form of literate communication; the vaudevillian Gene Green incorporated a half chorus of mock-Chinese scatting into his 1917 "From Here to Shanghai," and jazz saxophonist and arranger Don Redman scats on Fletcher Henderson's 1924 "My Papa Doesn't Two-Time No Time" (Columbia). We can even find earlier, though not as absolutely substantiated examples, such as Leadbelly's allegedly pre-blues performance style and Jelly Roll Morton's testimony: "Most people believe that Louis Armstrong invented scat singing. I must take that credit away from him because I know better. Tony Jackson and I were using scat for novelty back in 1906 and 1907 when Louis Armstrong was still in the orphan's home." (Actually, he wasn't even there yet.)

4. It was also selected by Dizzy Gillespie as the most primal Armstrong vocal for his homage, "Pops Confessin'," which combines this tune with the format from "Laughin' Louie." Well! What do you know about that?

KRIN GABBARD

ACTOR AND MUSICIAN: LOUIS ARMSTRONG AND HIS FILMS (1996)

Adapted from the book Jammin' at the Margins: Jazz and the American Cinema

Armstrong's twenty-three American feature films receive close scrutiny in the following essay by Krin Gabbard, which originally appeared as a chapter entitled "Actor and Musician" in his magisterial study Jammin' at the Margins: Jazz and the American Cinema *(1996). Gabbard draws heavily upon the terminology of semiotics—the study of signs and what they mean. To cite some basic examples of semiotic concerns, how does Armstrong hold his trumpet in a given scene, what does it signify, and what about his other gestures, qualities of gait, dress, dialogue with other characters? These signs are examined by Gabbard in the light of changing perceptions of Armstrong's sexuality, his significance as an African-American role model, and his overall achievement in terms of the debate about "art" versus "entertainment." He shows that such perspectives themselves are necessarily part of the discourse, the process of our speaking about a given topic that engages our attention at a given time and place in history, in short an area of research within cultural studies. —JB*

Louis Armstrong may have been as complex as the discourse that surrounded him. By contrast, Duke Ellington established a persona in his youth that filmmakers and the media could accept throughout his career, even if he had to endure regular affronts to his dignity. Although Ellington drifted in and out of critical favor with various constituencies, most of the public was aware of a single Duke Ellington, an urbane but earthy composer-musician-bandleader with a faux British accent. But Louis Armstrong was many things to many people. His mugging and laughing had little to do with the inner life of someone who could be brooding, stubborn, and outspoken. While the biographers may disagree about Armstrong's psychology, the disputes about his performance career have been even more dramatic. For some, the trumpeter achieved greatness with his 1920s recordings and then spent the rest of his life squandering his prodigious talent and thriving on show biz life. For others, he was a consummate artist who played and sang with wit and intelligence throughout his life. Still other critics have called into question the distinction between artist and entertainer, arguing that Armstrong's life and work stand as a strong counterargument to the empowering of serious "art" over mere "entertainment." Joshua Berrett (1992) has made this case especially well in his analysis of how Armstrong assimilated the opera arias that he quoted in his recorded solos during the 1920s and 1930s.

Regardless of how critics assess Armstrong's achievements, the issue has almost always been argued in terms of his trumpet solos and vocals. Virtually all of Hugues Panassié's (1971) book on Armstrong, for example, is given over to analysis of the recordings. In the first pages of the chapter on Armstrong in his *The Swing Era*, Gunther Schuller discusses the problems surrounding Armstrong's stardom; he then adds in a footnote, "While on the one hand, in the face of Armstrong's uniqueness, it may be futile to pass judgment on his post-1920s career, on the other hand—precisely because of his preeminent role in jazz—one must eventually come to grips with the totality of his life and work. This can only be done in a dispassionate way, which also takes into account Louis's personality and temperament, and the social-economic conditions within which he labored" (Schuller 1989, 160). After these words, however, Schuller devotes the rest of the essay to close readings of the trumpet solos, just as he had done earlier in the Armstrong chapter of his *Early Jazz* (1968).

Although many critics have followed Schuller in paying lip service to the nonmusical aspects of Armstrong's career, few have paid much attention to his roles in twenty-three American feature films. Especially today, when jazz canonizers have defined Armstrong as a revolutionary artist, his films are probably ignored to sidestep troubling questions about stage mannerisms that are invisible on the fetishized recordings. Better to remember him as the genius who improvised the stirring choruses of "Potato Head Blues" and "Weather Bird" than as the servile clown grinning at second-rate white actors. At least since the 1930s, however, audiences have probably known Armstrong best for his television and film appearances, including numerous shorts and soundies as well as the feature films. Even when Armstrong did not appear in person, his image graced cartoons such as "Old Mill Pond" (1936), "Clean Pastures" (1937), and "Swing Wedding" (1937), the latter a songfest for frogs who bear striking resemblances to Armstrong, Cab Calloway, Fats Waller, and

Stepin Fetchit. In Max Fleischer's Betty Boop cartoon of 1932, "I'll Be Glad When You're Dead You Rascal You," Armstrong appears first in a filmed performance with his band, then as a cartoon cannibal, and finally as a disembodied head singing the title song to Bimbo and Koko as they flee across an African plain.

Although Armstrong did not begin appearing regularly in Hollywood films until 1936, he listed his occupation as "actor and musician" on a passport application in anticipation of his first European tour in 1932 (Giddins 1988, 41). At that time his filmography consisted only of appearances in the nine-minute short *Rhapsody in Black and Blue* (1932), the lost low-budget American film *Ex-Flame* (1931), and the 1932 Betty Boop cartoon. But this listing of "actor" before "musician" may have reflected Armstrong's conviction that he was a performer rather than a mere maker of music, indeed a performer who had just broken into cartoons as well as into Hollywood films. Armstrong's words on a passport application can also be regarded as another example of how simple dichotomies break down when his entire career is considered. The actor and the musician were inseparable when Armstrong worked in front of an audience or a camera. His trumpet was never far when he acted in a film, and sooner or later it was at his lips. He was almost always called Satchmo or Louis Armstrong in his films, and later when he played Wild Man Moore in *Paris Blues* (1961) and Sweet Daddy Willie Ferguson in *A Man Called Adam* (1966), these were merely pseudonyms for Louis Armstrong. Many of the most important debates about Armstrong are played out as strikingly in his films as they are in any other aspect of his career.

Reading the Critics

Any study of the reception of Armstrong over the past seventy years invites the methods of what is now known as cultural studies, a collection of approaches that characterize novels, paintings, operas, comic strips, and other forms of cultural production not as stable objects into which artists have inscribed meaning but rather as sites where audiences create their own meanings (Grossberg et al. 1992). A film of Armstrong grinning and mugging has radically diverse meanings to audiences of different ages, races, and cultural values at different moments in history. In his several reviews of films with Armstrong during the 1950s, Bosley Crowther inevitably singled him out for praise, especially in films that Crowther otherwise held in contempt. For example, concerning *Glory Alley* (1952), Crowther wrote, "Every now and then, Louis Armstrong sticks his broad, beaming face into the frame and sings or blasts a bit on his trumpet. That makes the only sense in the whole film" (*The New York Times*, July 30, 1952). And here is Crowther on *High Society* (1956): "Mr. Armstrong beams as brazenly as ever and lets the hot licks fall where they may" (*The New York Times*, August 10,1956). But looking at the same films thirty years later, Donald Bogle, writing in *Toms, Coons, Mulattoes, Mammies, and Bucks,* saw "a coon and a tom all rolled into one" and placed his essay on Armstrong in a section called "Stepin's Step-Chillun" (Bogle 1992, 71–75).

These kinds of judgments tell us more about the critics than they do about Armstrong himself. Indeed, if we disregard most of the commentaries on the trumpeter's recorded solos, a number of concerns regularly surface in the critical literature. In this chapter I concentrate on three themes that I find especially important to an understanding of Armstrong's films: (1) attempts to place Armstrong somewhere on either side of (or above) the debate about art versus entertainment; (2) his sexuality and how it may or not have been expressed in his performances; and (3) "role model" arguments relating to his deportment on stage and the larger questions about his significance for African-Americans. Often these issues become intertwined in the critical debates. For example, Theodor Adorno combines (1) and (2) by arguing syllogistically that popular music-unlike true art-is castrating; Armstrong played popular music; therefore Armstrong is castrated. Critics who find evidence that Armstrong is "signifying" (regardless of whether or not they use that word) suggest that he was both (1) transcending the distinction between art and entertainment, and (3) becoming a hero to black people by showing them how to overcome demeaning conditions imposed upon them by the white power structure.

Artist or Entertainer?

Critics began bestowing lavish praise on Armstrong as early as 1928 (Collier 1988, 55). For most jazz writers, the trouble began in the late 1930s when Armstrong regularly worked with a conventional swing band and ventured beyond the vague boundaries of jazz by recording with the Mills Brothers, a gospel choir, and even with a group called the Polynesians. Although some critics today express pleasure in records such as "To You, Sweetheart, Aloha" (1936) and "On a Little Bamboo Bridge" (1937), jazz purists of the 1930s and 1940s felt betrayed. By the mid-1940s, Armstrong was held in contempt by many of the young beboppers as well as by the New Orleans revivalists who canonized his recordings of the 1920s but rejected most of what followed. Rudi Blesh (1976), for example, wrote in 1946 that Armstrong had abandoned "hot music," or true jazz, for the sensationalism and the easy popularity of "swing," a hybrid, bastardized form of jazz that Armstrong embraced as he moved away from the Hot Fives and Sevens to form a big band. As was often the case in Blesh's writings, the argument was phrased in apocalyptic tones:

> Had Armstrong understood his responsibility as clearly as he perceived his own growing artistic power—had his individual genius been deeply integrated with that of the music, and thus ultimately with the destiny of his race—designated leadership would have been just. . . . Around Louis clustered growing public cognizance of hot music and those commercial forces, equally strong and more persistent, which utilize the musical communications system of the phonograph record, the then new radio and talking motion picture, and the printed sheets of the Tin Pan Alley tunesmiths. And behind this new symbolic figure was aligned the overwhelming and immemorial need of his own race to find a Moses to lead it out of Egypt. (Blesh 1958, 257–58)

Writing in 1948, the Marxist critic Sidney Finkelstein also took a dim view of Armstrong's move toward swing, but he was more forgiving than Blesh. Finkelstein associated the simultaneously improvising New Orleans ensembles with a utopian, leaderless society; the cult of the soloist in front of a big band was for Finkelstein a symptom of capitalism and the commercialization of art. He conceded the following, however: "Had a genuine, musical culture existed in America, one capable of cherishing its talents and giving them a chance to properly learn and grow instead of destroying them, Armstrong might have been encouraged to produce a great American music. There was no such opportunity, however; instead, [there was] continual pressure to produce novelties, to plug new songs, or the same songs under new names" (Finkelstein 1988, 106).

James Baldwin dramatized the disdain toward Armstrong among beboppers in his 1957 story "Sonny's Blues" (Albert 1990), in which a black World War II veteran working as a schoolteacher confronts the desire of his younger brother to become a jazz musician. When his brother hits trouble explaining the kind of musician he wants to become, the older man intervenes:

> I suggested helpfully: "You mean—like Louis Armstrong?" His face closed as though I'd struck him. "No. I'm not talking about none of that old-time, down home crap." (Albert 1990, 189)

The younger brother eventually names Charlie Parker as a musician he aspires to imitate. In Baldwin's story the chasm between Armstrong and Parker becomes a metaphor for the cultural gap separating the brothers as well as for the revolution taking place among young African-Americans during the postwar years.

A few years after Baldwin's story, Amiri Baraka took a different view of Armstrong in his *Blues People* of 1963, regarding Armstrong not as the played-out representative of an obsolete music but rather as the "honored priest of his culture." Baraka distinguished Armstrong from Bix Beiderbecke, who was "an instinctual intellectual" with an emotional life "based on his conscious or unconscious disapproval of most of the sacraments of his culture." Armstrong, by contrast, "was not rebelling against anything with his music. In fact, his music was one of the most beautiful refinements of Afro-American musical tradition, and it was immediately recognized as such by those Negroes who were not busy trying to pretend that they had issued from Beiderbecke's culture" (Baraka 1963, 154).

In recent decades, critics have made increasingly extravagant claims in favor of Armstrong's music. The view that he was in decline after the 1920s has been rejected by some of the most eminent jazz critics. Dan Morgenstern (1972), for example, wrote that "Armstrong's mastery of his instrument and musical imagination continued to grow far beyond the threshold of the 30s." Even more recently, Stanley Dance (1993) has stated that Armstrong surpassed some of his classic recordings when he re-recorded them for the *Autobiography in Jazz* LPs in the 1950s. In an effort to recuperate all of Armstrong's career, Gary Giddins even defends the 1968 recordings of Disney songs, suggesting that Armstrong is having fun with his material in side remarks such as "Oh, the buckskin buccaneer" in his version of "The Ballad of Davy Crockett" (Giddins 1988, 203).

James Lincoln Collier tends to agree with the earlier appraisal of writers such as Blesh, identifying 1929 as the year in which Armstrong chose to become a popular entertainer and reach a larger audience beyond African-Americans. In his Armstrong biography, Collier attempts to psychoanalyze the trumpeter, presenting him as a tragic figure whose desire to please was completely inconsistent with romantic notions of the artist.

> Armstrong was clearly a man afflicted with deep and well-entrenched insecurity; a sense of his own worthlessness so thoroughly fixed that he was never to shake it off, even after he had become one of the most famous men in the world. But he could quench that relentless, sickening, interior assault on his self-respect, at least temporarily, by performing, standing up there before those dozens or thousands or millions of people and playing and singing and smiling and mugging and soaking up the healing applause, which for a moment pushed away the feeling that nobody liked him, that he was basically no good. And when he was offered the chance to earn ever larger doses of that healing balm, he could hardly have turned it down. (Collier 1983, 202–3)

Collier argues that the distinction between artist and entertainer—the dominant trope in recent discourse around Armstrong—would have been incomprehensible to a man who sought only to quench his desperate thirst for adulation.

At least for Collier, then, Armstrong would seem to be an unlikely character to appear in films where questions of jazz and art are debated. And yet he was cast in film after film where these issues were central to the plot. In *New Orleans* in the 1940s, *High Society* in the 1950s, and both *Paris Blues* and *A Man Called Adam* in the 1960s, Armstrong plays a crucial role in the film's debate about jazz as opposed to classical music or about the value of older jazz as opposed to newer jazz. My guess is that Armstrong held so much appeal for the mass audience that he made these kinds of discussions palatable. No one had to think too long about the issues when Armstrong himself was never making any pompous claims about being an artist. And if he was in fact an artist, he surely did not make anyone feel uncomfortable about so obsequious a fellow assuming that lofty position. Imagine Miles Davis, Thelonious Monk, or virtually any other modernist black jazz musician being extolled for his artistry; and then imagine how much differently white audiences might have reacted to the assertion.

Phallic or Castrated?

In *The Story of Jazz*, Marshall Stearns retells an anecdote about Armstrong that is especially relevant to his appearances in American films.

In emphasizing the immediacy of communication between jazz artist and audience, Stearns wrote, "There is a legend that, during the late thirties when Louis Armstrong recorded a series of wonderful performances, he was starting on his fourth honeymoon." (Stearns 1956, 280) This may be one of the first explicit attempts to associate Armstrong's music and persona with his sexuality; I have argued elsewhere that the jazz trumpet has always been an especially powerful means for expressing male sexuality, and Armstrong more than anyone else is responsible for perfecting the codes of that expression. Similarly, Gary Giddins has argued for Armstrong's ability to communicate sexuality in *Rhapsody in Black and Blue* (1932). In this early film appearance Armstrong is part of a fantasy dreamed up by an impoverished black man who imagines himself the "King of Jazzmania." By royal decree, Armstrong and his band perform for the king who sits on a throne in hypermilitary royal garb. Standing on a bizarre set covered with soap bubbles and dressed in leopard skins, Armstrong mugs his way through vocal choruses of "Shine" and "I'll Be Glad When You're Dead," but when he puts his trumpet to his lips, he becomes a different man. "He transcends the racist trappings by his indifference to every sling and arrow. . . . He's doing it not only with the magnificence of his music, but with his physical muscularity, his carriage, his boding sexuality ('comedian + danger'), the look in his eye" (Giddins 1988, 36).

Only a few years after the release of *Rhapsody in Black and Blue*, Virgil Thomson had kind words for Armstrong in a 1936 review of Hugues Panassié's *Le Jazz Hot*. Thomson wrote, "[Armstrong's] style of improvisation would seem to have combined the highest reaches of instrumental virtuosity with the most tensely disciplined melodic structure and the most spontaneous emotional expression, all of which in one man you must admit to be pretty rare" (Thomson 1981, 31). But Thomson added a curious historical comparison, suggesting that Armstrong resembled "the great castrati of the eighteenth century"; Theodor Adorno, in one of his several attacks on jazz and popular music, translated Thomson's remark to support his own claim that jazz brings about the castration of the listener, who ought to be listening to the more manly music of someone like Arnold Schoenberg (Adorno 1981, 130). For Adorno, the obsequious buffoon with the trumpet was anything but phallic.

The American film industry made a variety of attempts to contain Armstrong's sexuality in the 1930s and 1940s. Seldom was he able to assert himself as unequivocally as he had in *Rhapsody in Black and Blue*, if only because of the inevitable toll that aging took on his youthful vigor. Even more importantly, he does not seem to have updated the techniques he learned as a young man for expressing masculinity without threatening certain white men in his audiences. If, in fact, black audiences in the 1930s saw sexual power alongside the minstrel foolishness, few would recognize it in later decades when the media's images of black masculinity began to change.

Uncle Tom or Trickster?

Indeed, Armstrong's stage mannerisms lost their appeal for many when the civil rights movement made the old minstrel stereotypes untenable. Gerald Early argues that Armstrong had been a hero in the black community for several decades but that he lost a large portion of this audience when he played the King of the Zulus in New Orleans in 1949. When pictures of the trumpeter in blackface and a grass skirt were widely published, according to Early, many African-Americans felt that Armstrong was "holding the entire race up to scorn" (Early 1989, 296). Albert Murray has defended Armstrong against those who attacked him for appearing as King of the Zulus. Murray suggested that the critics outside of New Orleans confused Mardi Gras blackface with minstrelsy and that the specific ritual function of the King of the Zulus was "to ridicule the whole idea of Mardi Gras and the lenten season" (Murray 1976, 190). For Murray, Armstrong was simply playing the trickster once again.

Nevertheless, Armstrong continued to sing his theme song, "When It's Sleepy Time Down South," with its references to "darkies" and "mammies falling on their knees," right up until the end of his life, in spite of pleas from civil rights groups. Barney Bigard tells of a revealing incident that took place during the shooting of a film with Bing Crosby. Armstrong was told to substitute the word "folks" for "darkies" in his performance of "When It's Sleepy Time." Unwilling to change a lyric he had been performing nightly for decades, Armstrong left the set before the new words could be recorded. When he returned the next day, Bigard quotes him as saying to Crosby, "What do you want me to call those black sons-of-bitches this morning?" (Bigard in Martyn 1986, 123–24).

Even Armstrong's widely publicized denunciations of President Dwight D. Eisenhower and Arkansas governor Orval Faubus during the struggle to integrate Little Rock's public schools in 1957 did not entirely change his image, in spite of later attempts to give special significance to these statements. (Ralph J. Gleason, for example, begins a 1973 essay on Armstrong with the story of the Little Rock incident to make this the central, redeeming episode in a revised Armstrong biography [Gleason 1975, 3–35].) Shortly after Armstrong said that the American government could "go to hell" and that Eisenhower had "no guts," he was attacked by Sammy Davis, Jr., for appearing before segregated audiences (Collier 1983, 318). And in a notorious column following the fracas, Jim Bishop suggested that Armstrong's subsequent apology to Eisenhower may have been the result of a drop in ticket sales and "some empty tables at the Copacabana" (*New York Journal-American,* January 2, 1958: 17). Bishop did not acknowledge, however, that Armstrong only apologized after Eisenhower took action by sending federal troops to Little Rock to enforce court-ordered integration. Although Charles Mingus gave Orval Faubus a permanent role in jazz history with his 1959 composition "Fables of Faubus," Mingus was one of many boppers and post-boppers who did not bother to stand beside Armstrong when he publicly denounced official racism.

There is no question that Armstrong had a reverse influence on the black jazz musicians who were born during the Harlem Renaissance and came of age in the late 1930s and early 1940s. Thinking of themselves as artists rather than entertainers, some of the boppers adopted the aloof stage presence of the classical musician and of more restrained jazz artists such as Teddy Wilson. Even when Dizzy Gillespie danced and performed pelvic thrusts before audiences, his repertoire of stage business overlapped in no way with Armstrong's: his bowing and mugging had an element of fun but not servility. But for most of the boppers and for almost every jazz artist who has come of age since, a poker face has been obligatory; In his autobiography, however, Gillespie wrote, "If anybody asked me about a certain public image of him, handkerchief over his head, grinning in the face of white racism, I never hesitated to say I didn't like it. I didn't want the white man to expect me to allow the same things Louis did. Hell, I had my own way of 'Tomming' . . . Later on, I began to recognize what I had considered Pops's grinning in the face of racism as his absolute refusal to let anything, even anger about racism, steal the joy from his life and erase his fantastic smile. Coming from a younger generation, I misjudged him" (Gillespie 1979, 295–96). Miles Davis expressed a similar ambivalence in his autobiography when he included a photograph of Armstrong alongside pictures of Beulah, Buckwheat, and Rochester, all characters who can be associated with demeaning stereotypes of African-Americans. The caption reads, "Some of the images of black people that I would fight against throughout my career. I loved Satchmo, but I couldn't stand all that grinning he did" (Davis 1989). The opinion of an older trumpeter, the articulate Rex Stewart, is also worth quoting in this context:

> Some musicians consciously resent Louis' antebellum Uncle Tomism. The youngsters object to his ever-present grin, which they interpret as Tomming. This I feel is a misunderstanding. No matter where Louis had been brought up, his natural ebullience and warmth would have emerged just as creative and strong. This is not to say that even today, in an unguarded moment, a trace of the old environment, a fleeting lapse into the jargon of his youth will make some people cringe with embarrassment. (Stewart 1972, 42–43)

Acknowledging that Armstrong recorded inferior or highly commercial material at many moments throughout his career, Stearns argues that he was consistently able to rise above it with irony. Stearns singles out the 1931 recording of "All of Me" in which Armstrong parodies a British accent with the line, "I can't get on, *dee-ah*, without you!" On the one hand, according to Stearns, Armstrong is too embarrassed by the lame lyrics to sing them straight. "At the same time, by changes in the melody and by unusual accents in the rhythm, he makes the listener suddenly realize that he, Armstrong, is in full, double-edged control of the musical situation, embroidering beautifully on the stereotyped mask, and enjoying the whole affair hugely. In a word: he is the master—not of just the music but also of a complex and ironic attitude, a rare, honest way of looking at life" (Stearns 1956, 318–19). Stearns anticipates the comments of Ralph Ellison, who placed Armstrong in the tradition of the trickster: "Armstrong's clownish license and intoxicating powers are almost Elizabethan; he takes liberties with kings, queens and presidents; emphasizes the physicality of his music with sweat, spittle and facial contortions; he performs the magical feat of making romantic melody issue from a throat of gravel; and some few years ago was recommending to all and sundry his personal physic, 'Pluto Water,' as a purging way to health, happiness and international peace" (Ellison 1964, 67). Both Stearns and Ellison look forward to the more extensive discussion of African and African-American tricksters in Henry Louis Gates, Jr.'s *Signifying Monkey: A Theory of Afro-American Literary Criticism.* Gates mentions Armstrong only in passing, but he observes that "there are so many examples of Signifyin(g) in jazz that one could write a formal history of its development on this basis alone" (Gates 1988, 63).

In his scrupulous reading of Armstrong's several autobiographical statements, William Kenney has found evidence of signifying and even protest. Perhaps the most convincing example of how Armstrong "carefully orchestrated his story, creating edited versions of himself" (Kenney 1991, 38), is the account of his feelings for Bix Beiderbecke that appears in his second autobiography, *Satchmo: My Life in New Orleans*. After pledging his immense admiration for Beiderbecke, even calling him godlike, Armstrong adds, "Whenever we saw him our faces shone with joy and happiness, but long periods would pass when we did not see him at all" (Armstrong 1954, 209). For Kenney, this passage shows Armstrong slipping his own message past the ghostwriters and editors who controlled texts such as *Satchmo: My Life in New Orleans*. "He keeps his distance by offering a vaudeville stereotype of 'our' greetings to a third-party observer. At the same time, he indicates that while in Beiderbecke's physical presence, 'we' treated him respectfully, but, not 'seeing' him for long periods of time, 'we' were not obliged to pay him respect" (Kenney 1991, 51). Kenney also finds reasons for Armstrong's decision to reach out to popular audiences rather than to the small but discriminating coterie of jazz aficionados. For one thing, Armstrong had begun to worry as far back as 1928 that he would not be able to endure the physical hardships of playing the trumpet every day of his life at a virtuoso level. Lip problems would plague him throughout his life. Armstrong also recalled the fate of his mentor King Oliver, an excellent musical technician and a savvy businessman, but in no way an entertainer who played to the crowd. Oliver died in poverty. As a result, Kenney reasons, Armstrong consciously chose to become the showman who would dance, sing, joke, mug, and perform the popular hits of the day. In 1936 he began a lifelong association with Joe Glaser, the manager to whom he entrusted almost every aspect of his career. At least since the 1920s, Glaser had been urging the trumpeter to rely on showmanship rather than musical proficiency (Kenney 1991, 54). The changes brought on by Glaser may explain why the Armstrong in photographs from the 1920s with King Oliver and Fletcher Henderson seems so unfamiliar. As Stanley Crouch has written, "There we see an arrogant, surly young man who seemed to think himself handsome and was not to be fucked with" (Crouch 1978, 45).

Reading the Films

In most of the Hollywood films in which Armstrong appeared, he is a marginal figure. In films such as *Artists & Models* (1937), *Jam Session* (1944), *Here Comes the Groom* (1951), *The Beat Generation* (1959), and *Hello, Dolly!* (1969), he is set off from the plot in a single musical number so that he has virtually no interaction with the principal characters. In the Mae West vehicle, *Every Day's a Holiday* (1938), his character does not even have a name; he is simply a street cleaner who wordlessly enlists in the campaign of a political figure supported by West and who then leads a parade performing Hoagy Carmichael's "Jubilee." Sometimes he even appears to be outside the film. Throughout *High Society* (1956) and at the conclusion of *When the Boys Meet the Girls* (1966), he narrates the story with direct address to the audience. When he does play a role within a film's narrative, he is invariably cast as a trumpet player, even if it means awkwardly adjusting the nature of his role. In *Glory Alley* (1952) he is "Shadow," the trainer for the boxer hero Socks Barbarrosa and also the guide for the boxer's blind antagonist, "The Judge." Somehow the film makes trumpet playing relate to both of these occupations. In *Cabin in the Sky* (1943), Armstrong is the only musician in a group of six devils in the Hotel Hades, none of whom has any comparable distinguishing characteristics (with perhaps the exception of one devil played by Willie Best who sleeps through most of the sequence). It is also safe to say that the racial imagery in these films has not aged well. Joe Glaser seized any opportunity to find work for Armstrong, and if Glaser made no effort to ask if the movies were good for the Negro people, neither did Armstrong.

In his second full-length film, Armstrong has a speaking part in *Pennies from Heaven* (1936) as Henry, a musician hired to play in the "Haunted House Cafe." Henry and his men are invited to perform by Larry Poole (Bing Crosby), a self-styled "wandering minstrel" with no cash but with hopes of earning some by selling shares in his restaurant before it has opened. Larry has no personal need for money in this depression era fantasy, but he is determined to make a home for a young girl whom he has effectively adopted along with her grandfather. When Larry tells Henry that the musicians can have a 10 percent share in the restaurant, the trumpeter responds that there are seven men in the group, and "none of us know how to divide up ten percent by seven, so if you could just only make it seven percent." When Larry says, "Henry, you've got yourself a deal," Armstrong responds, "Thank you, Mr. Poole. I told them cats you'd do the right thing." In the following scene, however, the film does not persist in caricaturing Armstrong as stupid. "Gramps" has hopes of selling chicken dinners at the Haunted House Cafe by raising the birds in the backyard. To his chagrin, the two chickens in his yard have not multiplied. It is Henry (Armstrong) who points out that neither of the two birds is a rooster. Knowing that his job is dependent on the success of Gramps's meal plan, Henry then arranges for his musicians to supply Gramps with chickens.

Armstrong's big moment in *Pennies from Heaven* is his performance of "The Skeleton in the Closet," which he sings and plays with the usual gusto. Although the camera regularly shows the trumpeter in erect poses, even emphasizing his phallicism with high-contrast shadows of the trumpet pointed up at stark angles, the scene can be accused of activating racist stereotypes of the timorous black, easily terrified by graveyard images. When a dancer in a skeleton costume appears on stage, Armstrong's eyes bulge as he strikes a pose of trepidation. Those critics looking for signifying in this scene might note that Armstrong's reaction seems underplayed in comparison to the usual medley of exaggerated expressions that cross his face. They might also observe that his reactions have an aura of parody, perhaps allowing him some distance from the racist material. This first major appearance in a Hollywood film shows that Armstrong's mannerisms were already suited to anyone wishing to argue that he was working against the grain. It is possible that Bing Crosby, with whom Armstrong had already established a relationship, may have encouraged or at least tolerated the trumpeter's attempts to take liberties with the scripted material.

The end of Armstrong's sequence, however, is less ambiguous in its evocation of racist stereotypes. Shortly after "The Skeleton in the Closet," a sheriff enters the restaurant accompanied by three farmers. One of them points at the band and shouts, "There's the guys that stole our chickens." Armstrong jumps headfirst out a window saying, "Look out! The law gentlemen." The extent to which Armstrong signifies in *Pennies from Heaven* is very much in the eye of the beholder and is hopelessly complicated by backward glances through the distorting lens of history. And as Stanley Crouch points out in a personal communication (1995), Armstrong's humor is only problematic when contemporary racial sensibilities are invoked without regard to other contexts.

I am not blind to racist stereotypes nor do I misapprehend the limits of Hollywood conventions, but it is also important in discussions of this sort not to remove Armstrong from the context of styles of humor which

Negroes laughed at and which they still laugh at (that is, if you are aware of the remarkable similarities between the images in the world of classic minstrelsy—lazy, shiftless, dumb, buffoon, easily conned, roughneck, and so on—and those of black-written and black-directed music video satire). It is also essential—once we acknowledge the influence of Negroes on the conventions of American humor—to remember that the eye-rolling, hustling, and conning of Groucho Marx would play very differently to contemporary audiences if he had been a black comedian, as would the pomposity and imbecility of Laurel and Hardy, the drunkenness and determination not to work on the part of W. C. Fields, and so on. In short, much of what we consider "clean" white humor would be seen as demeaning and derogatory if the performers weren't white.

Artists & Models was directed by Raoul Walsh and released in 1937, but the one production number with Armstrong was directed by a young Vincente Minnelli, six years before he would direct Armstrong again in *Cabin in the Sky*. Most of the number is dominated by Martha Raye in dusky body makeup designed to give her a look more consistent with the stylized Harlem set populated by a large group of black actors and dancers. The sequence begins with a group of white "G-Men" arriving with machine guns in search of "Public Melody Number One," who is eventually revealed to be Armstrong. In this typically Hollywoodian conflation of violence and music, the "corrupting" aspects of jazz culture are playfully compared to the activities of gangsters. More importantly, the phallicism of Armstrong's trumpet is uniquely emphasized through its association with a gangster's gun. In Martha Raye's lyrics, the Armstrong figure is explicitly compared to famous gangsters: "Al Capone's a bundle of joy / Dillinger's a teacher's pet / Gattling's gun is only a toy / Compared to a note shot from a hot cornet." This acknowledgment and exaggeration of Armstrong's phallicism was daring in its time and probably could not have been filmed after race became more of a hot-button issue during the 1940s.

After Raye has compared him to Dillinger and Capone, Armstrong slowly emerges from the wings preceded auspiciously by his shadow. When he finally appears, he is attired in Hollywood's image of the overdressed gangster with a double-breasted suit and a bowler hat. With a stylized look of menace on his face, he shouts to the crowd, "Get under cover, you rhythm rascals, and run!" To the white men with their machine guns he sings, "Now look here, Mr. Hoover and your G-Men." Although he smiles and sings at other moments in the number, his dominant style of self-presentation is the mock-gangster pose. Meanwhile, Raye's body language is especially suggestive in the sequence, her dark skin presumably giving her license to engage in trucking, pecking, and other exaggerated gestures from black vernacular dance. As she moves and dances, her legs are almost always spread as widely as her tight skirt allows. According to Thomas Cripps, southern distributors raised objections to the interactions of Raye and Armstrong—although there is seldom even eye contact between the two, their proximity may have been too much for those devoted to racial segregation (Cripps 1977, 10). Undoubtedly, the fear of a sexual rapport between Raye and Armstrong was increased by the trumpeter's threatening posture, no matter how ironically the gangster-musician analogy was meant to be taken. A few months later, in *Every Day's a Holiday,* Armstrong was also able to inject a certain amount of sexual expression into his scene with some deft dancing in front of a parade.

In *Going Places* (1938), Armstrong was stripped of all sexual menace whatsoever. He did, however, have one of his largest acting roles as Gabriel, the groom for a racehorse named Jeepers Creepers, to which he sings the song of the same name. Rather than discharging his sexual energies in the proximity of a white woman, Armstrong is here asked to play and sing the title song to the horse. Jeepers Creepers the horse is known for his speed as well as for his hostility to riders. The plot, based on the Broadway show *The Hottentot,* revolves around the idea that the horse becomes so fond of Armstrong's rendition of "Jeepers Creepers" that he will submit to a jockey only when he hears the music. At the finale, Dick Powell, playing a romantic hero with no experience as a jockey rides the horse to victory while the trumpeter and his entire band drive along the course of the steeplechase playing the horse's favorite song. In one of the more inexplicable musical numbers in the film, Gabriel (Armstrong) leads an orchestra and sings "Mutiny in the Nursery" eventually joined by vocalist Maxine Sullivan and a host of black singers and dancers. Although Dick Powell and his costar Anita Louise later join in the singing, the film offers no explanation for a song about nursery rhymes, except perhaps to associate children's ditties with the infantilized black characters. The concept of an obstreperous horse fond of music was probably inspired by Howard Hawks's *Bringing Up Baby* (1938), in which a leopard called Baby responds positively to the song, "I Can't Give You Anything But Love, Baby." Similarly the combination of African-American music and horse racing was undoubtedly motivated by the success in 1937 of *A Day at the Races,* in which a horse responded to another trickster figure, Harpo Marx. In the earlier films, however, no black character was ever referred to as "Uncle Tom," the name that the film's two unsavory characters (Allen Jenkins and Harold Huher) use to address Gabriel.

Although he receives fourth billing in the opening credits, Armstrong appears for less than six minutes in director Vincente Minnelli's *Cabin in the Sky* (1943). This is the only film in which Duke Ellington and Armstrong both performed, although they are never in the same frame together. While Ellington appears as "Duke Ellington," the leader of a famous orchestra, Armstrong plays one of several devils in a scene at the "Idea Department" in the "Hotel Hades." Along with other black actors with small horns in their coiffures, he contemplates strategies for winning the soul of Little Joe, whose soul "The Lord" and "Lucifer, Jr." are competing to win. The sequence begins with Armstrong playing an unaccompanied solo on his trumpet until Lucifer, Jr. (Rex Ingram) bursts in and shouts, "Stop that noise!" Putting their heads together, the devils decide on a plan ultimately devised by "The Trumpeter," as Armstrong is called in the credits. The Trumpeter also insists that it was his idea to offer the apple to Eve in the Garden of Eden. After the brief sequence in hell, Armstrong is seen no more. In addition to his trumpet, Armstrong is distinguished from Lucifer, Jr. and the other four devils by his jive talk. Unlike the others, Armstrong uses phrases like "Well, all reet," and ends sentences with the vocative "man."

In his article on *Cabin in the Sky,* James Naremore makes an intriguing connection with the work of James Agee, who gave the film a negative notice when he wrote the unsigned review in *Time.* Basically, Agee objected to the demeaning of distinguished Negro actors, treated by the studio as "Sambo–style entertainers." The next year Agee would publish an article, "Pseudo-Folk," in the *Partisan Review* in which he denounced swing as a corruption of the true jazz produced by Negroes, "our richest contemporary source of folk art, and our best people en bloc." Like Rudi Blesh and many in the revivalist camp of the 1940s, Agee specifically cited the declining quality of Armstrong's work, but he also found evidence of the corruption of pure black folk art in Duke Ellington's slick compositions for big band, the "pseudo-savage" dancing of Katherine Dunham's troupe, and Paul Robeson's performance of Earl Robinson and John Latouche's "esthetically execrable 'Ballad for Americans.'" Naremore observes, "Although he never mentioned *Cabin in the Sky,* he [Agee] could hardly have come closer to describing it. Both Armstrong and Ellington were featured in the movie, and . . . both Dunham and Latouche had contributed to the original Broadway show" (Naremore 1992, 105). For Agee, as well as for many inside and outside the revivalist camp, Armstrong's participation in Hollywood's pseudo folklore was consistent with his embrace of industrialized popular music. But like Ellington, who was able to overcome the naive and racist dichotomies in *Cabin in the Sky* (although not in the opinion of Agee), Armstrong's exuberance and humor consistently place him outside the film's folklorist projects.

In 1944 and 1945 Armstrong appeared in three films, always in short performance sequences that could easily be excised in communities where sexualized black faces were not welcome on movie screens. In all three, *Atlantic City, Jam Session,* and *Pillow to Post,* his sexuality was explicit in ways that it had never been in earlier films. In *Jam Session* he plays a singing, trumpet-playing bartender who performs "I Can't Give You Anything But Love" to a line of elegantly dressed young black women. There is no question that his character would like to do exactly what the song says. In *Atlantic City* he performs with the lithe, picture-perfect Dorothy Dandridge, who is unrestrained in her erotic body language just before Armstrong enters the stage show at the Apollo Theater. As was not the case in his interactions with Martha Raye in *Artists & Models,* Armstrong appears fully cognizant of Dandridge's sexual presence; even as he holds his horn out straight, he cocks his eyes to watch Dandridge as she dances to his left. When Armstrong sings "Ain't Misbehavin,'" he addresses Dandridge directly with lines like "Your kisses are worth waiting for." The film also allows Armstrong to dip into his bag of tricksterisms; at one point during his trumpet solo, his eyes bulging with impertinence, he stoops down to blow his horn directly into a camera that seems to be placed at the level of his ankles. For a few moments the bell of his horn fills the screen.

In *Pillow to Post,* Armstrong again performs with Dandridge, this time at a roadhouse where she sings "Whatcha Say?" The number is staged so that Dandridge addresses the trumpeter with lyrics such as "Do I get that little kiss? Must you let me down like this?" Armstrong mimes shyness as the singer saunters closer, finally answering her questions by shouting his trademark expression, "Well, all reet!" Dandridge then sighs, "Oh, baby," and moves even closer. Armstrong feigns innocence and indignantly snorts, "Look out here, girl, don't you start that stuff here." He then smiles broadly before he blows the final high notes that end the number. At this time Hollywood was working much harder to contain black male sexuality than black female sexuality. In 1943, for example, the beautiful young Lena Horne was paired with Eddie "Rochester" Anderson (*Cabin in the Sky*) and Bill "Bojangles" Robinson (*Stormy Weather*), both of them long past the age when they could compete with her as leading men. But if *Pillow to Post* is any indication, the effort to repress black male sexuality was not as extreme as it had been just a few years earlier. What makes Armstrong's brief appearance in *Pillow to Post* especially interesting in this context is the presence of Willie Best, a black comedian busy during the 1930s and 1940s. Best is featured in *Pillow to Post* as "Lucille," the porter at the motel complex where the action takes place. Like Stepin Fetchit, Best played the most extreme stereotype of the shiftless, shuffling, slow-talking Negro. Although he makes a passing reference to "me and my girlfriend," we never see him in the company of a woman. His feminization is so overdetermined that at one point he even says that his two brothers also have female names. Compared to Willie Best's Lucille, the Armstrong of *Pillow to Post* is a strutting satyr. Although Armstrong and Lucille are never in the same scene, the film does implicitly pair the two black performers when Lucille plays reveille on a bugle. On the one hand, it is possible that Armstrong's familiarity to the mass audience made him less threatening and less in need of the drastic desexualization inflicted upon the black porter Lucille. On the other hand, the filmmakers may have regarded Armstrong's phallicism as problematic after all and consequently chose to pair him with an absurdly unthreatening black male. A similar choice may have been made three years earlier when Best danced ineffectually in two of the three-minute "soundies" that Armstrong filmed in 1942. Best was also paired with Armstrong in the Hotel Hades sequence in *Cabin in the Sky*—again, some racial logic in the minds of filmmakers must have required that the semisomnolent Best should balance out the exuberant Armstrong. Best defuses the phallicism of the trumpeter's erect image by appearing ineffectual, flaccid, often horizontal. Thus, it is Best, not Armstrong, who in the three-minute "Shine" gazes at the row of well-dressed, light-skinned black women, designated as desirable with both class and racial markers. The possibility that Armstrong's trumpet may symbolize something besides a trumpet is in a sense concealed by the antics of Best.

In the brief period that separated *Pillow to Post* (1945) from *New Orleans* (1947) and *A Song Is Born* (1948), the discourse of jazz changed drastically. Armstrong suddenly became useful when filmmakers began to accept arguments floated in the jazz press about the music being art. By casting a certified genius from jazz history both *New Orleans* and *A Song Is Born* achieved their goal of glorifying the white swing musicians that Americans had already embraced. Armstrong is applauded by royalty in *New Orleans* and associated with the generation of innovators who "took a reet jungle beat and brought it to Basin Street" in *A Song Is Born*. But as the representative of an earlier stage of the art form called jazz, his presence validates the primacy of Woody Herman, Tommy Dorsey, and Benny Goodman, musicians from a more "advanced" stage of the art.

Shortly after *New Orleans*, jazz and swing experienced a large decline in popularity. Following a brief moment as an artist in the movies, Armstrong was no longer needed to affirm that Americans were listening to the right music when popular taste embraced styles with fewer jazz inflections. In *The Strip* (1951), Armstrong's next film, no grandiose claims are made for the trumpeter in particular or for jazz in general as had been the case in his two earlier films. In fact, Armstrong and a band of canonized jazz greats are taken for granted and frequently ignored throughout the movie. *The Strip i*s a film noir, complete with a flashback structure and the kind of generic jazz score that was becoming typical for the genre. Armstrong performs several times as the leader of the house band at "Fluff's Dixieland," a posh club with a spacious bandstand and dancing waiters. The film stars a thirty-one-year-old Mickey Rooney in one of his early attempts to transcend the eternal juvenile who played opposite Judy Garland. As Stan, Rooney plays a drummer who takes a job with Armstrong's band, but not because he wants to play with Armstrong, Earl Hines, Jack Teagarden, and Barney Bigard, all of whom appear in the film; rather, he is interested in getting closer to a young woman who works as a dancer at the club. After the brief moment in the late 1940s when jazz was given a history, an aesthetics, and some degree of legitimacy, *The Strip* returns to a culture where the music is strictly for good times, providing at best a little solace now and then. Armstrong, who had been working with a New Orleans–style sextet for the past five years, was now a fixture in the revivalist camp, at least as far as the film is concerned—Fluff (William Demarest) refers to him as "Mr. Dixieland himself." Although he is frequently on camera as the plot develops, Armstrong and his band are confined within the musical numbers. Neither he, Teagarden, Hines, nor Bigard have any lines. Otherwise, this Armstrong is much like the one we know except that he has no control over who plays in his group. Stan is retained by Fluff, with no sign that he has consulted Armstrong (or his manager). At the end, Stan's would-be girlfriend dies, but the drummer finds solace in music, beating the drums with increasing conviction as the music of Armstrong and the band swells under the closing titles.

In *Glory Alley*, Armstrong is also a dispenser of solace for white protagonists, playing another of the strange hybrid roles that combined his public persona with a diegetic character. In this case, he plays Shadow, "the best trainer in the business," according to boxer Socks Barbarrosa (Ralph Meeker). Why the boxer's trainer plays a trumpet is never explained. Nor is the nature of Armstrong's second job as the apparent servant and guide for the Judge (Kurt Kasznar), a cantankerous blind man who is the father of Socks's love interest, a cabaret dancer played by Leslie Caron. Armstrong smiles a good deal as he escorts the Judge, and he is almost invariably given demeaning lines:

Judge: She could have been a great ballerina. You know what a ballerina is, Shadow?

Shadow: More or less, Judge.

Armstrong's first musical number takes place in the awkward space of a barroom frequented by the main characters, who smile benignly as the trumpeter walks among them singing the title song. When Armstrong switches to trumpet, the protagonist wanders to the other side of the bar and his voice-over obscures most of the trumpet solo. The film offers little space for the phallic Armstrong or the trickster Armstrong.

Although his scenes are brief, Armstrong was endowed with real phallic power when he appeared in two biopics, *The Glenn Miller Story* (1954) and *The Five Pennies* (1959). In both he is confined once again to nightclub sequences, largely isolated from the films' plots. In *The Glenn Miller Story* the hero interacts just this once with a black artist, as if Armstrong were preparing him for the sexual initiation of his wedding night. No longer identified with art, Armstrong is now brought in for his sexuality, however veiled this signification may be. Armstrong appears in a surprisingly similar scene in the Red Nichols biopic, *The Five Pennies*. Once again the hero and his girlfriend go up to Harlem to hear Armstrong, and once again the white musician gains sexual maturity after he plays with the black master. Armstrong's brazen treatment of Nichols in the subsequent scene is especially remarkable in light of his 1957 attacks on Eisenhower and Faubus. It is as if his outspoken political statements had spilled over into *The Five Pennies*, the first film he made after his highly publicized remarks on integration.

Later in *The Five Pennies*, Armstrong appears in another nightclub sequence, this time after Nichols has become established as a jazzman and has brought his young daughter to the club. Much in the spirit of the television variety programs in which both Armstrong and Danny Kaye (who plays Nichols) were at that time regulars, the two entertainers sing an elaborate version of "When the Saints Go Marching In" that associates jazz with classical music much more playfully than had been the case in the earnest *New Orleans*.

Nichols: Do ya dig Rachmaninoff?

Armstrong: On and off.

Nichols: Rimsky?

Armstrong: Of course a-koff!

Nichols: Ravel and Gustav Mahler?

Armstrong: Yeah, but don't forget Fats Waller.

The mid-1940s discourses of jazz as art have been replaced by the more familiar tradition of jazzing the classics, though here it seems more facetious than conciliatory.

In *The Five Pennies*, Armstrong functions primarily to validate Nichols's importance as a jazz artist. More importantly, he is on hand as evidence of the white protagonist's tolerant attitude toward blacks. At least since Jim in *Huckleberry Finn* (1885), a black companion indicates that the white hero has an independent spirit and a capacity to look beyond a person's color in spite of what society might think. These are the typical qualities of the independent hero of American myth who was and still is a staple of American entertainment (Ray 1985, 107).

Much the same can he said of Bing Crosby, who befriended Armstrong at least as early as 1930 when Crosby was in Hollywood filming *The King of Jazz* and making regular trips to Culver City, California, to hear Armstrong perform at Frank Sebastian's New Cotton Club. Although by all accounts the men shared a genuine friendship, the conventions of the film industry invariably placed Armstrong in the inferior position as the servile Negro in need of a white patron. Certainly this is what was dramatized in *Pennies from Heaven* and two decades later in *High Society*, when Dexter (Crosby) brings Armstrong and his group to Newport for a jazz festival staged by Dexter (not by George Wein). Dexter is also in Newport for the wedding of his former wife Samantha (Grace Kelly) to the social-climbing George (John Lund), but Dexter will be remarried to her at the finale just as in *The Philadelphia Story* (1940) on which the film is based.

High Society revives some of the discourse of jazz as art, but not, as

Bing Crosby and Armstrong in a still from *High Society,* 1956. Photo: Corbis-Bettmann.

in *New Orleans* and *A Song Is Born,* to bring white big bands in through the back door. Jazz was no longer a popular music in 1956, but it was developing the elite following that it retains today The jazz festival at Newport that allows Armstrong entry into the film had begun in 1954 and was a popular affair by the time *High Society* was released. The Newport Jazz Festival was one of many signs that a more affluent audience was taking the music seriously as an alternative to the increasingly infantilized music of the popular mainstream. At the same time, the jazz lover could be portrayed as more down-to-earth than those snobs who declared their preference for classical music. (Elvis Presley's denunciation of pretentious intellectual jazz fans in *Jailhouse Rock* was still a year away.) Dexter

(Crosby) is clearly on the winning side of this argument when his ex-wife tells him why she left him: "You could have become a serious composer or a diplomat or anything you wanted to be. And what have you become? A jukebox hero!" When Armstrong and Crosby together perform "Now You Has Jazz," their easy grace and humor reveal that Dexter has become something much more than a "jukebox hero."

At least for the white audiences of 1956, Dexter's proximity to Armstrong probably indicated that the white protagonist had character, a trait that jazz has been loaning out to American movie heroes in much more recent years, for example, to Clint Eastwood as the Secret Service agent in *In the Line of Fire* (1993), who relaxes by listening to Miles Davis records and playing jazz piano. Jazz has been the emblem of a special sensibility for equally unlikely characters, including Gene Hackman in *The Conversation* (1974), Warren Beatty in *Heaven Can Wait* (1978), and Dennis Hopper in *Backtrack* (1989), all of whom play jazz on a saxophone to express their inner feelings. In *The Fabulous Baker Boys* (1989), we know that Jeff Bridges is the more sensitive brother, at least in part because he has a picture of John Coltrane on his wall and because he plays jazz in a cellar with black musicians. In several of his films, Woody Allen has specifically used Louis Armstrong's music to bring depth to his characters. At the climax of *Manhattan* (1979), for example, the Allen protagonist lists Armstrong's recording of "Potato Head Blues" as one of the things that makes life worth living. Similarly, in 1994 no less than three Hollywood films used photographs of canonical beboppers to reveal a character's sensibilities. In *Renaissance Man* (1994), Danny DeVito has a photograph of Dizzy Gillespie on his wall; in *Wolf* (1994), a picture of Bud Powell sits on Jack Nicholson's desk; and in *Disclosure* (1994), the camera scans past an early photograph of Dexter Gordon on a wall in Michael Douglas's home. The audience is thus informed that all three men are sensitive and unconventional, even though there are no other references to jazz in any of these films. In *High Society*, Bing Crosby was one of the first of many slightly offbeat American film heroes to use jazz in general and Armstrong in particular as evidence of the subtleties in their souls.

Questions of art and jazz return with a vengeance in director Martin Ritt's *Paris Blues* (1961). If Duke Ellington and Billy Strayhorn were able to transform the film with the music they wrote for its final moments, then Armstrong becomes an even more problematic figure than he had been for jazz critics of the previous decades. In *Paris Blues*, Armstrong receives fourth billing for a part that is rather small but that carries much symbolic importance. The action of the film effectively begins with his arrival in Paris and ends with his departure. As Wild Man Moore, Armstrong's face is first seen on a poster in a train station in Paris where wildly cheering crowds have come to greet him. Also in the crowd is Ram Bowen (Paul Newman), the American jazz trombonist living in Paris who has come to show the trumpeter some music he has written. Moore (Armstrong) tells Bowen (Newman) that he looks good and suggests that Paris must agree with him, "What is it, the chicks or the wine?" He also says that he has heard good things about Bowen's performances in Paris and that some day he will drop by and "blow ya outta the joint." Not since *New Orleans* had an American feature film acknowledged the adoration that Armstrong had long been receiving in Europe, and in no previous film had another musician asked for his expert opinion. Armstrong appears comfortable in what was for him an unusual role—he brings good humor as well as authority to his scenes with Newman. It is also important, as the audience later learns, that Moore has agreed to take Bowen's music to René Bernard, apparently a grand old man of classical music in France.

Later on, when Wild Man Moore brings his orchestra to Bowen's club to challenge the trombonist and his sidemen, Armstrong stages a series of cutting contests with each member of the band. Although jazz enthusiasts are well aware of this ritual, it has seldom been dramatized in a fiction film. Without suppressing the phallic-aggressive aspect of the cutting contest, Armstrong brings a spirit of generosity to the practice, consistently registering joy as he engages each musician. Nevertheless, the script for *Paris Blues* is profoundly suspicious of any serious claims for jazz. The film evokes arguments about jazz and classical music, but it articulates them rather incoherently: a "serious" European composer (Bernard) is held up as the final arbiter of music written by a modernist jazz artist; the modernist jazz artist (Bowen) writes in the most advanced style of Duke Ellington but usually performs 1930s songs such as "Mood Indigo" and "Sophisticated Lady" that were seldom programmed by younger jazz artists in the early 1960s (as opposed to what younger artists have played in the 1980s and 1990s); to meet with the "serious" European composer, the modernist jazz artist must seek the help of an older jazz artist who plays in a decidedly pre-modern style; and as the modernist artist steels himself for a life of total devotion to art, the face of the older artist is covered over as if to symbolize the eclipse of "jazz" behind the forthcoming work of a composer who will stay in Paris to study theory, harmony, and counterpoint and presumably write something other than jazz. At worst, the film's idealization of a white hero alongside its denigration of Ellington and Armstrong is an especially insidious form of Hollywood racism. On the other hand, the idea that the white artist is the inheritor and resuscitator of a used-up tradition associated with Louis Armstrong is simply a more contemporary version of the same story that was implied in *New Orleans* and *A Song Is Born*.

Except for a brief appearance with Barbra Streisand in *Hello, Dolly!* (1969), Armstrong's last film was *A Man Called Adam* (1966). Sammy Davis, Jr., plays the trumpeter-singer Adam Johnson. As "Sweet Daddy" Willie Ferguson, an elderly trumpeter-singer very much like himself, Armstrong receives second billing in the credits, the highest listing he ever received in a fiction film. Unable to afford a hotel room, Ferguson has been temporarily moved into Adam's apartment by Nelson (Ossie Davis), the owner of a jazz club where Ferguson is performing. When Adam returns home drunk after petulantly and prematurely canceling a tour of club dates, he is outraged to find Ferguson there. Without acknowledging that he even knows who Ferguson is, Adam unceremoniously jettisons him into the hallway. The old man is rescued by the arrival of Nelson and Claudia (Cicely Tyson), a young, black, socially conscious woman, who is also Ferguson's granddaughter. The next morning Adam apologizes to the older trumpeter and assures him that he knows who he is. Accepting the apology, Ferguson makes a pitiful attempt at small talk, asking if Adam has ever heard of "Tree Top Jones." Adam replies, "Oh, of course. I play his 78s every morning before breakfast." Not catching the irony, Ferguson comments, "Yeah, he's a killer." When Adam's agent enters the apartment a few moments later, Adam accompanies him from the room while Ferguson is in midsentence.

Much of the old vocabulary of the war between the ancients and the moderns of the 1940s returns in several sequences, including one in which Adam sarcastically associates Armstrong with "true jazz." Finding Ferguson sitting alone by himself at a party Adam strikes up a conversation. The old trumpeter says that he feels uncomfortable among a youthful crowd, adding "seems like the people don't know what to say to me." Adam tells him, "Maybe it's just that they don't know what to say to a genius." Almost immediately after this encounter, Adam attacks Nelson for booking the Armstrong character: "What are you doing to that old man over there, huh? You know what you're going to do? You're going to break his heart, you and your 'true jazz.' You know what's going to happen, Nelson? He's going to play a while. He's going to be in. Then the novelty's going to wear off. The oddity's going to be gone. He won't be able to go back home again in the rice fields, and that sweet, nice old man's gonna be bumming drinks at bars up in Harlem."

Although Armstrong's character is given a degree of self-consciousness in *A Man Called Adam,* the trickster Armstrong never emerges except when he is performing on the bandstand. In his performance of "Back o' Town Blues," Ferguson (Armstrong) exchanges mock insults with his trombonist, Tyree Glenn. When the trumpeter sings, "I had a woman," Glenn exclaims, "So what! I had five!" Then, after Armstrong sings the line, "She had to run around," he adds as an aside to Glenn, "Like your daddy." This playful, confident performer is barely compatible with the tragic figure we later see sitting alone at a party feeling sorry for himself. Neither Armstrong the trickster nor Armstrong the artist have any place in a film that portrays the "true" black artist as introverted and self-destructive rather than ribald and outgoing. The film uses Willie Ferguson primarily for pathos—a slightly ridiculous old man whose smiling and clowning are transparently obsequious. The bitter, "tell-it-like-it-is" dialogue written for Adam becomes all the more topical thanks to Ferguson's pitiful attempts at humor and reconciliation. Nevertheless, Armstrong shows previously untapped resources as an actor in *A Man Called Adam.* The quality of Armstrong's performance adds an extra dimension to the pathos of the film and, like *Paris Blues,* shows Armstrong's ability to play the kind of serious role that never would have been offered to him in his youth.

"How 'Critical' Is It?"

The received wisdom about Armstrong was probably best expressed by Clive James in his *Fame in the Twentieth Century*—a series of BBC programs that were widely shown in the United States on PBS in 1993. Over scenes from *Rhapsody in Black and Blue* and the soundie, *When It's Sleepy Time Down South,* James makes the following judgments: "Louis Armstrong's brilliant trumpet solos were works of art from a sweatshop. The works of art were preserved on classic records, but white men controlled the record business and stole the money. To stay solvent, the artist had to become an entertainer. Louis Armstrong the revolutionary modern musician turned into Satchmo the showman . . . Armstrong detested the jungle bunny outfits. He didn't like playing Uncle Tom either. But it was the price of fame, and fame was the road to freedom."

It could just as easily be argued that Armstrong never thought of himself as an artist. As early as 1924, the trumpeter was singing and clowning with Fletcher Henderson's band in New York. (Because Henderson did not like his singing style, however, Armstrong's vocal breaks can be briefly heard at the end of one of the two surviving takes of "Everybody Loves My Baby" [1924] but nowhere else in his recorded output with Henderson.) Crowd-pleasing shenanigans also are abundant on records by the Hot Five and Hot Seven that are now canonized as serious "art" by most jazz writers. The argument that Armstrong "sold out" at some given historical moment is usually based on the automatic canonization of some earlier, edenic moment that can be fetishized but not examined.

Clive James has likewise misread Armstrong's racial politics. On the one hand, Armstrong did not detest wearing "jungle bunny outfits." When he dressed up in a grass skirt and blackface to be King of the Zulus in New Orleans at Mardi Gras in 1949, many black Americans may well have been scandalized, but Armstrong never apologized, insisting that it was an honor to be King of the Zulus. In this case, he liked the jungle bunny outfit, if that is what we wish to call it. On the other hand, Armstrong probably never thought of himself as an Uncle Tom either. By the early 1930s he was touring Europe and encountering a hero's reception, and he continued to be one of the two or three best-known Americans in the world until his death in 1971. He was right to pride himself on passing through doors that had always been closed to blacks. More revealingly, James has evoked the old art/entertainment distinction without acknowledging how easily it can be deconstructed. The duplicitous use that Hollywood has found for the discourse of art should tell us a great deal about the power relations actually at stake when arguments pro and con are made by critics. For a long time the BBC and PBS have invested deeply in keeping myths about "art" alive. James's series is typical of the BBC-PBS product that invites audiences to side with Armstrong the artist rather than with Armstrong the entertainer at the same time that audiences are invited to gaze at the "entertainer" in his "jungle bunny outfits."

More so than with most performers who retained their prominence through several decades, reactions to Armstrong have changed radically over the years. There are younger hipsters, both black and white, who first regarded him as a smiling buffoon with a white handkerchief, but who later came to admire him as a brilliant and original trumpet soloist. As a young man, my view of Armstrong changed from contempt to admiration when I began paying attention to the words of older jazz enthusiasts.

Conversely, some of the same black fans who mobbed Armstrong as a hero when he passed through Harlem in the 1930s probably found him something of an embarrassment in the 1950s. Today, his mannerisms are offensive to some young African-Americans. After showing footage of Armstrong in the 1930s to a large introductory class in film history I experienced something similar to the reactions described by bell hooks at showings of films depicting erotic love between black men.

> When I had Oberlin College show *Poison of Remembrance* to all the incoming freshpeople, during the scene where the two black men kissed in that film, a lot of the black males in the audience put their heads down. And when I went to the screening of *Young Soul Rebels*, when there were tender scenes of lovemaking and eroticism between black men, I remember the Rastas in the audience who were saying "Stop it, man, stop it!" That initially registers as a homophobic response, but it's also a response to seeing the public exposure of a certain kind of black male desire that is vulnerable. (hooks 1991, 177)

Although there was never anything explicitly homoerotic in Armstrong's self-presentation, his zeal to please surely suggested a similar vulnerability that today makes many young black people uncomfortable. In a culture that regularly castrates black men, many of them are unnerved by the sight of an African-American male who appears to accept his castration so readily. If Gary Giddins is correct—that black Americans in the 1930s lionized Armstrong because he communicated his sexuality in code while turning an obsequious face toward his white handlers—then it also must be true that Armstrong did not update his codes. Many in the black audience after the civil rights era ceased to recognize Armstrong's obsolete phallic codings and saw only what the white power structure was meant to see. I would not be surprised if first-time viewers find no evidence of Armstrong's sexuality in *Pillow to Post* or *The Glenn Miller Story,* although I hope that I have made the case that his sexuality is an issue in these films.

Can a case also be made that Armstrong was able to rise above the demeaning material he was regularly asked to perform? When he let his eyes bulge out or when he broke into an absurdly wide grin, was he overplaying to hide his real feelings? Was he saying to those whites in the audience who were uncomfortable with a black man's sexuality, "You may think this is me, but you'll never find the real thing underneath this mask"?

Undoubtedly, the answers to these questions will continue to change as the discourses of black and white America continue to change. While Armstrong may have overcome the soap bubbles and leopard skins of *Rhapsody in Black and Blue* (1932) simply with his carriage and the magnificence of his music, it is much more difficult to make this kind of argument for the out-of-place figure who wanders through *Glory Alley* in 1952. We can only speculate about how much of Armstrong's success was related to the reassurances he gave to white audiences who wanted to believe that his grinning visage was more typical of black people than were the menacing faces of young African-Americans that regularly showed up on the nightly news. Different constituencies at different historical moments have vacillated between seeing Armstrong as a trickster or as a Tom, just as Armstrong himself reacted differently to these discourses at different moments in his career.

Nevertheless, I would like to expand the comparison that Ralph Ellison (1964) makes between Armstrong and the witty jester of Elizabethan drama. In commenting on Stanley Edgar Hyman's lecture on trickster figures in American literature, Ellison charges Hyman with blurring distinctions between the various types of tricksters in order to group them all within the same archetypal structures. In the large literature on tricksters, most of it by folklorists and comparative anthropologists, a consensus has been reached that tricksters are liminal figures, identified with creative powers and the violation of taboos, especially sexual ones. As Enid Welsford has written, the fool "as a dramatic character stands apart from the main action of the play, having a tendency not to focus but dissolve. . . . He does not confine his activities to the theatre but makes everyday life comic on the spot" (Welsford 1966, xii). Barbara Babcock-Abrahams, in an attempt to synthesize the various trickster traditions, wrote:

> The tale of the trickster, picaro, or rogue is one of the oldest and most persistent cultural patterns of negation and one of the oldest of narrative forms. For centuries he has, in his various incarnations, run, flown, galloped, and most recently motorcycled through the literary imagination. Examples are legion. Hermes, Prometheus, Ture, Maui, Eshu-Elegba, Anansi, Wakdjunkaga, raven, rabbit, spider, and coyote are but a few from ancient and native mythology and folktale. And, in Western literature, one could cite Lazarillo de Tormes, El Buscon, Gil Blas, Felix Krull, Augie March, and of late the Butch Cassidys and Easy Riders of film. (Babcock-Abrahams 1975, 158)

As Ellison suggests, little of this really sounds like Louis Armstrong. Babcock-Abrahams does, however, make a distinction between "volitional and nonvolitional liminality." Obviously, Armstrong as a black American growing up in the early years of the twentieth century had his marginality forced upon him. Part of what makes him so interesting is how he coded his sexuality, surrounding it with highly unthreatening display in his singing and mugging. In this sense, he is most like the trickster whose extreme, hyperphallic behavior is balanced by conduct that tends to deny sexuality.

When Ellison implicitly compares Armstrong to Touchstone in *As You Like It* or the Fool in *Lear* he is, of course, invoking fictional characters to define a real one. Ellison may have based this comparison on an Armstrong who in many ways took on a life of his own as a fictional character. We see this trickster Armstrong most prominently when he parodies the potent gangsters in the "Public Melody Number One" sequence in *Artists & Models*. He was also claimed as a trickster in the remarkable "Swing Wedding," a cartoon produced by Hugh Harman and Rudolf Ising for MGM in 1937. Armstrong is one of several black performers who are faithfully—almost lovingly—portrayed as animated frogs. Although this cartoon feature is unquestionably dominated by racist stereotypes, the black entertainers are in some ways honored by the attention that has been lavished upon reproducing their images and habits of movement. As in "Public Melody Number One," Armstrong is narrativized here as a trickster figure. At least at the outset, "Swing Wedding" is about a marriage scheduled to take place between the female frog known as Minnie the Moocher and a male frog Smokey Joe, whose behavior is modeled closely on Stepin Fetchit. Because the groom is too slow to arrive at the wedding on time, a frog bearing a resemblance to Cab Calloway romances the female with his singing and dancing and eventually takes her to the altar himself. (Minnie and Smokey Joe are both characters in the lyrics of Calloway's theme song, "Minnie the Moocher," first recorded in 1931.) Frogs resembling Fats Waller and Bill "Bojangles" Robinson provide wedding entertainment.

The frog resembling Armstrong first appears playing his trumpet off to one side of the screen and speaking in the unmistakable Satchmo voice. Then, in praise of weddings, he sings one of his trademark songs from the 1930s, "Sweethearts on Parade." After Minnie has exchanged vows with the Calloway frog, the Armstrong frog encounters Smokey Joe as he is still making his way to the ceremony. Even though it is too late, the Armstrong character provokes Smokey Joe to compete with the Calloway frog by dancing for Minnie. Perhaps inspired by Smokey Joe's dance, the Calloway frog spins across the pond to lead his orchestra in a rendition of "Runnin' Wild." The Armstrong frog has effectively started a wild party that soon turns into chaos. The Waller frog smashes his piano, while the bassist in Calloway's band uses his instrument as a pogo stick. One of the musicians can even be glimpsed injecting himself with a hypodermic needle. At the cartoon's conclusion the Armstrong frog takes in so much breath for his trumpet playing that he puffs up to enormous size and floats into the pond. The last shot of the film is a close-up of his face as he utters, "Ah, swing." Like the Elizabethan fool, Armstrong disrupts from the sidelines, dissolving the action rather than focusing it. Armstrong was much too complex a man to be catalogued simply as a trickster or as an Uncle Tom, but his image was readily available, as when a trickster was needed for a fictional text, just as he was available three decades later when James Baldwin needed a symbol of obsolete black traditions for his story "Sonny's Blues."

Michele Wallace has written of Armstrong in a somewhat different but relevant context in an article about Michael Jackson: "My mother, who is a total fan of Jackson's, says he makes up words. But isn't that what black singers have always done? Ella Fitzgerald and Louis Armstrong simply made 'scatting' official. Henry Louis Gates calls this aspect of black culture 'critical signification.' It is a process in which black culture 'signifies' on white culture through imitating and then reversing its formal strategies and preconditions, thus formulating a masked and surreptitious critique. The perfect example is the relationship of 'jazz' to white mainstream music. But what I'm beginning to wonder is: how 'critical' is it?" (Wallace 1990, 86). For many young black people in the United States today, the answer is "not much." Wallace makes a much stronger case for the "cultural signification" achieved by Michael Jackson. But Jackson was born into an entertainment industry that resembled Armstrong's as much as a player piano today resembles a synthesizer.

Wallace is right that Armstrong's critiques of dominant culture may seem a little too "masked and surreptitious" today. Still, Armstrong ought to be read outside narrow notions of what constitutes a positive role model. In much of his self-presentation Armstrong plays on traditions of American humor that are not so easily separated into strictly white and black strands. Nor are these traditions so easily classified as demeaning or resisting. There are, however, legitimate questions about how Armstrong functioned within discourses of race and sexuality, and all of these issues are richly available for interpretation in his films. If we are to understanding the culture's impact on him, his films may actually be as valuable a resource as his recordings.

The American Feature Films of Louis Armstrong

Ex-Flame,	Director unknown,	1931 (Lost)
Pennies from Heaven,	Director Norman Z. McLeod,	1936
Artists & Models,	Director Raoul Walsh,	1937
Every Day's a Holiday,	Director A. Edward Sutherland,	1938
Going Places,	Director Ray Enright,	1938
Birth of the Blues,	Director Victor Schertzinger,	1941
Cabin in the Sky,	Director Vincente Minnelli,	1943
Jam Session,	Director Charles Barton,	1944
Atlantic City,	Director Ray McCarey,	1944
Pillow to Post,	Director Vincent Sherman,	1945
New Orleans,	Director Arthur Lubin,	1947
A Song Is Born,	Director Howard Hawks,	1948
The Strip,	Director Leslie Kardos,	1951
Here Comes the Groom,	Director Frank Capra,	1951
Glory Alley,	Director Raoul Walsh,	1952
The Glenn Miller Story,	Director Anthony Mann,	1954
High Society,	Director Charles Walters,	1956
The Five Pennies,	Director Melville Shavelson,	1959
The Beat Generation,	Director Charles Haas,	1959
Paris Blues,	Director Martin Ritt,	1961
When the Boys Meet the Girls,	Director Alvin Ganzer,	1966
A Man Called Adam,	Director Leo Penn,	1966
Hello, Dolly!,	Director Gene Kelly,	1969

Part Nine

LOUIS'S LEGACY

Armstrong's stature as the twentieth century's Gabriel is unassailable. But while he has been universally praised as the supreme trumpet titan, the divine Dippermouth, there are those who have perceived him as a sacrificial hero. In his provocative *Village Voice* piece of August 27, 1985, "Papa Dip: Crescent City Conquistador and Sacrificial Hero," Stanley Crouch concludes:

> Yes, Louis Armstrong was a real sacrificial hero, an innovator who led American music to a new land of artistry that he wasn't able to enter himself, too often presented in circumstances so beneath him that even his extraordinary talent couldn't lift everything. Before his heart attack, when he was still at the height of his mature skills, his crude manager Joe Glaser blocked Papa Dip from working with Gil Evans on an album of concerto arrangements, something Armstrong wanted to do after he heard Evans's work with Miles Davis on *Porgy and Bess*. There was much more he could have done. When we hear him in song on the Handy record that "from milkless milk and silkless silk, we are growing used to soul-less soul," there can be no doubt that Papa Dip is talking about things at the other end of the field from where he built his own monument, homemade and universal.

THE GIFT OF JOY

It was the year 1970. Still beholden to the mythic birth date of July 4, 1900, the world paid tribute to the living legend that was Louis Armstrong. A case in point was Down Beat *magazine, which dedicated its issue of July 9 to Louis, and included an eloquent editorial by Dan Morgenstern in which he said:*

We are proud to dedicate this issue of *Down Beat* to Louis Armstrong, the true King of Jazz. For more than half a century, this dedicated and beautiful man has been spreading joy on earth. Steadfastly, he has affirmed the eternal verities of love, beauty and goodness—as an artist and as a man. He is one of the few glories of our age. . . . . Long ago, Louis dedicated his life and art to a noble purpose. "It's happiness to me to see people happy," he has said, and he has turned millions on with his smile, his voice, and his horn.

—

And in a bouquet of tributes, "Roses for Satchmo," some eighty musicians filled the air with the song of praise, among them the following:

Jazz is not—never has been—a one-man show. But if I had to vote for one representative for jazz, that one would have to be Louis Armstrong.

—Art Hodes

. . . The joyful feeling he communicates always raised my hair. He really took me out and gave me the shivers. Such great feeling. He's like the first sculptor in music, a real monolithic sculptor, with his ability as an architect and his ability to communicate feeling and the whole range of emotions. . . . He's a whole man—the embodiment of the African praise singer and bard

—Roswell Rudd

Louis Armstrong could only happen once—for ever and ever. I, for one, appreciate the ride.

—Bobby Hackett

—

Shortly after his death in the early morning of July 6, 1971, Armstrong was the subject of countless loving tributes from the world over. The Soviet poet Yevgeny Yevtushenko celebrated him in a poem ending:

Do as you did in the past
And play.
Cheer up the state of the angels,
And so the sinner won't get too
unhappy in hell,
Make their lives a bit more hopeful.
Give to Armstrong a trumpet
Angel Gabriel.

—

Over twenty thousand letters of condolence came to Lucille Armstrong in Corona, Queens, from New Zealand, Rumania, Ghana, Ireland, and elsewhere. Envelopes addressed in such quirky fashion as "Mrs. Satchmo, Queens, N.Y., America" or "Lady Louis Armstrong, New York" made it to their destination. Although there were the predictable letters from political notables such as Richard Nixon, Nelson Rockefeller, George McGovern, and Coretta Scott King, not to mention from a cast of ambassadors and professional colleagues, what touches one most profoundly are those spontaneous outpourings of sympathy and admiration from more ordinary folk.

A Connecticut newspaper editor and his wife spoke for many when he wrote:

My wife and I are not show biz people, nor are we famous or well-known in any other degree . . . just two simple human beings who cried real tears when we heard of the passing of your husband, one of the greatest people who ever walked the face of this earth, let alone blew a trumpet . . . the human race has lost a fabulous human being. Your husband has often said that his music could be understood in any language, and right he was. What he never said was that his smile was just as understandable anywhere on earth.

—

And from New South Wales, Australia, came the tribute of one who was the recipient of the Polar Medal, Antarctica. Among his comments:

Only on Wednesday night I was attending my Returned Soldiers Club and the movie . . . happened to be *Hello Dolly!* When Satchmo appeared everyone stood and clapped, our strange way of showing that we remember him in grateful remembrance. I spent three years at the South Pole, Antarctica, and how his warmth made many a lonely cold Antarctic night so much enjoyable for us. . . .

ON CHANGING THE WORLD

Writing in the celebratory Down Beat *issue of July 9, 1970, the eminent jazz critic Martin Williams began his essay, "For Louis Armstrong at 70," as follows.* —JB

Of how many American artists can it truly be said that they have changed the world in their lifetimes? I am not sure about our writers, our painters, our concert composers, but I know it can be said of a number of our popular artists. Of Richard Outcault and the comic strip. Of D.W. Griffith and the film. And Louis Armstrong.

That may seem surprising, even incongruous, to those familiar with only the genial Satchmo of the television screen, the smiling singer and occasional trumpeter who seems to entertain tired businessmen so ably. But it's true.

Armstrong's music has affected all our music, top to bottom, concert hall to barroom. No concert composers here or abroad write for brass instruments the way they used to, simply because Armstrong has shown that brass instruments, and the trumpet in particular, are capable of things that no one thought them capable of before he came along. Our symphonists play trumpet with a slight, usually unconscious vibrato that is inappropriate to Beethoven or Schubert because Armstrong has had one.

We are likely to subdivide our popular music into a multitude of ill-defined categories—jazz, rock, soul—but Armstrong has affected them all. Armstrong introduced new ideas of rhythm, and because of them, Bing Crosby sings the way he sings. So Perry Como, Dean Martin, and all the rest sing the way they sing. And so Tony Bennett's or Andy Williams's or Steve Lawrence's latest record will have a rhythmic movement and momentum that we can identify ultimately as Armstrong's, and also will have effects and figures from the accompanying orchestra that may be as old as Armstrong's earliest recordings.

Next week's arrangement that accompanies the chorus of dancers in a popular TV show will be full of watered-down Armstrong—depend on it. Our most everyday rock-and-roll groups and our simplest rhythm-and-blues bands use his ideas constantly and probably unknowingly. Wherever his music has touched down in any part of the world, it has had its effect.

—

A STAMP FOR SATCHMO

The perpetuation of Armstrong's legacy has demanded enormous dedication and perseverance on the part of all concerned. In 1977 his simple three-story house at 34-56 107th Street in Corona, Queens—he lived there from 1943 until his death in 1971—was declared a national historic landmark; it became a city landmark in 1983. Then there is the rich cache of memorabilia recovered from the house—including some 650 reel-to-reel tapes, 84 scrapbooks, some 400 books and journals, thousands of photographs, and a number of unreleased recordings—that constitutes the core of the Louis Armstrong Archives at Queens College, City University of New York. Most important, in 1996 Queens College, which administers both the Louis Armstrong House and the Louis Armstrong Archives, signed a twenty-year agreement with the estate and the city of New York to convert the house into a museum and study center. Thus one of the most cherished dreams of Lucille Armstrong, Louis's fourth and last wife, was in the process of being realized some thirteen years after her death.

But perhaps even more compelling is the fourteen-year effort involved in having a postage stamp issued in Armstrong's honor. On September 7, 1995, the new postage stamp was finally unveiled as part of an event designated as "The Stamp Dedication at Satchmo's House," even though the New York celebration was pre-empted by a national first day ceremony on September 1 in New Orleans. The street in Corona was closed to traffic; there were sales and cancelations by mobile units of the Postal Service; music was provided by Arvell Shaw and the Louis Armstrong Legacy Band with guest artists Jimmy Heath and Clark Terry. Local dignitaries graced the scene.

Putting it all in perspective is a letter written in 1981 by Lucille Armstrong to the U.S. Postal Service. Armstrong became eligible for consideration ten years after his death. (The letter is now part of the Louis Armstrong Archives Series Vertical.) Lucille Armstrong's letter is followed here by an article by Roxane Orgill, originally published in The Wall Street Journal, *September 27, 1995.* —JB

December 10, 1981

Mr. John Litner, Senior Representative
for Governmental Relations, U.S. Postal Service
Washington, D.C. 20260
Dear Mr. Litner:

It has been brought to my attention that the U.S. Postal Service Citizens' Stamp Advisory Committee is considering recommending an issuance of a commemorative stamp in the name of my husband, Louis (Satchmo) Armstrong. I am very pleased.

Louis's dedication to his country as Ambassador Plenipotentiary of America's culture, jazz, is part of our history. During World War II, he gave his services at least once a week entertaining the GI's at Army camps, he performed at rallies to help sell War Bonds. After World War II,

Louis Armstrong pictorial postmark design winner Rafael Hernandez with his father (left) and Postmaster William Rogers (right) at the unveiling of the Louis Armstrong stamp at Louis Armstrong's Corona home, September 7, 1995. Photo courtesy of the Louis Armstrong House & Archives, Queens College/CUNY.

I accompanied him on all his world travels. From 1951 to 1970, the year before he died, we traveled Europe and each alternate year we would visit the countries of the Middle East and the Orient. I remember an interesting incident occurred in 1956 while touring Australia, the Far East and Africa, at the start of a 45-concert tour arranged with the U.S. Government and Pepsi Cola sponsorship. The press wrote, "Nairobi has taken Louis Armstrong to its heart; what a wonderful ambassador Satchmo is for his country." Further along on that same trip, when Louis stepped off the Congo River ferry from Brazzaville, the rival forces of Joseph Mobutu and those loyal to Patrice Lumumba joined together to welcome him. Then again at the stadium, over 100,000 of the enemies and the foe came to enjoy and share the performance. They had stopped shooting; they didn't want any stray bullets to hurt Louis.

In the 60s, his South American trip was overwhelming. The crowds were so enthusiastic wherever we went that Louis had to call Yogi Berra back in the States to ask for a catcher's mask to fend off the fans who wished to touch his face and lips.

I also recall most vividly on one of the trips through Eastern Europe, Louis performed twice a day at a theatre in Prague. One evening among the hundreds of fans who came backstage to meet Louis were some people who told us they had come all the way from Poland via the underground and didn't know how they were going to make it back. During the same tour, the concert in Budapest drew 90,000 fans stomping and clapping; it was most thrilling. They were familiar with all of Louis's hits as his voice was heard in every corner of the globe via The Voice of America.

His contribution to the peoples of the world on behalf of the State Department and the United States of America is a vital part of our country's history. After he died, it took a staff of secretaries and myself over two years to answer the notes and letters of condolence that poured in from heads of state, as well as the man on the street from every country on the face of the earth.

Rather than continuing to relate all the reasons why Louis should be honored in this fashion by his own country, I will include some of the quotes made during and after his lifetime. Duke Ellington said, "Louis was the epitome of jazz; he is what I call an American Standard, an American original." Henry Pleasants, musicologist and author, "A living legend for over half a century, not just to his own black people, nor to the American people as a whole, but to millions of people around the world." Andre Hodeir, foremost French jazz critic, "Louis Armstrong's importance to musical history is difficult to overestimate." Gunther Schuller, President of the New England Conservatory of Music: "Amstrong's music transcended its implications; this was music for music's sake, not for the first time in jazz, to be sure, but never before in such brilliant and unequivocal form." Bing Crosby: "He is the beginning and the end of music in America."

His was a life of complete dedication to his music, the joy of performing, and to America and its people. I feel that as the wife of Louis Armstrong for over 30 years, the world would love and cherish this stamp as a tribute to one who has given so much of himself, his music, his heart, to the world, his fans.

Most sincerely,
Lucille Armstrong (Mrs. Louis)

ROXANE ORGILL

Satchmo's Stamp of Approval

New Orleans—At the recent unveiling of the Louis Armstrong 32-cent commemorative stamp, 90-year-old Adolphus "Doc" Cheatham sat with the mayor and other dignitaries, fingering the valves of his silver trumpet all through the speeches. When the New Orleans Postal Jazz Ensemble struck up "What a Wonderful World," he could wait no longer. Cutting into the clarinet solo, he pointed the bell of his horn toward heaven and sent a message to Satchmo.

The message was probably "Thank you." When Mr. Cheatham got to Chicago in the '20s, a kid from Nashville with a dollar and change in his pocket, he found the doors closed. New Orleans musicians had all the jobs. He spoke to Armstrong, and the doors opened.

Such stories about Armstrong are legion. He touched many, many people, not only as a musician—the trumpet player who originated the jazz solo, the singer who could transform a silly pop song into art music—but as a man.

Then why did it take 14 years to get his image onto a piece of prephosphored paper measuring 1.56 by 1.23 inches, coated on one side with water-activated gum? How come Elvis got there first, not to mention Howlin' Wolf?

It was certainly not for lack of public interest.

In 1981, the first year that Armstrong was eligible as a stamp subject (you must be dead at least 10 years), his widow, Lucille Armstrong, wrote a letter to the senior representative for governmental relations at the U.S. Postal Service: "It has been brought to my attention that the U.S. Postal Service Citizens' Stamp Advisory Committee is considering recommending an issuance of a commemorative stamp in the name of my husband, Louis (Satchmo) Armstrong. I am very pleased." In two single-spaced pages, she made her case, noting his status as an unofficial ambassador of goodwill, who brought temporary peace to the Congo simply by showing up to play his horn.

The Postal Service noted her suggestion, as it does 40,000 suggestions received each year. Anyone can suggest a stamp subject to the Citizens' Stamp Advisory Committee, a 15-member body appointed by the post-master general, provided the subject is "interesting and educational" and meets 12 other criteria. The committee reviews every suggestion before making recommendations to the postmaster, who makes the final decision.

To bolster the argument, the late Mrs. Armstrong and her friend Phoebe Jacobs, now vice-president of the Louis Armstrong Educational Foundation, mounted a signature campaign. With help from ASCAP, the Actor's Fund, several elected officials, musicians Quincy Jones, Marian McPartland and Benny Carter, producer George Avakian, and the student bodies of the two Louis Armstrong schools in Queens, N.Y., to name just a handful of the parties, they amassed half a million signatures in six years, Mrs. Jacobs estimates.

The Postal Service has no record of them.

"The file only goes back to 1987," said Postal Service spokesperson Monica Hand. "That's not to say they never existed," she added.

But the Postal Service does have a stack of correspondence from Donald Marquis, curator of the jazz collection at the Louisiana State Museum here in Armstrong's hometown. After the Duke Ellington stamp came out in 1986, Mr. Marquis and the New Orleans Jazz Club president, Bill Farrell, Jr., decided it was Louis's turn. Mr. Marquis put a stack of petitions atop a display case, and every three or four months, he mailed a batch of signatures to Washington. When the Postal Service decided in late 1994 to honor Armstrong with a stamp, following the lead of Burkina Faso, Chad, Dominica, Gabon, Guyana, Madagascar, Mali, Niger, Rwanda, Senegal, St. Vincent and Tanzania, Mr. Marquis did a tally. He had collected 38,765 names from all 50 states and 62 countries.

Sadly, the petitions may have had little effect. "I don't think the number of signatures is what brought the issue to the forefront," says Virginia Noelke, president of the Citizens' Stamp Advisory Committee. "He has been on our agenda consistently since he was eligible." (Don't tell that to the Swedish visitor who took the petition home and got 85 friends to sign it.)

What may have turned the tide in Washington was a bit of market research conducted by the Postal Service in 1994, which revealed Armstrong to be the most requested male subject. A new format helped also, Ms. Noelke said. The Legends of American Music series began in 1993 with Elvis Presley, and continued with other rock 'n' roll figures, Hank Williams and country musicians, "Oklahoma!" and Broadway shows, Ethel Merman, Bessie Smith, Nat King Cole, Billie Holiday and other pop, blues and jazz singers.

At the ceremony, held in Armstrong Park and hosted by the ever-eloquent Wynton Marsalis, fans wondered aloud whether Armstrong's turn would have come sooner had he not spoken out against the U.S. government during the Little Rock, Ark., school troubles of 1957. When Governor Orval Faubus refused to integrate the schools and President Eisenhower did nothing to interfere, Armstrong raised his voice, politically, for the first time. "The way they are treating my people in the South, the government can go to hell," he told the press. "The President has no guts." (Later, when Eisenhower ordered troops to Little Rock to enforce the law, Armstrong sent him a congratulatory telegram: "If you decide to walk into the schools with the colored kids, take me along, Daddy. God bless you.")

"Why else would they do Elvis Presley before Louis?" asked one admirer. The official answer, from Ms. Noelke, was that Presley's enormous fan club put such pressure on the Postal Service, via TV and newspaper stories, that the committee felt compelled to put the King on a stamp. As it turned out, the Elvis stamp is the single most popular U.S. commemorative, with a record 500 million print run, of which an astounding 124 million stamps were never used, but saved. The Armstrong stamp, by contrast, has a 150 million print run.

None of this seemed to matter one whit to Mr. Cheatham, who came to blow his horn in tribute to a pal, and ended up blowing listeners away with his sound, strong and delicate, like a spider's web, and the elegance of his phrasing. He closed out a busy week with a concert in the Blue Room of the Fairmont Hotel (formerly the Roosevelt, once famous for its radio broadcasts), where he played marvelous duets with New Orleans's current favorite resident trumpeter, Nicholas Payton, who is about 70 years his junior. Mr. Payton's sound is bright and aggressive, in contrast to Mr. Cheatham's sweet horn. The elder musician sat back, grinning, as Mr. Payton took his first solo, blowing hard and high, and sounding just a little like Satchmo himself.

THE C ABOVE C ABOVE
HIGH C

First performed at the Nuyorican Poets Café in New York's East Village (mid-May to July 6, 1997), Ishmael Reed's play The C above C above High C *presents a provocative intermingling of history, legend, and scandal. It harks back to 1957, when Armstrong, stereotyped as an Uncle Tom, had his showdown with President Dwight Eisenhower over the issue of integration at Central High School in Little Rock, Arkansas. Mr. Reed's Armstrong "sinks sharp barbs into [J. Edgar] Hoover" and chastises the president for his bigotry; the play meanwhile surrounds Armstrong with sharply profiled portrayals of his two major wives—a liberated Lillian Hardin and the strong but more home-bound Lucille Wilson. Both of these women serve as a foil for the devastated, alcoholic Mamie Eisenhower, who has lost her man to Kay Summersby. There is at the same time an evocation of the jazz of the era and its heroin addicts in the person of "Be-Bopper"—a character ready to disdain tradition and dismiss all that Armstrong is perceived to represent.*

What follows are excerpts from an interview conducted with Ishmael Reed in Oakland, California, June 24, 1997. —JB

Berrett: *What has Louis meant to you in your life, and have your perceptions of him changed in recent years?*

Reed: My perceptions of Louis Armstrong have changed over the years, since in the 1950s I was devoted to the new music, bebop. The party line for beboppers was that Louis Armstrong was an Uncle Tom and that his music was quaint. We didn't listen very much to Louis Armstrong. I just revisited a book by Dizzy Gillespie where he said he didn't listen to Louis Armstrong at all. That was the feeling in the '50s.

In the late '60s and early '70s I did some research on New Orleans culture and began to change my mind about Louis Armstrong, that he was really a bearer of tradition.

Berrett: Anything more recent that prompted the writing of your play?

Reed: In the 1980s I read a book by Gary Giddins called *Satchmo.* . . . [Giddings] sought Louis Armstrong's file under the Freedom of Information Act, and it was revealed that Louis Armstrong got into trouble with the government for saying that Dwight Eisenhower was gutless for not assisting the students in integrating Central High School in Little Rock. That brought him into conflict with J. Edgar Hoover and the Justice Department. There were files on Louis Armstrong. He also lost engagements. . . . 1957 was a very pivotal year. These three notions—that I dismissed Louis Armstrong as an Uncle Tom in the 1950s, then began to reevaluate his music and his importance to American culture in the 1970s, and then the Gary Giddins revelations—led to this play.

Berrett: Speaking of J. Edgar Hoover, what impelled you to portray him as a black transvestite?

Reed: . . . Anthony Summers . . . repeats rumors and suspicions in Washington, D.C., that J. Edgar Hoover was not really white, and Gore Vidal, the novelist, goes so far as to say that Washington society never accepted him as [i.e., becasue he was] a black man. That [portrayal] was not a case of nontraditional casting, as one critic said. . . .

Berrett: What has been your experience with the reception of the play? Has it been performed in venues other than the Nuyorican Poets Café?

Reed: The play was selected to be performed at the National Black Theater Festival that's going to be held in August [1997] in Winston-Salem, North Carolina, and also there's a move here in Oakland on the part of the Oakland Arts Council to bring it to Oakland in 1998.

—

Berrett: Do you listen to much of Armstrong's actual music?

Reed: I've been listening to [Armstrong's music] in recent years. I'm just amazed by his range and his subtlety. And also you can hear how he really shaped modern music, even though he had conflicts with the beboppers. If it [had] not been for Louis Armstrong's quality of improvisation there would have been no bebop. Someone even described swing as orchestrated Armstrong. Also, his influence on modern musicians—that should have been a tip-off for me. Billie Holiday is as hip as they come—one of the icons of modern jazz—yet she is obviously influenced by Armstrong. His influence is all over the place.

Berrett: Are you happy with the play in its present form? Are you going to do any revising?

Reed: I did revising until even after the first performance. I had a very good cast; they went out and did some research that I found very useful. For example, the first actress who played Kay Summersby (Susan Carr) found a biography that I couldn't obtain in Oakland . . . so I was able to add about a dozen lines in the scene between Kay Summersby and Eisenhower that were based on reading that book. The cast went way beyond merely acting. They contributed to the research. One actress who played Mamie Eisenhower was able to get us actual footage of things that we really needed, tapes, and things regarding Armstrong. . . .

Berrett: What's your feeling about your portrayal of Mamie Eisenhower? What is the separation between fact and fiction?

Reed: There isn't all that much separation between fact and fiction in the play. I think two scenes, the scenes between Kay Summersby and Eisenhower and the scene between Eisenhower and Louis Armstrong, are made up, obviously. But a lot of the lines and the comments are based upon fact. For example, Eisenhower did have a racist attitude towards school integration; he was a supporter of the Confederacy, made racist remarks about African-Americans, about Asians. According to a book called *Nixon's Piano,* which I used in my research, he was known for making racist jokes. But, at the same time he stood up to the mob. I went back to look at the newspaper clippings . . . it was so rare that an American president would use troops against citizens that the newspapers of the times were always referring to Shays's Rebellion. . . . . Yet he did it against the Southerners, and he stood up for law, which is quite different from modern politicians, who wait to see the polls. . . .

A QUILT FOR THE FUTURE

PS 143 is located at 34-74 113th Street, six short blocks from the Louis Armstrong House in Corona, Queens, New York. Formerly the Meadow School, it officially changed its name to the Louis Armstrong School in May 1977. In addition, there is also the Louis Armstrong Middle School (IS 227) at 30-02 Junction Boulevard in East Elmhurst. Both schools adopted the Armstrong name with the full blessing of Lucille Armstrong. Marianne Veidt, a dynamic, dedicated teacher at PS 143, retired in January 1997 after thirty-two years of service. Excerpts from a March 27, 1997 interview with her follow.—JB

About three years ago [around 1994] I got involved with the Queens Museum of Art. . . . . The head of their education department, Sharon Vatsky, was interested in getting a neighborhood collaboration going with the museum. Because of our proximity she thought there might be something we could do in education using the facilities of the museum. The Smithsonian, [which] had a traveling exhibit on the legacy of Louis Armstrong . . . was to open in the Queens Museum of Art because Louis had come from Corona. We wrote a federal Institute of Museum Services grant . . . for the children to get involved with that whole exhibit, and what we did was train fifteen fourth-graders and fifteen fifth-graders to be docents at the museum. They went to workshops, they saw the exhibit before it was open to the public, they knew what was going to be in it, they learned about Louis . . . they did all kinds of activities to get them involved with Louis Armstrong; that was a year-long project.

One of the activities that I did with them was the making of the quilt. We brainstormed what parts of Louis's life we would like to illustrate in a quilt. I had done quilting before. The last time I had a class, in 1986, I entered the New York Mets contest; they had a contest called "Teamwork," and I had made a quilt on the Mets. We won citywide and had a barbecue with the Mets, and the kids and their parents were invited. . . . A purist in quilting would look at that and say it's not really a quilt; it's more of a patchwork banner, but we called it quilting for our purposes. We brainstormed with the thirty children—what squares they would like to do, what they thought was representative of Louis. We talked about his life span, his music, where he was born, the cities he went to . . . Chicago, New York, Hollywood. We wanted to do one on the records, one on his films, and we came up with these ideas for the quilt, and we made patterns, we cut magazine pictures, made a little pattern— just they way you'd make a dress—and made all the pieces out of felt. Boys and girls worked together, and we did it in our spare time. I met with them; they took their own little square home and worked on it. I ended up doing most of the sewing, but I did teach them some of the overhand stitches, and things like that. Then we had to put it together. I think there were twenty-five panels.

It's a Title I school, which means most of the families are on assistance; it's a low socio-economic area. . . . Shortly after Louis's death we asked Mrs. Armstrong if we could change the name of the school to honor Louis. She gave her permission, and we put in our petition to the Board of Education. While she was alive Lucille used to come to the school and award our top medal at graduation, the Louis Armstrong Achievement Award. We have a plaque in the school, a bust by James Counts, a painting by Elton Fax— commissioned by our PTA—and this was all done in her lifetime.

Every year they [the Louis Armstrong House] have their concert "Pops Is Tops," and they invite children from our school. I was always in charge arranging the trips; they sit in Louis's yard and they are able to listen to his music.

That very famous picture that's always used with Louis sitting on the stoop playing the horn, and the children are there. Well, two of them were in my class—Willie Johnson, and he's got a brother, Johnny, but Willie's the little one holding the horn. At the end of the grant that I had with the museum . . . when I made the quilt we filled our gymnasium . . . with all the projects the children had made during the year, and all my personal memorabilia that I have of Louis. He [Willie] came; he still lives in the neighborhood across the street from where Louis was . . . he came that night.

Unfortunately I never knew Louis myself. I was working at the school when he was still alive. This Willie Johnson brought me a signed portrait of Louis, a black-and-white photo where he wrote "To Miss Viedt" [*sic*]— and I yelled at the child because he spelled my name wrong. I said, oh my God, how long are you in my class and you don't know how to spell my

Louis Armstrong with neighborhood children on the steps of his home in Corona, New York. Photo: Louis Armstrong House & Archives at Queens College/CUNY.

name! That's a treasure I have because I never met him myself. I really got interested in all this after his death when we started to know Lucille; she used to come to the school quite often.

⟡

When Lucille was alive Phoebe Jacobs [vice-president of the Louis Armstrong Educational Foundation] used to come with her to the school. . . . I used to do all these big extravagant shows for Black History Month. . . . We had a weeklong celebration. One year when Lucille was around she used her influence to get friends of Louis to come . . . got us a piano player and some musicians. . . . Jimmy Heath lives right across the street from the school.

Ethnically the school has changed. We are more than 80 percent Hispanic now, and so I was even more determined in the last few years to see that Louis was not forgotten, because Latinos love jazz, but they just don't know. So many children, you'd say to them: "Who is your school named after?" And they'd look at you . . . didn't have the vaguest idea, because they're not born here and they really don't know. We're doing the best we can to perpetuate his memory through the school; that's a living landmark to him.

Chronology

1901

Aug. 4   Born in area of Jane Alley, New Orleans to Mary Albert and common-law husband, William Armstrong. Baptized three weeks later into Catholic Church; father has already abandoned mother.

1906

"Second lining," that is, follows brass bands in parades.

1907

Begins attending Fisk School for Boys and starts working for Russian-Jewish Karnofsky family in junk business; Karnofskys help buy his first cornet.

1908–10

First ventures into Storyville, delivering coal to cribs; likely hears Joe Oliver playing at Pete Lala's Cabaret. Possible first contact with Oliver, the latter as member of marching ensemble, the Onward Brass Band.

1912

Drops out of Fisk School middle of fifth grade. Joins vocal quartet as tenor. Attracts attention of Bunk Johnson, Black Benny, and Sidney Bechet.

Dec. 31   Arrested for firing pistol into sky, locked up overnight in New Orleans Juvenile Court House.

1913

Jan. 1   Sentenced to Colored Waif's Home; there becomes bugler and plays in band.

1914

June 16   Released from Waif's Home to custody of father and stepmother; moves with them to heart of the Battlefield, at Miro and Poydras Streets; cares for two younger stepbrothers.

late 1914   Rejoins mother Mayann and sister at Liberty and Perdido Streets. Brought by Black Benny to National Park to sit in with Kid Ory's band. Begins playing at Henry Ponce's honky-tonk.

1915–16

Delivers coal for C. A. Andrews Coal Company, while continuing at Henry Ponce's; tonk later closes.

Aug. 8, 1915
Second cousin Clarence born; becomes primary breadwinner for Mayann, Mama Lucy, and Clarence. Sells newspapers; brief spell as a pimp; regularly employed by Kid Ory. Bonds with Joe Oliver.

1917

Nov. 12
Prostitution declared illegal in Storyville. Armstrong departs for Houma, La., to work in funeral band. Returns to New Orleans to rejoin Mayann; plays in Henry Matranga's tonk; hauls coal; purchases first Victrola and jazz and opera records.

1918

Registers at local draft board.

June
Joe "King" Oliver leaves for Chicago; takes Oliver's place in Kid Ory's band. Creates sensation at Pete Lala's doing the Shimmy; song and dance routine becomes known as "I Wish I Could Shimmy Like My Sister Kate." Rivalry between Creole reading musicians of Robichaux Orchestra and "hot" musicians of Kid Ory's band. Joins Oscar Celestin's Tuxedo Brass Band. Attracted to prostitutes at Brick House; becomes involved with first wife, Daisy Parker.

1919

Noticed by Fate Marable; offered place in Marable's reading orchestra aboard Mississippi riverboat *Sidney* of Streckfus Steamboat Line. Plays alongside Baby and Johnny Dodds and Johnny St. Cyr.

1920

June–Sept. Works boat excursions out of St. Louis; based in New Orleans rest of year.

Summer Meets Bix Beiderbecke in Davenport, Iowa.

1921

Sept.
Leaves Fate Marable; returns to New Orleans. Works in Tom Anderson's Cabaret Club; with Zutty Singleton; also with Tuxedo Brass Band and other groups.

1922

Continues association with Oscar Celestin and Kid Ory.

Summer Marriage to Daisy Parker ends.

Aug.
Receives telegram to join "Papa Joe" Oliver at Lincoln Gardens, Chicago, as second cornet.

Aug. 8 Leaves New Orleans aboard the 7 P.M. Illinois Central.

1923

Continues at Lincoln Gardens through late Feb.; then tours Illinois, Ohio, and Indiana.

Apr. 5   First recordings, for Gennett, in Richmond, Indiana; returns with Oliver's band to Chicago.

1924

Jan.   Based at Lincoln Gardens.

Feb. 5   Marriage to Lillian Hardin in Chicago.

Feb.– early June   Tours Illinois, Indiana, Pennsylvania, Ohio, Michigan, and Wisconsin with Oliver.

June   Leaves Oliver, works briefly with Ollie Powers's band in Chicago.

Sept.   Joins Fletcher Henderson Orchestra at Roseland Ballroom, New York.

Oct. 7   First recording with Henderson; ten days later records with Sidney Bechet, for Okeh. Begins backing blues singers, including Sippie Wallace, Josephine Beatty, and Clara Smith.

1925

Jan. 14   Records with Bessie Smith; with Fletcher Henderson at Roseland Ballroom until May 31.

Summer   Tours Connecticut, Maine, Maryland, Massachusetts, and Pennsylvania with Henderson.

Fall   Active in studio with Clarence Williams and Perry Bradford.

Nov.   Leaves Henderson; joins Lil Armstrong at the Dreamland Café, Chicago.

Nov. 12   First Hot Five recordings.

Dec.   Engagements with Erskine Tate's Orchestra at Vendome Theater; orchestra plays for silent movies, including overtures and operatic excerpts.

1926

Continues at Dreamland; records with Erskine Tate; also with singers Sippie Wallace, Hociel Thomas, and others. Hot Five sessions interspersed among sessions with vocalists and acts such as Butterbeans and Susie.

Apr.   Joins Carroll Dickerson Orchestra at Sunset Café; meets Joe Glaser. Works with Dickerson and Tate for balance of year.

1927

Leaves Dickerson and leads own big band, "Louis Armstrong and his Stompers," at Sunset Café.

Apr.   Begins doubling with Clarence Jones's Orchestra at Metropolitan Theater; also leads at Sunset and works other venues.

1928

Works with Clarence Jones and Carroll Dickerson for most of year.

May   Brief stint with drummer Floyd Campbell aboard SS *Saint Paul* out of St. Louis.

June–July   Last recording sessions with Hot Five; June 28 session with Earl Hines features "West End Blues."

1929

Regularly featured at Savoy Ballroom, Chicago, with Carroll Dickerson Orchestra; appears in Detroit and St. Louis.

Mar.   Brief return to New York guesting with Luis Russell's band; in Chicago involved with producer-manager Tommy Rockwell.

mid-May   Begins series of touring one-nighters with Dickerson; rehearses in Philadelphia for Vincent Youmans show *Great Day*.

June 24   Begins four-month residency at Connie's Inn, New York. Same month first appears in *Hot Chocolates* show at Hudson Theater on Broadway.

July 19, 22   Records "Ain't Misbehavin'" and "What Did I Do to Be So Black and Blue?"; more theater work follows.

1930

Jan.–Feb.   With Luis Russell's band; appearing in Washington, D.C., Baltimore, and Chicago.

Feb.–May   With Mills Blue Rhythm Band; dates in New York, Baltimore, Philadelphia, Pittsburgh, Detroit, and Chicago.

July   Starts as cabaret soloist at Frank Sebastian's Cotton Club in Culver City, California.

Aug. 19   Records "I'm Confessin'," in Los Angeles, recording shows Bing Crosby influence.

late   Films *Ex-Flame* (now lost).
Aug.–Oct.

1931

Mar.   Busted for smoking marijuana, spends nine days in Los Angeles City jail; enter Johnny Collins, fixer-manager.

Apr.   Begins residency at Show Boat, Chicago; threatened there at gunpoint.

mid-May   Leaves Chicago with Collins and band, tours from Illinois to West Virginia.

Summer   New Orleans.

Sept.–Oct.   Swings through Texas, Oklahoma, Tennessee, Missouri, Ohio; "backfiring affidavits" in legal suit brought by Tommy Rockwell.

1932

Jan.–Feb.   Theater dates in Boston, New Haven, Jersey City, and New York. Appears in California at Frank Sebastian's Cotton Club.

July–Oct.   Departs New York bound for England aboard SS *Majestic;* opens at London Palladium July 18; tours the U.K.; then returns to New York.

Nov. 26–   At Lafayette Theater in *Hot Chocolates;* balance of year with Chick Webb's
Dec. 2   band in Philadelphia and Washington, D.C.

1933

Jan.   Joins band organized by Zilner Randolph; tours Illinois, Kentucky, Indiana, and Nebraska.

mid-July   In Philadelphia with Hardy Brothers' Band.

late July   Leaves New York bound for England and Europe aboard SS *Homeric;* showdown with Johnny Collins in mid-Atlantic (Jack Hylton becomes his manager during September).

July 28   Broadcasts on BBC from London Palladium, then tours the U.K.

late Fall   Tours Denmark, Norway, Sweden, and Holland; back in London in December.

1934

Apr.   Moves to Paris for long vacation.

Nov.   Appears at Salle Pleyel; befriended by Hugues Panassié, Stephane Grappelli, Django Reinhardt, and others. Tours Belgium, Switzerland, and Italy.

1935

Jan. 24   Returns to New York; career in financial disarray.

May (?)   A handshake agreement in Chicago with Joe Glaser leads to final managerial change.

July 1   Opens in Indianapolis with new band directed by Zilner Randolph; tours Midwest and South.

Oct. 29   Begins residency at Connie's Inn, New York.

Nov.   Featured in *Vanity Fair.*

1936

Feb.   Again featured in *Vanity Fair,* with classical violinist Fritz Kreisler.

Mar.   appears at Apollo Theater and at Metropolitan in Boston.

May   Begins theater tour with band, visiting Pittsburgh, Detroit, St. Louis, Chicago, and Kansas City.

Aug.	Films *Pennies from Heaven* in California.
Sept.–Dec.	Tours West Virginia, Chicago, Savannah, St. Louis, Youngstown, and Akron; publication of *Swing That Music*.

1937

Jan.	Enters Provident Hospital, Chicago for minor throat surgery; tours Nebraska, Massachusetts, and Pennsylvania; in New York in early April.
Apr. 9	Begins hosting national radio program, *Fleischmann's Yeast Hour,* as replacement for singer Rudy Vallee.
May	Appears at Chicago's Regal Theater and New York's Apollo; films *Artists & Models* in California.
Late May	Tours Connecticut, Pennsylvania, Massachusetts, and the South.
Oct.	Returns to California to film *Every Day's a Holiday;* performs there November and December.

1938

late Jan.	Concludes residency at Cotton Club in Culver City.
Jan. 28–Mar. 9	Grand Terrace, Chicago; dates in Indianapolis, Pittsburgh, New York, and Cincinnati.
June–Sept.	Tours South, including New Orleans; after August 17 filming *Going Places;* late September starts tour of Mississippi, Louisiana, Alabama, and Georgia.
Sept. 30	Divorces Lil Hardin.
Oct. 11	Marries Alpha Smith in Houston. Performs in New Orleans, Memphis, Kansas City, Detroit, Chicago.
Oct. 19	Plays all-star jam session in New York on WNEW.
Dec.	New York's Apollo; also guest vocalist at Paul Whiteman's Christmas Eve Concert in Carnegie Hall.

1939

Feb. 20	Records with Casa Loma Orchestra on Decca; records "Happy Birthday" tribute to Bing Crosby.
Oct. 14	Appears with Benny Goodman Orchestra at Waldorf Astoria.
Nov. 29	Opens at Rockefeller Center as Bottom in *Swingin' the Dream.*
Dec. 18	Broadcasts from Cotton Club, New York.

1940

Apr. 5	Ends Cotton Club residency.
Apr. 10	Records with Mills Brothers in New York.
May 27	Reunites with Sidney Bechet for Decca session.

Aug.–Dec. Tours Alabama, Georgia, South Carolina, and Iowa; Mississippi and Florida.

1941

Performs at military bases; June in Ontario, Canada.

Oct. 21 Broadcasts from Grand Terrace, Chicago; again on November 27.

1942

Aug. Ban on recording threatened by Petrillo's American Federation of Musicians takes effect; records "soundies" based on such hits as "When It's Sleepy Time Down South" and "Shine."

Sept. 2 Records for *Cabin in the Sky*.

Oct. 12 Marries Lucille Wilson in St. Louis.

Dec. 25 Plays Fort Benning, Ga.

1943

Mar. Makes permanent home at 34-56 107th Street, Corona, N.Y.

Apr. 23 Films *Jam Session*. Active on Armed Forces Radio Service.

Nov. 7 Broadcasts on NBC.

1944

Jan. 18 Appears in jam session at Metropolitan Opera House, New York, as winner in first *Esquire* jazz poll. New band formed under Teddy McRae.

Apr.–May Sessions with Dexter Gordon and Velma Middleton.

June Films *Atlantic City*.

Aug. Records big band arrangements in Los Angeles with Teddy McRae, Dexter Gordon, Dorothy Dandridge, and others; films *Pillow to Post*.

Dec. 7 Midnight V-disc recording session with all-star cast, including Jack Teagarden, for distribution to military bases.

1945

Jan. 17 Second *Esquire* all-American Jazz Concert in Municipal Auditorium, New Orleans; simulcast coast-to-coast with Benny Goodman and Duke Ellington Orchestra.

Feb. 11 WNEW Fats Waller Memorial Show, New York.

Feb. 13 Broadcasts from the New Zanzibar. AFRS performances throughout the year.

1946

Jan. 10 Concert of *Esquire* all-American Award winners, including Johnny Hodges, Duke Ellington, and Billy Strayhorn.

Apr.–Aug.	Tours; residencies at Aquarium and Apollo, New York, Regal and Savoy Ballroom, Chicago.
Aug.–Oct.	Performs and records with Billie Holiday and his own big band in Los Angeles.
Sept. 5–Oct. 8	Films *New Orleans* in Hollywood.

1947

Feb. 8	Appears at Carnegie Hall with Edmond Hall Sextet and his own big band.
Feb. 18	WNEW broadcast with Jack Teagarden and others.
Apr. 26	"This Is Jazz" broadcast moderated by Rudi Blesh.
May 17	Town Hall, New York, concert featuring both Louis Armstrong Quartet and the All Stars.
June 19	NBC broadcasts performance with All Stars at New York's Winter Garden Theater; coincides with world premiere of *New Orleans*.
July 16–17	Films *A Song Is Born*.
Aug. 9	Giants of Jazz concert in Los Angeles with Tommy Dorsey, Benny Goodman, and others.
Aug. 13	All Stars debut at Billy Berg's, Hollywood.
Nov. 30	All Stars in concert, Symphony Hall, Boston.

1948

Feb. 22–28	All Stars in concert at Nice Jazz Festival, France.
Mar.	Broadcasts from Zürich, Switzerland.
June 2–12	Broadcasts from Ciro's, Philadelphia.
early Sept.	Broadcasts on WCAU and KYW in Philadelphia.
Oct. 29	Civic Auditorium, Pasadena, California.
Nov. 23	WPIX-TV, New York.
Dec. 11	Damon Runyon Cancer Research ABC broadcast from Chicago's Blue Note.

1949

Feb. 21	In San Francisco for *Bing Crosby Show;* appears on cover of *Time* with feature story on role as King of Zulus in Mardi Gras.
late Mar.	Broadcasts with All Stars from Hollywood's Empire Room.
June 11	On *Eddie Condon Floor Show,* NBC-TV; same on August 27, September 3 and 10.
Oct.–Nov.	With All Stars in Zürich, Marseilles, and Trieste, Italy.

1950

Jan. 18   San Francisco for Bing Crosby's *Chesterfield* TV show.

Jan. 27   All Stars broadcast, San Francisco.

Apr. 25   U.S. Treasury Department guest-starring with All Stars; again on May 7.

June 26   Appears with Sy Oliver's orchestra, New York.

Late Aug.   With Louis Jordan and his Tympany Five; with Ella Fitzgerald and Sy Oliver orchestra.

Oct. 10   Part of Ted Steele's "Cavalcade of Bands" in New York.

Dec. 17   On *The Big Show*, TV show with Bob Hope and Tallulah Bankhead.

1951

mid-Jan.   Films *The Strip*.

Jan.–Feb.   On Bing Crosby's *Chesterfield* TV show; Vancouver, British Columbia, Canada, with All Stars; Gene Norman's Just Jazz Concert, Pasadena, California; with Gordon Jenkins orchestra in Los Angeles.

Apr.–July   All Stars concerts.

Sept. 25   New York, Milton Berle's *Texaco* TV show.

mid-Nov.   Films *Glory Alley*.

Nov. 23   With Ella Fitzgerald and Dave Barbour's orchestra, Los Angeles.

Nov. 28   With Bing Crosby on *Chesterfield* TV show, Los Angeles.

1952

Jan. 1   With Frank Sinatra on CBS-TV.

Feb. 1   With All Stars in Vancouver, Canada; March 19, Denver, Colorado.

June 8   "U.S. Royal Tire TV Showcase."

June 28   *Abbott and Costello* TV show.

Oct.   West Berlin, Hamburg, Lausanne, Florence, Brussels, and Dortmund with All Stars.

Dec. 20   *Tallulah Bankhead* TV show, New York.

1953

late Feb.–   With Sy Oliver's orchestra, Detroit; then tours with the All Stars; July and
June   August at Blue Note, Chicago.

June 5–   Films *The Glenn Miller Story*.
Sept. 21

Dec. 31   With All Stars in Yokohama, Japan.

1954

Jan. 16   Club Hangover, San Francisco, with All Stars.

Jan. 20   Broadcasts on CKNW, Vancouver, Canada.

Feb.–Dec.   Tours with All Stars; in August *Ebony* publishes "Why I Like Dark Women"; publication of *Satchmo: My Life in New Orleans* by Prentice-Hall.

1955

Jan.–Feb.   Crescendo Club, Los Angeles; Absinthe House, New Orleans.

Feb. 26   *Horace Heidt* TV show, New York.

Apr.–May   With All Stars in New York.

May 15   *Ed Sullivan Show.*

June 4   "All Star Parade of Bands," NBC.

Oct.–Dec.   Tours in Sweden, Amsterdam, Rome, and Milan with All Stars.

1956

Jan.–May   With All Stars in Los Angeles; films segments of *High Society.*

May 24   Accra Airport, Ghana; performs with some of All Stars and local musicians.

June 1   With All Stars at Medinah Temple, Chicago, for Multiple Sclerosis concert.

July–Aug.   Voice of America broadcasts Newport Jazz Festival; *Ed Sullivan Show*; performs with Leonard Bernstein, Ella Fitzgerald, and Oscar Peterson.

Sept. 17   "Producer's Showcase," NBC-TV, New York.

Dec. 18   Performs with Royal Philharmonic Orchestra in Royal Festival Hall, London, in benefit for Hungarian and Central European Relief Fund.

1957

Jan.   *Danny Kaye Show; Ed Sullivan Show.*

July–Aug.   Newport Jazz Festival; performs with Ella Fitzgerald, Oscar Peterson, and others.

Sept. 18   In Grand Forks, North Dakota, speaks out against U.S. government regarding handling of events in Little Rock, Ark.: "government can go to hell"; cancels State Department–sponsored tour.

Oct. 13   *Ford Edsel* TV show.

late Oct.   Performs with Oscar Peterson, Herb Ellis, and others; Los Angeles, National Tuberculosis Association concert with All Stars; tours with All Stars of South America.

Dec. 30   NBC *Timex Show* with All Stars. United Artists releases *Satchmo the Great,* documentary by Edward R. Murrow and Fred Friendly.

1958

Feb. 4   With Sy Oliver's choir and orchestra, New York.

Apr. 30   NBC *Timex Show,* New York.

July 7   With All Stars at Newport Jazz Festival.

Sept.–Oct.   With All Stars in Los Angeles; films *The Five Pennies.*

Oct. 22–   Films *The Beat Generation.*
early Nov.

Nov. 10   NBC *Timex Show,* Bal Harbour, Florida.

1959

Jan. 1   With All Stars at Frank's Steakhouse, Queens, New York.

Jan. 7   With Dizzy Gillespie on "Timex All-Star Jazz Show," CBS-TV, New York.

mid-Jan.–   Tour dates in Sweden, Copenhagen, Antwerp, Amsterdam. Hamburg,
late June   Vienna, and Spoleto, Italy.

June 22   Stricken with heart attack and hospitalized in Spoleto, Italy.

early July   Returns to U.S.

Aug.   Returns to performing; appears with Dukes of Dixieland; with All Stars as part of Playboy Jazz Festival.

Sept. 20   *Ed Sullivan Show,* Las Vegas.

Sept. 27   New York, the *Bing Crosby Oldsmobile* TV show; tours through the rest of year.

1960

Jan. 1   Appears on *Bell Telephone Hour,* NBC-TV, New York.

Mar. 22   Broadcasts on Voice of America.
–26

June 7   Appears on *CBS World Series of Jazz,* TV show.

June   With Bing Crosby in Los Angeles.
28–30

July 1   Newport Jazz Festival with All Stars.

Oct.   Lusaka, Zambia.

mid-Dec.   Records and films for *Paris Blues* in Paris.

1961

Jan. 19   *Chevrolet* TV show.

early Feb.   TV shows in Munich and Berlin.

Apr. 3   Performs with Duke Ellington, Trummy Young, Barney Bigard, and others.

June   Broadcasts from Sunnybrook Ballroom, Pottstown, Pa.

July 2   *Ed Sullivan Show,* New York; again on October 15 and December 17.

July 4   Newport Jazz Festival.

Sept. 12   Performs in New York with Dave Brubeck, Joe Morello, and others.
–13

1962

Feb.–Apr.   Tours Europe; with All Stars in Stockholm, Sweden; broadcasts with All Stars from Hamburg; *Ed Sullivan Show* from army base in West Berlin; Stuttgart and Munich; Manchester, England; Rome, with All Stars; Nice, France.

June 29   *Ed Sullivan Show,* New York.

July 7   Newport Jazz Festival.

July 19   *Steve Allen Show,* NBC-TV.

Dec. 14   *Ed Sullivan Show* from Guantanamo Naval Base, Cuba.

Dec. 31   With All Stars at Cocoanut Grove, Los Angeles.

1963

Mar.–May Tours Australia and Japan with All Stars.

July 2   Newport Jazz Festival.

Dec. 3   With All Stars plus strings records "Hello Dolly!" for Kapp Records in New York.

1964

Jan. 13–17 *Mike Douglas Show* with All Stars.

Mar.   In Beth Israel Hospital, New York, for treatment of acute swelling in lower right leg.

Mar. 22   *What's My Line?,* NBC-TV. Plays dates in Las Vegas later in March.

Apr.–Nov. With All Stars. Week of May 9, "Hello, Dolly!" displaces the Beatles as number one on the pop charts; Armstrong and All Stars playing Puerto Rico.

1965

Feb.   With All Stars on *Bell Telephone Hour,* NBC-TV, New York; with All Stars in Miami, Florida.

Mar.   Broadcasts from Prague; performs in East Berlin and Höchst, Germany.

Apr. 9   In U.S., takes off six weeks for dental surgery.

May 1   *Hollywood Palace* TV show, Los Angeles.

May 25   Flies to England for concert tour.

June 4   Palais des Sports, Paris.

late July	Films *When the Boys Meet the Girls.*
Sept. 17	Voice of America broadcasts All Stars from Monterey Jazz Festival.
Oct.	*Dean Martin Show,* Los Angeles; again on December 9; plays New Orleans for first time in 12 years.
Nov. 4	*Shindig,* ABC-TV, New York; again on November 11.
Nov. 22– early Dec.	Films *A Man Called Adam.*
Dec. 27	*I've Got a Secret,* NBC-TV, New York.

1966

until July	Sporadic playing with All Stars; also stint with Guy Lombardo's Orchestra; through late summer performs in New Jersey.
Nov. 3	*Dean Martin Show.*
Nov. 16	*Danny Kaye Show.*

1967

Apr. 24	With All Stars on NBC "Grammy" TV show in New York.
May 11	With All Stars on *Johnny Carson Show;* again on August 16.
late May	Bout with pneumonia.
June 25 –27	CBS *Kraft Music Hall* TV show.
July	Tours Ohio, Atlantic City, Dublin, Antibes, St. Tropez, Majorca, Copenhagen, and Juan-Les-Pins, France, with All Stars.
Sept. 14	"All That Brass," with Herb Alpert and Tijuana Brass in New York.
Dec. 20	"Operation Entertainment," ABC-TV, from Fort Hood; again December 21 from Killeen, Texas.
Dec. 30	With All Stars in Miami on *Jackie Gleason Show.*

1968

Jan. 1	With All Stars at Tropicana Hotel, Las Vegas.
Feb.	San Remo Festival, Italy; tours with All Stars in Pennsylvania, Maine, Mexico, New York.
early May	On set of *Hello Dolly!*
June	New Orleans Jazz Festival; "What a Wonderful World" a top hit.
July	On BBC program *Desert Island Discs;* with All Stars on BBC-TV; on Voice of America; with All Stars in Las Vegas.
Sept.–Dec.	In Beth Israel Hospital, New York, suffering from shortness of breath and acute heart failure; swelling of belly, legs, and face.

1969

Jan.   Briefly released from Beth Israel. Reenters in February, remains there until April.

Mar. 31   Shocked by sight of Joe Glaser in coma, begins writing about Karnofsky family and early years in New Orleans.

June 6   Death of Joe Glaser.

Oct. 28   Records film soundtrack for *On Her Majesty's Secret Service* in London.

1970

Jan. 13   *Dick Cavett Show*, ABC-TV.

Feb. 11   On *David Frost Show*.

Feb. 13   On *Johnny Carson Show*; again on April 3.

late May   New York, "Louis Armstrong and His Friends," with arrangements by Oliver Nelson.

early June   On TV shows with Mike Douglas and David Frost.

July 10   Newport Jazz Festival with Bobby Hackett and others.

July 29   *Dick Cavett Show*.

Aug.   *David Frost Show*; Nashville, Tenn., with Nashville Rhythm Section.

Oct. 10   On *Johnny Cash Show*.

Oct. 22   *Flip Wilson Show*.

Oct. 29   Astoria, London, for charity concert.

1971

Jan. 23   On ABC-TV with Pearl Bailey.

Jan. 29   At National Press Club, Washington, D.C., with Tyree Glenn and others.

Feb.   *David Frost Show; Dick Cavett Show*.

Mar.   *Johnny Carson Show*; against doctor's orders plays two-week engagement with All Stars in Waldorf Astoria's Empire Room.

late Mar.–May   Suffers heart attack on March 15 and reenters Beth Israel Hospital; kept in intensive care until mid-April. Insists on discharging himself on May 6.

July 6   At approximately 5 A.M. dies in sleep at home in Corona, New York.

Selected Discography of Recommended CD Reissues

Portrait of the Artist as a Young Man, 1923–34
Columbia/Legacy 57176 (4-CD set)
Released 1994

The Complete RCA Victor Recordings
RCA 09026-68682-2 (4-CD set)
Released 1997

The Complete Decca Studio Recordings of Louis Armstrong and the All Stars
Mosaic MD 6-146 (6-CD set) (available from Mosaic Records, 35 Melrose Place, Stamford, CT 06902)
Released 1993

The Essence of Louis Armstrong
Columbia/Legacy CK 47916
Released 1991

The Hot Fives, Vol. I
Columbia Jazz Masterpieces, CK 44049
Released 1988

The Hot Fives and Hot Sevens, Vol. II
Columbia Jazz Masterpieces, CK 44253
Released 1988

Rhythm Saved the World
Decca GRD-602
Released 1992

Satchmo the Great
Columbia/Sony CK 53580
Released 1994

Stardust
Portrait RK 44093
Released 1988

The California Concerts
Decca GRD 4-613 (4-CD set)
Released 1992

The Great Chicago Concert, 1956
Columbia/Legacy C2K 65119 (2-CD set)
Released 1997

The Complete Louis Armstrong and Duke Ellington Sessions
Roulette CDP 7938442
Released 1990

The Complete Ella Fitzgerald and Louis Armstrong
Verve 314 537 284-2 (3-CD set)
Released 1997

Louis Armstrong Plays W. C. Handy
Columbia/Legacy CK 64925
Released 1997

Louis Armstrong and Earl Hines
Columbia Jazz Masterpieces, CK 45142
Released 1994

Louis Armstrong with Oscar Peterson
Verve 833293-2 (2-CD set)
Released 1987

Louis Armstrong and His All Stars: Satch Plays Fats
Columbia/Sony CK 40378
Released 1994

16 Most Requested Songs
Columbia/Legacy CK 57900
Released 1994

Toyama Yoshio: What a Wonderful World, American Classic
Columbia COCC-13558
Released 1996

Selected Bibliography

Adorno, Theodor. "Perennial Fashion: Jazz." In *Prisms,* trans. Samuel Weber and Sherry Weber. Cambridge, Massachusetts: MIT Press, 1981.

Albert, Richard N., ed. *From Blues to Bop*. Baton Rouge, Louisiana: Louisiana State University Press, 1990.

Armstrong, Louis. *Swing That Music*. New York: Longmans Green, 1936 (reprint, New York: Da Capo, 1993).

———. "My Kicks in Europe," parts 1–4, *The Melody Maker,* June 28, July 12, August 23, August 30, 1952.

———. "Why I Like Dark Women," *Ebony,* August 1954.

———. *Satchmo: My Life in New Orleans*. New York: Prentice-Hall, 1954 (reprint, New York: Da Capo, 1986).

———. "Daddy, How the Country Has Changed!" *Ebony,* May 1961.

Babcock-Abrahams, Barbara. "A Tolerated Margin of Mess: The Trickster and His Tales Reconsidered." *Journal of the Folklore Institute* 11 (1975): 147–86.

Baraka, Amiri. *Blues People*. New York: Morrow, 1963.

Bechet, Sidney. *Treat It Gentle*. (reprint, New York: Da Capo Press, 1976).

Berrett, Joshua. "Louis Armstrong and Opera," *The Musical Quarterly* 76, no. 2 (Summer 1992): 216–41.

Bergreen, Laurence. *Louis Armstrong: An Extravagant Life*. New York: Broadway Books, 1997.

Blesh, Rudi. *Shining Trumpets*. New York: Knopf, 1946. Rev. ed. 1958 (reprint, New York: Da Capo, 1976).

Bogle, Donald. *Toms, Coons, Mulattoes, Mammies, and Bucks: An Interpretive History of Blacks in American Films*. New York: Viking Press, 1992.

Borneman, Ernest. "Bop Will Kill Business Unless It Kills Itself First: Louis Armstrong," *Down Beat,* April 7, 1948.

Caffey, H. David. "The Musical Style of Louis Armstrong, 1925–1929." *Journal of Jazz Studies* iii/1 (Fall 1975): 72–96.

Chilton, John. *Sidney Bechet: The Wizard of Jazz*. New York: Oxford University Press, 1987.

Collier, James Lincoln. *Louis Armstrong: An American Genius*. New York: Oxford University Press, 1983.

———. *The Reception of Jazz in America: A New View*. Brooklyn, Institute for Studies in American Music, 1988.

Cripps, Thomas. *Slow Fade to Black: The Negro in American Film, 1900–1942*. New York: Oxford University Press, 1977.

Crouch, Stanley. "Laughin' Louis," *The Village Voice*, August 14, 1978.

Dance, Stanley. Review of *The Complete Decca Studio Recordings by Louis Armstrong and the All Stars* (Mosaic), *Jazz Times*, November 1993.

Davis, Miles, with Quincy Troupe. *Miles: The Autobiography*. New York: Simon & Schuster, 1989.

Early, Gerald. *Tuxedo Junction: Essays on American Culture*. New York: Ecco Press, 1989.

Ellison, Ralph. "Change the Joke and Slip the Yoke." In *Shadow and Act*. New York: Random House, 1964.

Feather, Leonard. *From Satchmo to Miles*. New York: Stein and Day, 1972.

Finkelstein, Sidney. *Jazz: A People's Music*. New York: Citadel, 1948 (reprint, 1988).

Friedwald, Will. *Jazz Singing*. New York: Charles Scribner's Sons, 1990.

Gabbard, Krin. *Jammin' at the Margins: Jazz and the American Cinema*. Chicago: University of Chicago Press, 1996.

Gates, Henry Louis, Jr. *The Signifying Monkey: A Theory of Afro-American Literary Criticism*. New York: Oxford University Press, 1988.

Giddins, Gary. *Satchmo*. New York: Doubleday, 1988.

Giddins, Gary, Dan Morgenstern, and Stanley Crouch. "Armstrong at 85," *The Village Voice*, August 27, 1985.

Gillespie, Dizzy, with Al Fraser. *To Be or Not to Bop*. Garden City, New York: Doubleday, 1979.

Gleason, Ralph J. "Louis Armstrong." In *Celebrating the Duke and Louis, Bessie, Billie, Bird, Carmen, Miles, Dizzy, and Other Heroes*. Boston: Little, Brown, 1975.

Glenn, Tyree. "Unforgettable Satchmo," *Reader's Digest*, December 1971.

Goffin, Robert. *Horn of Plenty: The Story of Louis Armstrong*. New York: Allen, Towne & Heath, 1947.

Grossberg, Lawrence, Cary Nelson, and Paula Treichler, eds. *Cultural Studies*. New York: Routledge, 1992.

Hadlock, Richard. *Jazz Masters of the 20's*. New York: Macmillan, 1965.

Hammond, John, with Irving Townsend. *John Hammond on Record*. New York: Summit Books, 1977.

Hardin-Armstrong, Lillian. *Satchmo and Me*. Riverside RLP 12-120.

hooks, bell, and Isaac Julien. "States of Desire," *Transition* 53 (1991): 168–84.

Jones, Max, and John Chilton. *Louis: The Louis Armstrong Story*. Boston: Little, Brown, 1971.

Kenney, William Howland. "Negotiating the Color Line: Louis Armstrong's Autobiographies." In *Jazz in Mind: Essays on the History and Meaning of Jazz,* edited by Reginald T. Buckner and Steven Weiland. Detroit: Wayne State University Press, 1991.

"Louis the First," *Time,* February 21, 1949. (Cover story, on Armstrong as King of the Zulus in Mardi Gras.)

Martyn, Barry, ed. *With Louis and the Duke*. New York: Oxford University Press, 1986.

Miller, Marc H., ed. *Louis Armstrong: A Cultural Legacy*. New York: Queens Museum of Art, and Seattle: University of Washington Press, 1994.

Morgenstern, Dan. Liner notes, *Louis Armstrong: Chicago Concert*. Columbia CS 36426, 1956.

———. Liner notes, *Louis Armstrong V.S.O.P., Vol. I*. Epic EE 22019, 1972.

———, ed. *Down Beat* (special issue), July 9, 1970.

———, ed. *Down Beat* (obituaries), September 16, 1971.

Murray, Albert. *Stomping the Blues*. New York: McGraw-Hill, 1976.

Naremore, James. "Uptown Folk: Blackness and Entertainment in *Cabin in the Sky*," *Arizona Quarterly* 48, no. 4 (1992): 99–124.

Panassié, Hugues. *Douze Années de Jazz*. Paris: Editions Corréa, 1946.

———. *Louis Armstrong*. New York: Charles Scribner's Sons, 1971.

Pinfold, Mike. *Louis Armstrong*. New York: Universe Books, 1987.

Pleasants, Henry. *The Great American Popular Singers*. New York: Simon & Schuster, 1974.

Porter, Lewis. *Louis Armstrong and Sidney Bechet in New York, 1923–1925*. Washington, D.C.: Smithsonian Recordings RO 26, 1981.

Ray, Robert B. *A Certain Tendency of the Hollywood Cinema, 1930–1980*. Princeton, New Jersey: Princeton University Press, 1985.

Rose, Al. *Storyville, New Orleans*. Tuscaloosa, Alabama: University of Alabama Press, 1974.

Schuller, Gunther. *Early Jazz: Its Roots and Musical Development*. New York: Oxford University Press, 1968.

———. *The Swing Era: The Development of Jazz, 1930–1945*. New York: Oxford University Press, 1989.

Shapiro, Nat, and Nat Hentoff. *Hear Me Talkin' to Ya*. New York: Rinehart, 1955.

Stearns, Marshall. *The Story of Jazz*. 1956 (reprint, New York: Oxford University Press, 1970).

Stewart, Rex. *Jazz Masters of the 30's*. New York: Macmillan, 1972.

Stowe, David W. *Swing Changes: Big Band Jazz in New Deal America*. Cambridge, Massachusetts : Harvard University Press, 1994.

Stratemann, Klaus. *Louis Armstrong on Screen*. Copenhagen: JazzMedia, 1996.

Taylor, Jeffrey. "Louis Armstrong, Earl Hines, and "'Weather Bird.'" *The Musical Quarterly* 82, no. 1 (Spring 1998), 1–40.

Teagarden, Jack. "The World's Greatest Horn Player," *Varsity*, December 1948.

Thomson, Virgil. "Saving Music." In *A Virgil Thomson Reader*, 28–32. New York: Dutton, 1981.

Wallace, Michele. "Michael Jackson, Black Modernisms and "'The Ecstacy of Communication.'" In *Invisibility Blues: From Pop to Theory*, 77–90. New Year: Verso, 1990.

Welsford, Enid. *The Fool: His Social and Literary History*. Cambridge, Massachusetts: Harvard University Press, 1966.

Westerberg, Hans. *Boy from New Orleans*. Copenhagen: JazzMedia, 1981.

Williams, Martin. *Jazz Masters of New Orleans*. New York: Macmillan, 1967.

Permissions

Part One: Do You Know What It Means to Miss New Orleans?

Louis Armstrong. "The New Orleans Jewish Family." Reproduced with permission from the Louis Armstrong House and Archives at Queens College/CUNY.

Joshua Berrett. "Louis Armstrong and Opera." *The Musical Quarterly,* Summer 1992. Reprinted by permission of Oxford University Press.

Part Two: I'm a Ding Dong Daddy

Lewis Porter. "Louis Armstrong and Sidney Bechet in New York, 1923–1925." Reprinted from *Louis Armstrong and Sidney Bechet in New York, 1923–25,* by Lewis Porter. © 1981 Smithsonian Institution. All rights reserved. Used by permission.

Lil Hardin-Armstrong. "Lil and Louis: Satchmo and Me." Transcribed from Lil Armstrong, *Satchmo and Me,* Riverside RLP 120120. Used by permission of Fantasy, Inc.

Max Jones. "Lil Armstrong, Royalties, and the Old Songs." *The Melody Maker,* April 8, 1967. Used by permission of IPC International Syndication.

Dan S. Ingman. "England's Welcome to Louis Armstrong." *The Melody Maker,* August, 1932. Used by permission of IPC International Syndication.

Hugues Panassié. "Louis Armstrong at the Salle Pleyel." Translated by Joshua Berrett from *Douze Années de Jazz* (Paris: Editions Corréa, 1946). Original French source courtesy of Louis Panassié.

Part Three: You Rascal You

Louis Armstrong. "Tommy Rockwell." Reproduced with permission from the Louis Armstrong House and Archives at Queens College/CUNY.

Louis Armstrong. "Groovin' High on Gage," excerpt from unpublished manuscript "The Satchmo Story." Reproduced with permission from the Louis Armstrong House and Archives at Queens College/CUNY.

Louis Armstrong. "Johnny Collins." Reproduced with permission from the Louis Armstrong House and Archives at Queens College/CUNY.

Louis Armstrong and George Avakian. "Contention with Collins." Reproduced with permission from the Louis Armstrong House and Archives at Queens College/CUNY.

Part Four: Memories of You

Louis Armstrong. "Early Years with Lucille." Reproduced with permission from the Louis Armstrong House and Archives at Queens College/CUNY.

Lucille and Louis Armstrong. "Lose Weight the 'Satchmo' Way." Reproduced with permission from the Louis Armstrong House and Archives at Queens College/CUNY.

Part Five: Red Beans and Ricely Yours

Louis Armstrong. Letters to Leonard Feather, Beatrice Armstrong, Frances Church, Madeleine Berard, Lucille Armstrong, and Joe Glaser. Reproduced with permission from the Louis Armstrong House and Archives at Queens College/CUNY.

Part Six: Do You Know What It Means to Miss New Orleans

George T. Simon. "Bebop's the Easy Way Out, Claims Louis." *Metronome,* March 1948. Used by permission.

Louis Armstrong, Barney Bigard, Ernest Borneman, and Mezz Mezzrow "Bop Will Kill Business Unless It Kills Itself First: Louis Armstrong." *Down Beat,* April 7, 1948. Used by permission.

Orrin Keepnews. "*Changer* Editor Also Blasts Wolff." *Down Beat,* July 15, 1949. Used by permission.

Louis Armstrong. Letter to Dizzy and Lorraine Gillespie. Reproduced with permission from the Louis Armstrong House and Archives at Queens College/CUNY.

Part Seven: Bourbon Street Parade

Ron Welburn. "Interview: Russell 'Big Chief' Moore." Excerpts from interview transcripts reprinted by permission of the Institute of Jazz Studies, Rutgers University, Newark, administrators of the Jazz Oral History Project as established by the National Endowment for the Arts.

Joshua Berrett. "Interview: Arvell Shaw." Reproduced with permission from Arvell Shaw.

Patricia Willard. "Interview: Barney Bigard." Excerpts from interview transcripts reprinted by permission of the Institute of Jazz Studies, Rutgers University, Newark, administrators of the Jazz Oral History Project as established by the National Endowment for the Arts.

Patricia Willard. "Interview: Trummy Young." Excerpts from interview transcripts reprinted by permission of the Institute of Jazz Studies, Rutgers University, Newark, administrators of the Jazz Oral History Project as established by the National Endowment for the Arts.

Dan Morgenstern. "Commentary," excerpt from liner notes to *Louis Armstrong: Chicago Concert,* Columbia CS 36426. Reprinted with permission from the author.

David H. Ostwald. "Louis Armstrong, Civil Rights Pioneer." *The New York Times,* August 3, 1991. Copyright © 1991 by The New York Times Co. Reprinted by permission.

Part Eight: High Society

Will Friedwald. "Mr. Satch and Mr. Cros." Copyright © by Will Friedwald, from his book *Jazz Singing,* New York: Macmillan, 1990. Used by permission of the author.

Krin Gabbard. "Actor and Musician: Louis Armstrong and His Films." Excerpt from *Jammin' at the Margins: Jazz and the American Cinema.* Copyright © 1996 by Krin Gabbard. Reprinted with permission from the University of Chicago Press.

Part Nine: Louis's Legacy

Martin Williams. "For Louis Armstrong at 70." *Down Beat,* July 9, 1970. Reprinted with the permission of *Down Beat.*

Lucille Armstrong. "Armstrong Postage Stamp, 1995." Louis Armstrong Archives Series Vertical. Reproduced with permission from the Louis Armstrong House and Archives at Queens College/CUNY.

Roxane Orgill. "Satchmo's Stamp of Approval." *Wall Street Journal,* September 27, 1995. Reprinted with permission from the author.

Joshua Berrett. "Interview: Ishmael Reed." Reproduced with permission from Ishmael Reed.

Joshua Berrett. "Interview: Marianne Veidt." Reproduced with permission from Marianne Veidt.

Index

Note: Page numbers in *ital* indicate photographs.

MGM, 79, 231
Middle East, 173–74
Middleton, Velma, 97, 126, 128, 144, 176, 179, 180
Miles, Flora, 15
Milhaud, Darius, 59, 61, 67
Mills Brothers, 204
"Milneburg Joys," 129
Mingus, Charles, 210
Minnelli, Vincente, 215, 217
"Minnie the Moocher," 231
minstrelsy, 209, 215, 250
Mississippi River excursion boats, 13, 16–20, 164
Mobutu, Joseph, 242
"moldy fig" (term), 139, 152, 167
Mole, Miff, 46
Monk, Thelonious, 139, 154, 207, 250
Montmartre (Paris), 68
"Mood Indigo," 169, 225
Moore, Al, 163, 164, 165
Moore, Russell ("Big Chief"), 160
    interview with, 161–63
Morgenstern, Dan, 28, 140, 160, 177–86, 196, 206, 237
Morton, Jelly Roll, 31, 200n.3
Moulin Rouge (Las Vegas), 134
movies. *See* films
Mozart, Wolfgang Amadeus, xiii
"Mr. Satch and Mr. Cros" (Friedwald), 190, 191–200
Multiple Sclerosis Society, 177, 183
Murray, Albert, 209
Murrow, Edward R., 183, 187
Muse, Clarence, 181
Musical Quarterly, The (publication), 24–29
"Mutiny in the Nursery," 216
"My Papa Doesn't Two-Time No Time," 200n.3

N

Naremore, James, 217–18
National Black Theater Festival (Winston-Salem, N.C.), 247
Negro, An Anthology (Cunard ed.), 56
New Basin Canal, 16

New Connie's Inn (New York City), 118
New Cotton Club (Culver City), 28, 79, 80, 222
Newman, Paul, 225
New Orleans, 108, 119, 129
    Armstrong commemorative stamp ceremony in, 243–46
    Armstrong's departure from, 19
    Armstrong's return to, 120–22
    Armstrong's youth in, xi, xii, 1, 4–12, 12–18, 24–26, 75–76, 88
    choice musicians, 11–12
    clarinet tradition, 33, 35
    Italian neighborhoods, 27
    jazz greats, 147
    jazz revival, 139, 159–60, 166, 181, 182, 204, 220
    jazz solos, 34–35
    Mardi Gras, 124, 125–26, 130, 209, 228
    parade bands, 11–12, 14–15, 26, 120, 166
New Orleans (film), 162, 169, 181, 222, 223, 233
    Armstrong on, 129–30
    Armstrong's role in, 207, 209, 219–20, 225, 226
    publicized premiere of, 139, 160
New Orleans Jazz Club, 244
New Orleans Rhythm Kings, 59
Newport Jazz Festival, 160, 185, 222, 223
    Armstrong birthday celebration, 178–80
New York City
    Armstrong designated landmarks, 240
    Armstrong's stints in, 33–35, 40–41, 77–78, 83, 84
    See also Corona; Harlem
New York Herald Tribune 46
New York Times, 31, 86, 186–88, 204
Nice jazz festival, 144, 147, 166
Nichols, Red, 221–22
Nicholson, Jack, 224
Night at the Opera, A (film), 29, 198
Nixon, Richard, 238
Noble, Ray, 54